George Baxter

THE BIRD WATCHER'S DIARY

Designed to Increase the Pleasures of Birding
A Compendium of Bird Lore • Tips for Birders
A Permanent Record of Your Bird Sightings

By
EDGAR M. REILLY
Senior Scientist, Zoology, Emeritus, New York State Museum
and
GORTON CARRUTH
Editor, *Our Living World of Nature*

Foreword by
DEAN AMADON
Curator of Birds, Emeritus, American Museum of Natural History

A HUDSON GROUP NATURE BOOK

1817
HARPER & ROW, PUBLISHERS, New York
Cambridge, Philadelphia, San Francisco, London
Mexico City, São Paulo, Singapore, Sydney

We dedicate this book to our wives,
Alice B. Reilly and Gisèle Carruth

FIRST EDITION

Designed by Pam Forde Graphics

We gratefully acknowledge permission to reprint the following copyrighted materials: Page 52, "What do you mean, let's go South? This is South!" © Punch/Rothco. All rights reserved. Page 72, "Real birds don't eat milo." By permission of the artist, Sandy Dean. Page 116, "The National Geographic Special is on!" © 1982. Reprinted by permission of Ladies' Home Journal and Joseph Farris. Pages 184 and 190, illustrations reprinted by permission of the artist, Bill Colrus, and Mulvey Associates, Inc.

LIBRARY OF CONGRESS CATALOGING-IN-PUBLICATION DATA

Reilly, Edgar M.
   The bird watcher's diary.

   "A Hudson Group nature book."
   Includes index.
   1. Bird watching.   2. Birds.
I. Carruth, Gorton.   II. Title.
QL677.5.R45   1986   598'.07'234   86–18359
ISBN 0–06–096092–2 (pbk.)

87 88 89 90 91 MPC 10 9 8 7 6 5 4 3 2 1

FOREWORD

I am pleased to recommend this book to everyone interested in birds, from beginners whose interests are confined to feeding birds outside their windows to birders who spend many days in the field. To my knowledge, the week-by-week arrangement is unique in a book about birds, not only because it provides space for keeping records, as in any diary, but especially because it enables the authors to include a wide variety of detailed information that maintains interest and attention at the maximum.

The authors are uniquely qualified to write an authoritative, wide-ranging popular book about birds—their characteristics, their biology, their way of life, their hazards and enemies, and their conservation. Dr. E. M. Reilly, who has had a long association with the Laboratory of Ornithology at Cornell University, is perhaps the country's premier interface between amateur bird watchers on the one hand and professional ornithologists on the other. Gorton Carruth, a former director of the Saw Mill River Audubon Society in Westchester County, New York, has been an editor and publisher of books on birds for 30 years.

I must mention that Dr. Reilly in his many years as a zoologist at the New York State Museum in Albany served as a sort of ombudsman dealing with endlessly diverse public inquiries about birds. He has also lectured widely to local bird and garden clubs and has written numerous articles for nature and conservation magazines. He has had time nevertheless to pursue his scientific specialty of zoogeography. He wrote the first draft of much of the fifth edition of the official *Check-list of North American Birds*, a project under the direction of Dr. Alexander Wetmore, at the time secretary of the Smithsonian Institution. In addition, Dr. Reilly wrote the authoritative and useful *Audubon Illustrated Handbook of North American Birds*.

Gorton Carruth brings a comprehensive editorial background to *The Bird Watcher's Diary*. He edited the popular series of ecologically oriented nature books —14 volumes in all—*Our Living World of Nature*, published in conjunction with the *World Book Encyclopedia*. He supervised publication in the United States of the important *New Dictionary of Birds* as well as *Hawks, Eagles, and Falcons of the World*, of which I am coauthor.

It is no surprise, then, to find in *The Bird Watcher's Diary* discussions ranging from the details of avian anatomy to the most practical methods of attracting birds and providing for their needs. Read this book for pleasure; the profit in knowledge and understanding will accrue quite without effort.

Dean Amadon
Curator of Birds, Emeritus
American Museum of Natural History
Lake Placid, Florida, 1986

PREFACE

During the more than fifty years that we have been watching birds, there has been a remarkable growth of interest in birds. Not only do increasing numbers of birders visit state, provincial, and national parks and wildlife refuges, but additional millions of Americans and Canadians feed wild birds at home. Perhaps it is this interest in feeding and watching birds that has led many thousands of people of all ages and walks of life to take a keen and deep interest in identifying birds, to travel in order to see birds different from those seen near home, and to study the behavior and life cycles of birds.

The Bird Watcher's Diary developed from our belief that beginning bird watchers would profit from a book that would help nurture their growing interest. In our professional lives—though for us birding is as much avocation as vocation—and in our work in museums especially, we have been asked thousands of questions about birds that are not generally answered in field identification guides or in other books found at home. This diary supplies answers to the questions most frequently asked. What are the best foods for birds? When should one start feeding—and stop? What are the best kinds of feeders? The best kinds of bird houses? In addition, the diary introduces the reader to the biology of birds and explains how birds fly, produce eggs, raise nestlings, and get along in their world. There is information on the scientific names and English names of birds. Readers learn how to identify birds and where to go to increase their chances of seeing birds. But beyond our goal of introducing the beginning birder to the fascinating study of birds is the intention of raising serious questions about the survival of wild birds in the present environment.

Birds live according to a natural calendar, which to some extent corresponds to the weeks and months of our own year. We decided that a convenient way of organizing a book about bird watching was to progress through the seasons week by week, introducing a timely topic each week. Another reason for developing a diary format was to encourage beginning birders to keep daily records of the birds they see. Ornithologists have great need of accurate information on the behavior of birds, and even a beginner can be helpful in this respect.

While we describe much bird behavior during the weeks in which it is observed, other activities, both avian and human, must be discussed out of season, because the schedule, particularly in spring and autumn, becomes too crowded. In recognition of this situation, we have provided a table of contents and an index to help readers find discussions of topics they wish to consult regardless of the time of year.

Above all we have tried to make this diary as interesting and as much fun as bird watching itself.

Everyone who has joined us in birding has contributed to this book. Among those others who have helped us especially, by providing information about birds in their local areas, are: Walt and Rebecca Anderson, Eugene, Oreg.; Dr. Kay Ball, Edmonton, Alta.; Patricia Bergey, Norman, Okla.; David Booth, Lake Charles, La.; Helen Carson, Billings, Mont.; Dr. E. A. Dillard, Jr., Texas City, Tex.; Bebe Fitzgerald, Billings, Mont.; Dr. George Grube, Dana College, Blair, Nebr.; Billie Hicks, Joliet, Mont.; Julian Huynean, Teaneck, N.J.; Steve Labuda, Alamo, Tex.; Janet M. McGee,

Lawton, Okla.; D. Weir Nelson, Ely, Iowa; Janice O'Keefe, Dodge City, Kans.; Bob Pennylegion, Holiday, Fla.; Galen L. Pitman, Lawrence, Kans.; Esther Serr, Rapid City, S.Dak.; Drs. Walt and Sally Spofford, Portal, Ariz.; Karen Steenhof, Boise, Idaho; Egon and Sue Wiedenfeld, Comfort, Tex.; Mrs. Doris Winship, Rockport, Tex.; Betty Wyatt, San Jose, Calif. We offer them our thanks.

We thank also John Rice and Peter Loewer for their drawings and Manfred Milkuhn for his maps. These gentlemen worked under the pressure of a short schedule, and we are grateful for their patience and understanding. We are indebted to Pam Forde, who designed and produced our book. She worked long and hard to bring together its many elements. It is difficult to imagine how the diary could have come into being without her dedication and, yes, her interest in birds. We thank too Hayden Carruth and Raymond V. Hand, Jr., for their computerization of the text, which made editing of it easier and more accurate.

We owe special thanks to Eugene Ehrlich, our colleague in The Hudson Group, who read every word several times, asked innumerable questions in his quest for clarity, and suggested textual changes that improved the text greatly. We are grateful for his help and interest.

We thank Dean Amadon, our friend and fellow birder for many years. Dean read the text, offered many valuable comments, and stood ready always to help us.

We hope that none of our friends and colleagues will be embarrassed by any errors they may discover: These mistakes are ours, not theirs. Finally, we would like to have suggestions from our readers for improving *The Bird Watcher's Diary*, especially its coverage of birds in their own localities.

HOW TO USE THE BIRD WATCHER'S DIARY.

First of all it must be made clear that you can begin using this diary at any time of year and go on using it year after year. When you identify birds for the first time, make a record of where and when you see them. In the list of birds seen in the United States and Canada, which begins on page 204, note the date and place of each first sighting and the page of the diary on which you record weather conditions and the bird's habitat and behavior. Each week of the diary provides space for such record keeping. There you may also note the arrival and departure dates of birds at your feeders as well as information about the kinds of food they eat.

We have made many other suggestions about information useful to record (see "Record keeping" in the index), and we hope you will find that this diary—like any other—will increase in value with each passing year as you personalize it with descriptions of your birding experiences.

For the spelling of bird names, please turn to page 144.

CONTENTS

BIRDS IN WINTER

ACTIVITIES. Begin recording in this diary the behavior of birds at your feeder. As the year advances you will see changes not only in the kinds of birds you see but also in behavior and plumage. And next year, when the cycle begins again, you will be able to compare what you see then with notes of this year. You might begin your observations by noting the food each species prefers and then the ways in which the species feed. Which species feed at your tray one individual at a time? Which feed many at a time? Which species hog the tray, not sharing with others? You will observe that some species are feistier than others, sneaking a morsel despite the presence of a bigger or threatening bird.

BIRDS IN WINTER. Spring and summer are associated with an abundance of birds, but paradoxically, the driving snow and plummeting temperatures of winter may also make for highly productive bird watching. Trees are bare, and fields, swamps, and marshes open up for good viewing, so birders can enjoy some of the best bird watching of the year. The fun is heightened further since in winter many unfamiliar species from farther north may be seeking an easier life in a less harsh environment.

Since the availability of food is more critical for survival of birds than how far the temperature drops, winter feeders sometimes attract unfamiliar birds, which overcome their wariness of house and yard to search for food. For example, though flowers and insects are absent, hummingbirds can survive in freezing temperatures as long as they have food, and birds that could be basking in southern climes will stay up north because a feeder supplies plentiful food. One of our feeders supported a Carolina Wren over an entire winter far north of its normal range, and another fed a Rufous-sided Towhee long after other members of the species had left the area. Each year, more people put out bird food, so in many areas more and more birds are making their first appearances at feeders, among them Red-bellied Woodpeckers, Verdins, Gray Catbirds, Rock and other wrens, Varied Thrushes, Phainopeplas, Bronzed Cowbirds, Lark Buntings, Chipping Sparrows, and Song Sparrows.

Winter adaptations. Seeing how birds adapt to severe weather in their natural habitats makes this season interesting for all birders who look for birds in sheltering woods and protected niches. Ruffed Grouse often plunge deep into snowbanks, where the snow protects them against cold and wind. House Sparrows have been seen crowded together under eaves or in the lee corners of homes, barns, and other man-made structures. Lark Buntings, Vesper Sparrows, and Dickcissels also seek such winter shelter.

KEEPING WARM. *Northern Bobwhites huddling together for protection against winter cold.*

COMINGS AND GOINGS.
Excitement is added to winter birding when you spot a rare northern species that has moved south in search of better wintering conditions. The rare and elusive longspurs are among these northern birds, but you will need sharp eyes to spot them, since they wander far south only in singles or pairs. Look for them in flocks of wintering birds, such as Horned Larks or Water Pipits, which you can find in fields and along beaches. The Lapland Longspur may be reported in some years from all the southernmost states. If you see one, get the news out. The sighting may be a once-in-a-lifetime event.

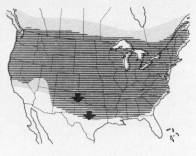

Farthest extent south: ▤ *Lapland Longspur*
▒ *Snow Bunting*

NOTES

Brown Creepers form a circle head to head on the sheltered sides of large trees. Small birds often seek protection within vacant woodpecker nesting holes, sometimes as many as a dozen or more in the same barracks. When they emerge, some show bent tail feathers from a night spent at the bottom of the pile.

Much is yet to be learned about how birds along open coasts or in large open fields protect themselves against winter storms. They are known to seek shelter in hollows among the dunes and fields, but they do not always use the same hollows day after day. In windstorms, field birds hug the ground, keeping their heads turned into the wind. When driving your car along country lanes during snowstorms at night, your headlights may pick up flocks of Horned Larks, Snow Buntings, Lapland Longspurs, or other birds that have been flushed from a road cut. In forests and brushland, much natural cover is available for birds— even the lee sides of large trees or shrubs may suffice. But shelter from storms may not afford enough protection if predators are active and if the cold has made birds less alert than they should be. Though some 20 to 30 percent of the wintering bird population may perish each winter, this is only normal attrition. Their populations are soon replenished in spring, when birds return to their breeding territories.

Hibernating birds? Though the body temperatures of birds are higher than those of most mammals and their hearts beat at a faster rate, some birds become torpid for brief periods in winter. During cold weather, when food becomes short, the heartbeats of hummingbirds huddled in rock crevices may slow to one-tenth of normal, and their body temperatures may drop below 50° F, less than half of normal. Some members of the nighthawk and whip-poor-will families have also been known to become torpid, and other species may have developed this ability as well. But these are certainly special cases. True hibernation is a long-term winter affair, lasting at least two to three months, and the Common Poorwill of the western United States is the only bird known to

SEEKING SHELTER. *A hibernating Common Poorwill snuggled away from the wind in a crevice of a rock wall. In harsh winter weather, Ring-necked Pheasants and other ground-dwelling birds often take shelter under lean-tos built by caring birders.*

practice true hibernation. In the southwestern United States, the Poorwill has hibernated deep in rock crevices for at least three months, with its body temperature at about 40° F.

Importance of shelter and food. Severe winter storms inevitably kill many birds. Why not provide shelter for them and enjoy watching the birds come and go? A long structure with a narrow open side, interior perches, and a roof can be nailed to the sheltered side of a tree or building to provide a winter roost. Another kind of shelter is also welcome. Piles of twigs arranged on the ground as a lean-to, with its open end facing south or away from the prevailing wind, will provide welcome refuge for grouse, quail, pheasants, larks, and others during rough weather.

Finding adequate food is the most important survival strategy birds must employ in winter. When ponds and marshes are frozen, ducks, herons, and others move to open water, where the temperature is apt to be just as low but an adequate food supply is available. Certain berries and other fruit, such as rose hips, become more palatable to birds after the fruit has been thoroughly frozen. During winter, such foods sustain American Robins and Northern Mockingbirds as well as other species.

Birds appreciate food most when they find it in a feeder after a winter storm. Suet and other high-protein foods are especially welcome. (See page 10 for information about the best kinds of foods.) Even in southern areas, severe storms may make it difficult for birds to find adequate food, so feeders and shelters can be havens. In all regions, when the high winds of a storm have subsided, you may see at your feeder members of a species new to you that have been driven far from their regular habitats. So the winds, snow, ice, and cold can produce a bonanza for bird watchers.

A WINTER SHELTER. *It can be about 4 to 6 inches square and about 15 inches high. Cut the hole about 2 inches from the bottom.*

JAN 8–14

WINTER
FEEDERS

ACTIVITIES. Once you have identified a bird at your feeder, make detailed notes of the shapes of its tail and wings, bill, feet, and eyes. Can you guess from these features how the bird makes its living? A good way to find out is to read its life history (see pages 174–177). Develop the habit of describing these features not only for species around home but also for species you see on walks along the beach and through fields and woods. You will soon observe species sharply different from those that come to your feeder; in short, birds that have evolved different styles of living will be found in different habitats.

According to the United States government, about 60 million people in the U.S. actively feed wild birds. We do not know how many people in Canada do so, but we expect that about 5 to 6 million maintain feeders. Birds do not need to be fed, but feeding permits a larger percentage to survive in the wild, especially in times of natural food shortage. We feed birds because we like to watch them, observe their antics, note arrivals and departures of different species, enjoy their songs and calls, and learn their habits.

WINTER FEEDERS. Long before the invention of writing, people recognized birds as harbingers of spring. In the primitive agriculture of the distant past, knowing when to begin planting gave farmers a schedule that enabled them to take full advantage of the growing season. The earliest written records, about 3000 B.C., mention birds in the fields. Temple priests used such records of natural events to help forecast times for planting. The shamans were the keepers of such traditions, and watching for the first arrivals of certain species of birds led easily to putting out food and other attractions to draw the omen-birds into view. Even today, primitive peoples almost everywhere in the world follow such natural events as the first arrivals and last departures of migrating animals as a method of marking seasons or scheduling farming activities.

Birds appear in Stone Age rock drawings, in ancient Egyptian and Mesopotamian carvings, and in Greek and Roman art, where they are shown being fed by humans. During the Middle Ages, people of Europe placed food for birds in evergreen trees to welcome the birds back from the warmer south—a practice that may have led indirectly to our modern practice of decorating Christmas trees.

By far the most common reason for feeding birds now is that it offers a convenient way to observe and enjoy them. For the beginning bird watcher, feeding offers an entertaining way to learn how to identify different species. For the more advanced birder and for the ornithologist, attracting birds to a feeder provides a natural environment in which to study bird behavior. At the Laboratory of Ornithology at Cornell University, for example, quantities of feed are shoveled out daily throughout the year. This is done partly to make sure there are birds to entertain visitors to the Cornell Laboratory and partly to enhance its bird sanctuary as a living laboratory. Most bird sanctuaries maintain feeding stations to attract birds, even where natural food is usually plentiful in winter.

COMINGS AND GOINGS. West.

Here is a real challenge for birders. The Pacific Loon, formerly considered a subspecies of the Arctic Loon and fairly common, is now accepted as a full species. This reduced the status of the Arctic Loon to that of a rare straggler. But positive identification of the Arctic Loon in winter can be made only with the bird close at hand, since its definitive field marks are known only for the breeding plumage. The keen of vision will also identify Common and Red-throated loons and, along the northern Pacific coast of Canada, the Yellow-billed Loon.

▬▬ *Combined winter ranges of Arctic and Pacific loons along marine coasts and nearby inland waters*
• *Accidental occurrences*

NOTES

A HANDOUT. *A Tufted Titmouse will accept sunflower seeds from a hand held near a feeder.*

Feed stores do not always label seeds as reliably as one would wish, so learn to identify seeds yourself in order to get just what you want for your birds.

Should you feed the birds? Undertaking to feed birds raises the important question of responsibility. Birds come to rely on feeders for part of their winter food. Feeders also become an enticement for birds to remain in an area at a time when they normally would disperse or move south to find a natural supply of food. Ornithologists believe some seed-eating species, such as the Northern Cardinal, Tufted Titmouse, Bushtit, and Scrub Jay, have extended their winter ranges and increased in numbers because of the abundant supply of food at feeders.

To avoid abandoning birds to the peril of an inadequate winter food supply, you must answer certain questions: Can you tend feeders almost every day? Can you fill them with enough food to last during times when you must be away, or are there several reliable feeders nearby? If you cannot answer such questions affirmatively, you probably should not start up a feeder, especially if you live where natural food may be in short supply in winter.

Some birders oppose all feeding, claiming that birds become dependent on handouts. But home feeders have become so prevalent over the United States and Canada that this system of supporting birds cannot be abandoned. Besides, it is a method of attracting birds for people who might otherwise not see and get to know them.

Types of food. Commercially packaged wild birdseed is generally satisfactory in every part of the United States and Canada. Composed for relatively large regions, this food is not always suitable for birds of a particular local area and inevitably includes much inexpensive, comparatively unpalatable seed. This is not the fault of the commercial packagers, since putting together customized recipes for local areas is impractical.

You should first put out packaged food to determine which seeds your birds prefer. Then you can buy the preferred seeds from a grain and feed market and make your own mixtures. Just be sure the seed you buy is clean and polished.

Like humans, birds may avoid certain food if it is not just right for them. Sunflower seeds and cracked corn lose quality if left in sacks or cans over the summer, so birds returning to a feeder in autumn may ignore them. Then, too, insects may infest stored seed and create distasteful dirt and fecal matter. If you scatter this old seed on the ground away from the base of your feeder, it probably will be eaten but may also attract pests.

There are special mixtures for particular types of birds, but before buying them it is wise to check range maps in a field guide or bird book to be sure species you wish to attract occur in your area. Be patient. The birds may not be attracted immediately.

One way to select seeds that are best for your feeders is to put out several trays, each containing a cupful of a particular kind of seed. Notice which types attract the most birds as well as which attract your desired species. After a day or two, measuring the seed remaining in each tray will identify the preferred seed. Commonly available seeds and foods are listed on pages 10 to 12.

For years while working at a museum, we dissected many of the dead birds brought to us by the public and never found one chickadee or titmouse with peanut butter compacted in its crop. Our experience does not mean that this problem never occurs, but it is probably rare. Mixing peanut butter with cornmeal or small seeds, even milled oats, will reduce chances, if any, of a compacted crop. Small seeds from a feeder rarely go down the throat or windpipe of larger birds and choke them, but this can happen even while they are eating wild seeds in woods or fields. It is a risk birds have to take. You cannot stand by with a first-aid kit, waiting for an accident to occur.

Pests. Feeders attract more than just the birds you wish to see. Starlings, House Sparrows, and grackles, for example, and even large numbers of House Finches or Evening Grosbeaks may become tiresome. The larger species can be barred by providing only small openings as access to the feeder food. (Chicken wire may be useful.) Some commercially sold feeders work as advertised, but none can be considered effective against all pests. Bees, wasps, and ants are attracted to food—bees and wasps in particular like fats melting in the sun. Larger mammals, such as opossums, raccoons, skunks, dogs, foxes, cats, porcupines, deer, and bears may be reasonably controlled—as long as your bears are reasonable—by cleaning the area around feeders and keeping foods that attract these mammals well beyond their reach.

For ingenuity and resourcefulness, squirrels are a separate class of pests. Squirrel-proof feeders on the market work well enough most of the time, but we have seen only two feeders that fully merited the name. One was atop a 14-foot chrome-plated steel pole—the tray had to be lowered each time a refill was required. And the post was checked frequently for rust spots that might furnish squirrel toeholds. The other was on a post with an inverted cone beneath acting as a barrier to climbing squirrels. Both were well away from overhanging trees and buildings.

Do not spread poisons around to kill pests. Mouse poison looks like bird food and kills birds as well as mice. Some poisons that kill rats and mice may easily kill the hawks and owls that eat the rodents. The populations of hawks and owls are already too low, so the populations of pests they feed on are on the increase.

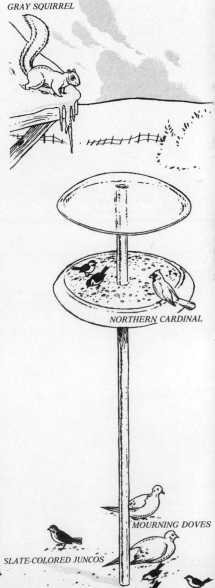

A SQUIRREL-PROOF FEEDER. *Squirrels unchecked can eat birds out of house and home.*

GRAY SQUIRREL

NORTHERN CARDINAL

MOURNING DOVES

SLATE-COLORED JUNCOS

AMERICAN TREE SPARROW

BLACK-CAPPED CHICKADEES

FOODS THAT ATTRACT BIRDS

Canary seed
Liked by sparrows, finches, blackbirds, chickadees, titmice, doves, quail, etc. Low on protein and minerals. Needs addition of other seeds and foods.

Cheese
American, cottage, cream, and others. Eaten by many birds. Put some out to see which birds like it.

Corn
Finely cracked to whole kernel. Favored by many feeder visitors. Spread on the ground, attracts doves, blackbirds, various sparrows, and finches. Whole kernels eaten avidly by larger species, such as doves, jays, pheasants, partridge, and quail. Mix cracked corn with peanut butter and fats.

Fruit
Bananas, dates, fresh and cooked apples, orange sections nailed to trees or feeders, pears, grapes, and cherries. Use in spring, summer, fall—and when winter weather allows. Fruit attracts robins, thrushes, mockingbirds, orioles, tanagers, and others. Use it if you want to see summer birds at your feeder.

Hay floor sweepings or chaff
In rural and suburban areas you may be able to gather your own with the permission of barn owners. Chaff, which contains many grass and weed seeds, is one of the best bird foods.

Melon seed
Cantaloupe, watermelon, squash, pumpkin, papaya, etc. Save such seeds—many birds like them. We use a coarse comb to separate seeds from pulp, then dry them in an oven at low heat before bagging for storage in a dry, cool place. Doves, jays, chickadees and relatives, nuthatches, cardinals, Pyrrhuloxias, sparrows, and finches relish such food.

Millet
Several species and varieties available from feed and grain establishments: Browntop, Foxtail (Golden, German, Hungarian), Pearl, and Cattail are favored by doves, finches, sparrows. Proso Millet comes in white, red, and yellow. White is chosen as bird food by most people, but the birds hardly notice the difference. For many birds, millet is one of the most favored food seeds, after oil seed (black sunflower seed). If your birds prefer white millet, mix it with sunflower and other seeds to prevent waste.

Nutmeats
Almonds, black or white walnuts, coconuts, hickory nuts, peanuts, and pecans. Cracked and chopped, they are highly nutritious, a good energy source. Birds will eat Brazil nuts if you crack them and chop the meat.

Safflower seed
Very good for many birds, but expensive and sometimes hard to get.

Sorghum (milo)
Eaten by doves, House Sparrows, blackbirds, finches, and others. Forms a good percentage of scratch feed, which is an inexpensive mixed seed food consisting mostly of cracked wheat and cracked corn.

QUICK REFERENCE TO BIRD FOODS

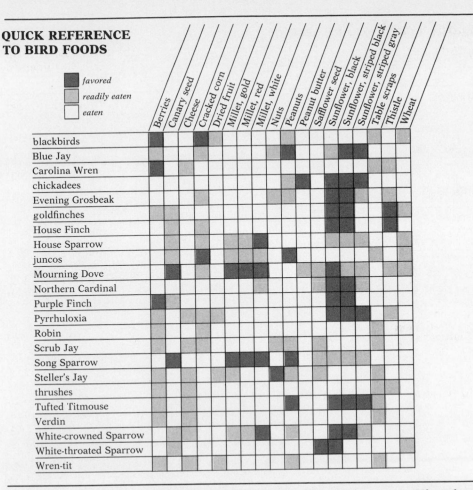

Sunflower seed

Three main varieties are sold in feed stores: 1. Oil seed, or Perdovic, smallest of the three and number one on the feed list. 2. Black-and-white striped seed, favored slightly over the next variety. The finches, Song Sparrows, White-throated and White-crowned sparrows prefer other seeds, possibly because of the stout husk. 3. Gray-and-white striped seed, still one of the best food seeds. Starlings are unable to crack the husks of the second and third varieties.

Thistle seed

More properly Niger, an expensive, sometimes hard-to-obtain small black seed imported from Africa (mainly Ethiopia). It is apparently a favorite of many birds: finches, redpolls, siskins, doves, chickadees and relatives, towhees, juncos, and sparrows. Thistle seed is best served from hanging feeders, which thwart some of the larger pest species.

Wheat

Highly nutritious food for birds, even though they seem to prefer corn. It is eaten by quail, partridge, doves, jays, chickadees and kin, blackbirds, cardinals, finches, and sparrows. Cracked wheat forms part of scratch feed and makes an excellent additive in any seed mixture.

OTHER FOODS AND SUPPLEMENTS

Animal fats Bacon drippings, cooked and cracked animal bones, etc. Place out of reach of dogs, cats, raccoons, and the like.

Berries Almost any kind. When young are in the nest, berries will attract thrushes, mockingbirds, catbirds, bluebirds, waxwings, and others.

Bread crumbs Bits of toast and bread are not a favored food but are eaten, especially in winter.

Dog food Soaked dog biscuits, dry food (be sure to moisten), and canned dog food will attract robins, thrushes, wrens, jays, grackles, etc. Robins and other thrushes have survived cold snaps in winter on this regime. We have not tried any of the cat foods, but they may serve as well.

Eggs Serve leftover scraps of egg dishes to birds. They like egg raw or cooked in any fashion. Crack or grind the shells and place on feeder because many birds appreciate this mineral supplement, especially during breeding seasons.

Mealworms Not worms, but the larval forms of Flour Beetles. Great treats for many birds in spring and early summer when young are in the nests. May be bought in pet stores and some feed stores. Place mealworms in edged dishes or trays so they cannot crawl away.

Minerals Almost all animals require minerals in their diets. Some of the required minerals, usually entering the body as a mineral salt, are calcium, phosphorus, magnesium, sodium, iodine, iron, copper, manganese, sulfur, and their compounds. Birds may obtain minerals from grit, which is sold at grain or pet stores, but they are also present in ashes, sand, ground seashells, fish bones, and fine gravel. A small amount on or near a feeder will suffice. Many seed-eaters require fine gravel or sand to grind food in their crops to a size easily digested, but in some areas gravel and sand may be hard to reach through winter snow and ice.

Suet Plain suet is a treat for many birds. But suet and other animal fats may be rendered, and various seeds, grains, bits of fruits, peanut butter, etc., stirred in. Once cooled, suet can be placed on feeders or in suet racks. Try different mixtures till you find the ones your birds favor, but remember that their preferences may reflect seasonal variations.

Spaghetti Left over from meals, chopped fine, and served on the feeding tray, spaghetti is popular with many bird species. The kind of sauce does not matter: We once forgot to discuss spaghetti sauce on a radio program, and you would not believe how many phone calls we received. Robins will even eat long strands as though they were worms, but do not put out long spaghetti strands when temperatures are below freezing.

Table scraps Pie crusts, doughnuts, muffins, bread, etc.

Water. Birds appreciate a supply of water, especially when the natural supply is frozen. (They are able, with some effort, to use snow and ice as a water supply.) If you put out a water dish in winter, you will need a thermostatically controlled heater and waterproof electric outlet. These are available in farm supply stores or at stores that sell birdhouses, feeders, and supplies. Garden supply stores also sell water basins equipped with circulating water pumps that attract birds by keeping the water in motion. A plastic container leaking water drop by drop may be installed over a simple birdbath and achieve the same effect during the warmer months—it will need only to be kept filled and is especially attractive to warblers.

WINTER WATER. *A Blue Jay drinking from a watering dish kept at temperatures above freezing by means of a thermostatically controlled heater.*

When food appears plentiful—any amount in a feeder indicates this to birds—much of it seems to be wasted. This is a phenomenon that has evolved to ensure that there will be enough seed for the following year's plants. If you fill your feeders sparingly several times each day, and not at night, you will eliminate some of the apparent waste. But because nature recycles almost everything, nothing is actually wasted.

Where to place the feeder. If you plan to have only one feeder, you will want to place it where you can watch the feeding birds. If only one such place is available and your beloved cat or dog sleeps there, you had better give up. Birds at feeders like escape hatches—plantings into which they can dart to avoid cats, dogs, hawks, and other predators. For this reason, do not place your feeder out in the open. Again, do not place it where it will get full sun or full shade all day. And do not put the feeder where winds blow continually.

If you have plenty of open space, try to establish a ground-level feeding station for birds that have some protective coloring, such as quail, pheasants, Roadrunners, various blackbirds, Northern Mockingbirds, and juncos. In open areas, make sure there is a wide view so birds can see and escape from their predators. Having done this, place another feeder closer, where you can observe it easily. An ideal sanctuary is a garden spot with a comfortable bench not far away so you have a view of birds at their bath or feeder. (One backyard we know near Phoenix, Arizona, is crowded with flowering plants attractive to hummingbirds and other garden birds. It draws 20 or more species at a time.)

If your open feeding area attracts birds that in turn may attract bird hawks (Cooper's, Sharp-shinned, or Goshawk), you may lose some of your more common birds, but that is also part of bird watching. You are not establishing a feeder to see such events, but life has its own rules, and you will see yet another part of nature that is necessary and interesting.

You should not supply moldy or tainted foods—especially table scraps—nor leave wet food on feeder trays, where they can turn rancid or moldy. Food trays should be cleaned frequently, especially after rain or snow.

JAN 15–21

BIRD EVOLUTION

ACTIVITIES. Winter is a good time to watch for owls. The records of your bird club may tell you which species are reported regularly and where. Since owls generally use the same wintering grounds year after year, some clubs have marked their maps for "winter owl territory." Presence of an owl is often revealed by raucous crows trying to drive it off. Short-eared, Snowy, and Pygmy owls do fly in the daytime; nocturnal owls, naturally, are seen most easily at dawn and dusk. At the appropriate hour, you can sometimes call owls into view by playing a recording of their calls over and over. Incidentally, keep an eye on your bird feeder. One winter an Eastern Screech-Owl came regularly to our feeders, hunting for deer mice that fed on leftover seed.

FLASH NEWS. A recently discovered fossil, almost certainly that of a bird, is about 75 million years older than Archaeopteryx. *It has been named* Protoavis.

ARCHAEOPTERYX. The first-known bird, shown above in a reconstruction, probably could fly but likely not for great distances. Comparing the skeleton of this ancient bird with that of a modern pigeon shows that the sternum of Archaeopteryx, *to which flight muscles were attached, was comparatively small. This is a good indication that sustained flight was not fully developed. On the other hand, the rachises of its major flight feathers were not centered. This is a good indication that the evolution of flight had begun.*

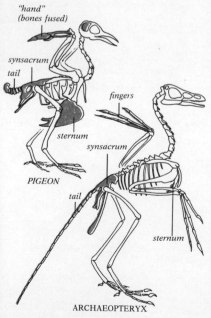

"hand"
(bones fused)

synsacrum

tail

fingers

sternum

synsacrum

PIGEON

tail

sternum

ARCHAEOPTERYX

BIRD EVOLUTION. In 1861, a remarkable fossil was found at Solnhofen, near Munich, in what is now West Germany. The site was a quarry of fine-grained, lithographic limestone about 140 to 150 million years old. The fossil animal had visible feathers, making it the most ancient bird identified, the *Archaeopteryx lithographica*.

Five other specimens have since been found, all of the same species. But this does not mean no other bird species lived in that distant past, nor does it mean that *Archaeopteryx* was the first bird. Evolution of its feathers and of its other birdlike features must have taken a long time, and *Archaeopteryx* must have had its birdlike ancestors.

It is hypothesized that the earliest bird lived as long as 250 million years ago. Since there is no proof that *Archaeopteryx* is a direct ancestor of any particular group of modern birds, it is possible that another ancient species, yet undiscovered, is more closely related to modern birds. Scientists have been arguing the point ever since the 1861 discovery, and the matter may never be settled, since fossils from so long ago will probably always be rare, and those of flying birds rarer still. To complicate things more, recent articles in a scientific journal suggest that the feathers of an *Archaeopteryx* in the British Museum are a clever hoax. The fact that there are at least five other *Archaeopteryx* specimens seems to argue against the possibility that all are fakes and indicate that *Archaeopteryx lithographica* certainly existed.

While the skeleton of *Archaeopteryx* resembles the skeletons of small dinosaurs, its avian characteristics help differentiate it. Like the skeletons of modern birds, some of the fossil bones were already fused. Moreover, as a hello to its kin across millions of years, the second and third digits of the hand were beginning to fuse. In modern birds, these finger bones plus a tiny remnant of the thumb are fused into a single bone. (See pages 28 and 47 for an explanation of this adaptive modification.) The rachises (shafts) of the major flight feathers were not centered but located toward the outer part of the vane.

COMINGS AND GOINGS. West.

A chance at seeing oceanic birds usually means a trip out to sea. From October to June, for example, thousands of Black-footed and Laysan albatrosses course well off the Pacific coast, heading in a southerly direction. But on shore after a strong Pacific storm, you may spot a wind-blown waif flying along beaches or bluffs. You may even find the remains of a bird that lost its struggle to make its way back to its fierce, beloved ocean. As an aid in positive identification, photograph the bird or at least measure its wings and tail. Keep eyes peeled also for shearwaters, petrels, and storm-petrels.

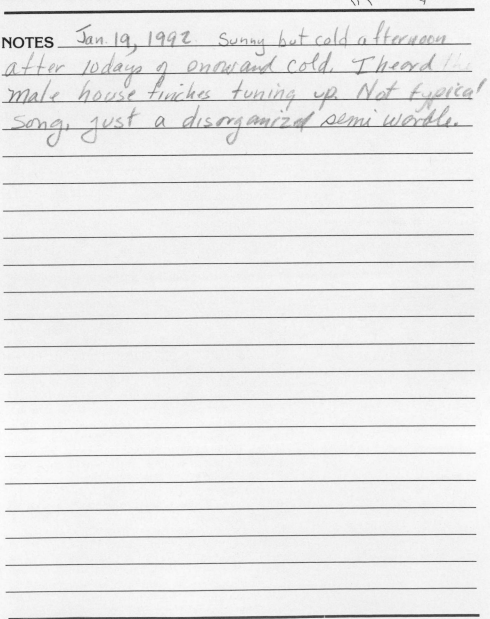

Offshore ranges: ➡️ *Black-footed Albatross*
- - -➡️ *Laysan Albatross*
Farther north later in the year

NOTES Jan. 19, 1992. Sunny but cold afternoon after 10 days of snow and cold. I heard the male house finches tuning up. Not typical song, just a disorganized semi warble.

Geography of evolution. Fossils have been found of about 35 species of birds dating from the end of the Cretaceous Period, 65 million years ago. (Throughout the world there may actually have been 3000 to 4000 species.) Among these 35 were specialized forms, such as swimmers, ternlike birds, and even flightless species. Today, there are about 9000 species of living birds, more than any other class of terrestrial vertebrates—amphibians, reptiles, and mammals. Taking into account species that became extinct over the millennia, there probably have been more than 60,000 species. In terms of numbers of species, therefore, birds have been remarkably successful.

The process of speciation. Speciation is the evolution of one living form into another. It requires separation of a breeding population from others of its kind, and it is important that the isolated group be large enough to reproduce itself. Colonial birds, such as terns and gannets, may not breed until a flock has reached a certain size, and it is unlikely any species will survive when its numbers have been reduced to one female and one male. Even though two birds may live in the same area and roost together, their pool of genes would be too small for their descendants to withstand emergencies or to supply the variety needed to overcome environmental factors.

Geographic isolation tends to produce genetically controlled variation. Offshore islands at distances too great for regular flights from the mainland by small birds will be occupied nevertheless by such birds when they are carried there by high winds. In time, colonies founded by such wind-waifs may begin to differ noticeably from mainland populations.

If it is by geographic isolation over time that populations are separated into species, how does this occur? A storm may blow a flock to an island it cannot leave, or a widespread population of birds may become divided by persistent incursion of the sea or by the action of glaciers. Relatively recent species of birds, for example, have developed on oceanic islands that never were connected with any continent. Consider the Galápagos Islands and Hawaii, where the resident species of Darwin's Finches and Hawaiian Honeycreepers, respectively, are well documented. Over time, probably hundreds of thousands of years at least, the isolated populations began to develop structural and behavioral characteristics that distinguished them from the original mainland populations, which themselves were undergoing change. Eventually, the differences between populations made the isolated birds unable to breed with the original populations.

But speciation takes a very long time. The Red-shafted Flicker and the Yellow-shafted Flicker almost made it when the original population of a single species (Northern Flicker) became separated into two populations. This happened over 15,000 years ago and was caused by a long tongue of a continental glacier. When the ice melted about 12,000 years ago, the reds and yellows met again and interbred readily, showing that they were still one species, even though the

16

Red-shafted Flicker, unlike the Yellow-shafted Flicker, today lives mainly west of the Rockies.

Just as differences between individuals within a species—brothers or sisters, for example—are the result of inheriting different genes, so the differences between species require a different mix of genes. The mix is so different that even closely related species, such as the Downy and Hairy woodpeckers, have lost the ability to interbreed. Differences in the genetic code are sometimes the result of mutations, sudden changes in individual genes. But mutations usually result in nonadaptive, even lethal changes, so the bird does not reproduce successfully and pass on the mutation.

Sufficient variety in genes from individual to individual must persist under environmentally selective forces for a long time for speciation to occur. An isolated population, because it does not have the same mix of possible genes as the original population, tends to go off in its own developmental direction, with genes different from those of the original population. This results in what are called adaptive changes. Over hundreds of millions of years, speciation has produced such remarkable differences as those between the Scintillant Hummingbird of Costa Rica and Panama and the Ostrich. The former is one of the smallest and the latter the largest of birds.

A BASILISK-LIKE LIZARD
OF THE EARLY MESOZOIC

Modern ornithologists and zoologists have little doubt that birds arose from reptiles. They believe that during the Triassic, the first division of the Mesozoic Era, birds and dinosaurs shared an ancestor in a group of primitive reptiles known as thecodonts. Among the Pseudosuchia, a suborder of the thecodonts, was a reptile named *Euparkeria,* whose bones closely resemble those of *Archaeopteryx.* No fossil of an animal halfway between *Euparkeria* and *Archaeopteryx* has yet been found, but most scientists believe it would look much like *Euparkeria.* The latest hypothesis, reflecting evidence offered by Dr. John Ostrom of Yale University, is that birds arose from pseudosuchian ancestors, more precisely through a side branch, the Coelosauria, having many features present in birds. But fossils of so-called missing links are rare. The ancestral animals, replaced by more successful descendants, became extinct.

THE BIG DEBATE AMONG EVOLUTIONISTS *concerns whether the reptiles from which birds arose were lizardlike creatures that ran swiftly over the ground with forelegs outstretched for balance or whether they scurried up trees and along tree branches. In other words, did birds develop wings that helped them run better, or did the wings help them move better from branch to branch and tree to tree?*

Consider the modern evidence. Basilisks are tropical lizards with proportionately long hind legs. They run across the surfaces of streams and ponds while reared up on their hind legs, going so fast that the observer sees only the splashes of their feet on the water. Large arboreal lizards move slowly and carefully, and small ones are so light that when they drop from a height, the fall is slow and does little damage—not unlike the fall of an ant. The Flying Dragon of the East Indies does not fly at all. It glides along, using a wide fold of skin on each side supported by special ribs. But these animals bear no relation to birds, whether fossil or living, so one can say there are valid arguments for both paths of development.

The evolutionary tree. Scientists have classified birds in gradations from those they consider the most primitive to those they consider the most advanced. Reflecting the belief that human intelligence is the highest yet attained, ornithologists have placed crows, considered the most intelligent of living birds, at the top of the avian hierarchy. Originally, they considered the flightless land birds as the simplest in structure. But when they studied the Ostrich, rheas, emus, cassowaries, kiwis, and tinamous, they learned that, except for the tinamous, these birds no longer needed the special anatomy developed for flight. Their flight mechanisms had atrophied, so of course their anatomy seemed simpler. Close study showed that these birds have a long and complicated evolutionary history dating perhaps more than 80 million years back into the Upper Cretaceous.

Paleontologists have discovered possible ancestors of many groups of living birds. Several birds of the Mesozoic, including *Archaeopteryx*, had teeth, but species eventually evolved that did not. The early birds first had to evolve certain other improvements, including better wings, appropriate methods of eating, and anatomy adapted to life off the ground. In the Cretaceous, there still were toothed birds but they looked much like today's herons, geese, and gulls or terns; some had fewer and lighter teeth. About 65 million years later, in the Eocene, the first epoch of the Tertiary Period, modern bird families began to appear: penguins, loons, pelicans, rails, gulls, hawks, and owls along with birds apparently unrelated directly to any surviving species, such as *Diatryma, Gastornis,* and *Eleutherornis,* the last a possible ancestor of the modern ratites. (Ratites, which lack keels on the sternum or breastbone, include most of the present flightless birds.) *Eleutherornis,* a fragmentary fossil, was a flightless bird with much reduced wings, a moderately keeled sternum (see page 29), and other features indicating a position midway between flying birds and ratites.

Now it is time to board a time machine and go back about 10 million years. Look about you. You see many birds that look familiar. You probably cannot identify all the species, but you know some of them: Common Loon, Whooping Crane, Blue-winged Teal, Bufflehead, Ruddy Duck, Sharp-shinned Hawk, Red-tailed Hawk, Spruce Grouse, Ruffed Grouse, Wild Turkey, Killdeer, Willet, Common Flicker, Downy Woodpecker, Phoebe, Eastern and Western kingfishers, Horned Lark, Barn Swallow, Purple Martin, Steller's Jay, American Crow, Raven, Red-breasted Nuthatch, thrashers, Mockingbird, Catbird, bluebirds, thrushes, American Robin, vireos, warblers, Northern Oriole, grackles, Song Sparrow, and Evening Grosbeak. The birds show minor differences, for

The Greater Roadrunner has a medium-depth keel and can fly. But it spends most of its time running on the ground. It has an animation artist as its press agent, who unfortunately gives people erroneous ideas about the accomplishments of the species. A member of the cuckoo family, the Greater Roadrunner lives on the ground in the dry country of the Southwest. Its song is a series of vehement coos and oohs. And it can run swiftly. Though it does not run as fast as the animated cartoons suggest, it can indeed outrun coonhounds and other dogs. The Greater Roadrunner eats lizards, snakes, scorpions, centipedes, and large spiders. Its personality makes it a welcome visitor, so if you live in the Southwest, place long strips of meat in your ground feeders to attract this interesting species.

example, in their songs, which may not resemble those of their descendants we hear today.

Now move ahead, stopping 10,000 to 12,000 years before the present. Look about. Most species we know now are probably on the scene.

FOSSIL HISTORY OF BIRDS

ERA	PERIOD EPOCH	BEGAN	FIRST APPEARANCES OF MAJOR GROUPS
CENOZOIC	QUATERNARY RECENT	Began 11,000 years ago	Today's c.9000 species. Perching birds are dominant.
	PLEISTOCENE	2,000,000 years ago	All modern orders and families present. Extensive dispersals and extinctions. Widespread continental glaciers.
	TERTIARY PLIOCENE	13,000,000 years ago	Probably largest ever number of bird species present. Rise of western New World mountains, grasslands, and deserts.
	MIOCENE	25,000,000 years ago	Most orders and families of today's birds present. Some families become extinct. Warm, dry climate gradually cooling.
	OLIGOCENE	36,000,000 years ago	Grebes, shearwaters, petrels, gannets, boobies, storks, falcons, turkeys, parrots, pigeons, goatsuckers, swifts, Old World warblers, and sparrows first appear. Climate drying; vast forests springing up.
	EOCENE + PALEOCENE	65,000,000 years ago	Major evolution of birds. Penguins, rheas, loons, albatrosses, pelicans, ibises, flamingos, hawks, grouse, cranes, gulls, terns, auks, cuckoos, owls, kingfishers, chickadees, starlings. Modern mammals rise. North Temperate Zone tropical.
MESOZOIC	CRETACEOUS	130,000,000 years ago	Toothed birds, *Hesperornis* and *Ichthyornis*, appear and die out. Dinosaurs peak and then disappear. Early inland seas and swamps; late mountain building.
	JURASSIC	180,000,000 years ago	The first known bird *Archaeopteryx* appears. Pterosaurs, the largest dinosaurs, and small primitive mammals present. Cycads and conifers common.
	TRIASSIC	220,000,000 years ago	Possible ancestor of *Archaeopteryx*, the Pseudosuchia, present. Dinosaurs and egg-laying mammals appear. Many deserts.
PALEOZOIC	PERMIAN	270,000,000 years ago	Reptiles increase, amphibians decrease. Much glaciation in arid climate.
	CARBONIFEROUS	350,000,000 years ago	Coal Age. Many amphibians present. Reptiles appear.
	DEVONIAN	400,000,000 years ago	Fishes dominate. First amphibians and trees appear.
	SILURIAN	425,000,000 years ago	Early fishes present. First insects and land plants appear.
	ORDOVICIAN	500,000,000 years ago	Vertebrates appear. Much land under water.
	CAMBRIAN	600,000,000 years ago	Many invertebrates. Mild climate.

THE OUTER BIRD

ACTIVITIES. A good way to sharpen your birding eye when observing activity around your winter feeder is to write out descriptions of two or three species, as is done below on this page, and see if your friends can identify them from your descriptions. If your friends are not birders, try anyway, but give them a field guide to consult. Make your descriptions as correct as you can, using the correct names for the parts of a bird (see page 22). You may find yourself describing a rarity, an individual bird you can always tell apart from others of its species. For example, we once observed a Black-capped Chickadee with two white feathers in its cap. Learning to identify individual birds is difficult, which is one reason why ornithologists band birds.

THE OUTER BIRD. A friend knows you are interested in birds. He sees you in the supermarket and says, "I just saw this little bird in my garden. It had red sides, yellow on the top, and I think it had some black around the bill. What is it?" In fact there is no such bird. But, though you would need a lot more information before you could reliably identify it, your friend did see a bird. True birders might say they saw a strange bird in a tree: smaller than a House Sparrow; small sharp bill; tail, wings, and above yellowish brown; face, throat, and below yellow; cap black. This description would enable you to identify the bird: a Wilson's Warbler.

When you see an unfamiliar bird and go to experts for identification, they may not be able to help you unless you know how to describe a bird. Professional birders, experienced amateur birders, museum personnel, and ornithologists depend on information from birders to expand their knowledge of birds. Unfortunately, much information birders supply is less than useful because of inaccuracies and uncertainties. It takes an instant to make a mistake, and it may take years to correct it.

Topography of birds. Modern field guides include diagrams similar to the one we show on page 22, which labels the parts of birds useful in providing accurate descriptions. Familiarity with these terms will help you understand the descriptions of birds supplied in books and help you describe birds to others. It is good practice to use such a diagram while describing a familiar bird.

SEE IF YOU CAN IDENTIFY THIS BIRD: *It is the size of a House Sparrow, with a pinkish conical bill, black lores (the spaces between eye and bill), black streak above the eye and narrower black streak below, white crown and eye stripe (superciliary). Underparts, aural region (cheeks), sides and nape of the neck, and undertail coverts are gray. Back, shoulder, and rump are a somewhat darker gray, with brown streaks on the back. Tail is a darker, brownish gray, and wings are brownish with darker brown toward the tips of the primaries, secondaries, and other wing feathers. The bird has two whitish wing bars, and its legs are pinkish. Your field guide will help you identify this bird as a* White-crowned Sparrow.

COMINGS AND GOINGS.

East. Winter is a good time for oceanic birding off the Atlantic coast. Moving northward year-round—but most easily spotted in winter—are Audubon's and Greater shearwaters, the former sometimes wandering into the Gulf of Mexico. Of the albatrosses, only the Yellow-nosed and Black-browed have been reported in visual sightings to have reached the Atlantic coast. They may also be spotted in any season, so after an Atlantic storm go out quickly to search the coastal areas. At all times be alert for surprises. On July 14, 1976, a Greater Shearwater was seen heading upriver near Albany, New York. Bewildered and exhausted, it was captured later in Lake Champlain, near Burlington, Vermont.

Year-round ranges: • *Reports of Yellow-nosed Albatross*
➤ *Greater Shearwater*
▪■➤ *Audubon's Shearwater*

NOTES
_____

_____

_____

_____

_____

_____

_____

_____

_____

_____

_____

_____

_____

_____

_____

_____

_____

_____

_____

_____

_____

_____

In describing a bird to an expert, some birders try to say how big the bird is in inches. It is better to state that the stranger is as big as (or smaller or bigger than) a House Sparrow or an American Robin or an American Crow, since most people know the sizes of these birds. The shapes of birds also help. For example, you soon learn that a Rock Dove or Mourning Dove is chunkier than the American Robin. Incidentally, a dove is frequently misidentified as a Kestrel despite the fact that like other hawks, the Kestrel has a chunkier head. Expert birders ask themselves questions: Did the bird walk or hop on the ground? Did it have a long tail, that is, longer or shorter than its body? Was its bill as long as or longer or shorter than its head?

Beginning birders frequently forget to describe bills and feet. Illustrations here show the shapes of some bills and feet to help you make identifications. (See page 42 for wing shapes.) Learn also to note the presence or absence of wing bars, rings about the eyes, brightly colored lores, and special markings on tail or wings. When you have learned these kinds of identifying characteristics, you also will be able to recognize birds whose appearance and plumage have changed during their annual molts.

Field marks. The distinctive markings of bird plumages, noted in field guides, are known as field marks. The phrase "upper tail coverts white," for example, is a field mark of a Northern Flicker or

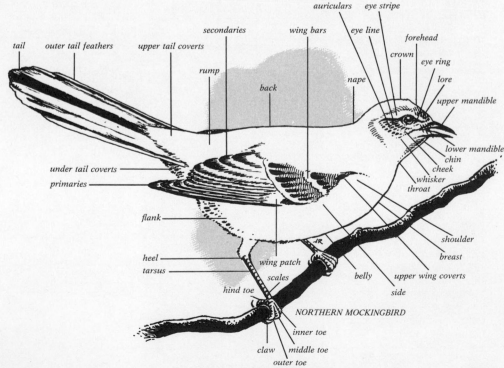

NORTHERN MOCKINGBIRD

White-rumped Sandpiper. Silhouettes of birds on the ground or in flight also are field marks. Field marks help you identify birds far away or flying by —at least to family or genus if not to species.

Shape, relative size, and other aspects of bills, legs, wings, tails, and other parts of a bird body have evolved as a result of the way the bird lives. Sharp talons and powerful legs indicate a predator; long legs, a wader; long bill, a prober of shorelines or flowers; and webbed feet, no matter how small the webbing, swimming birds. The bills, legs, and feet illustrated in this section show their great variety and indicate their functions. In the section on flight, the shapes of wings and tails are discussed in relation to functions. Since ears usually are hidden by feathers, called ear patches or auriculars, many people mistakenly assume that birds have poor hearing. True ears, hidden as they are, add no visible identification aids to birders in the field, but the so-called ears or horns of owls and other birds—they bear no relation to ears— are helpful field marks.

The legs of swimming birds usually are closer to the rear of the body than are the legs of land birds. When on land, many swimming birds walk or perch almost erect. Some, like the penguins, lie on their bellies and sled over ice and snow, using their feet as propellers. Such birds are awkward walkers.

Special feathers, such as crest plumes, decorate certain birds—some throughout the year, others only during courtship or breeding. Some birds, like the frigate birds and certain Ptarmigans and prairie chickens, have featherless sacs on the throat or sides of the throat, but these brightly colored aids to courtship are rarely visible except in breeding season, when the males inflate them like balloons. A frigate bird will often fly about with its large red sac fully inflated. (Remember, only the males sport these air sacs.) The Pelecaniformes—pelicans and their relatives—are recognizable also by their patches of bare skin at the throat, bright or dull and inflatable. Tropicbirds, frigate birds, boobies, gannets, cormorants, and anhingas all belong to this order, but only a few species have inflatable sacs.

HEAD OF CEDAR WAXWING

Crests occur in species too numerous to list, but all are shown in field guides. They may be large and prominent or so small as to be barely noticeable. Plumes are long feathers extending from heads, rumps, tails, even wings. They may be brightly colored or flagged by partial vaning at or near the tips of the feathers. Plumes make some birds easy to identify, but remember that they are not always worn throughout the year, nor are they always worn by immature birds. Crests, however, are present in adults year round except during molts. Some plumes arise from crests, as with Gambel's Quail.

Bills. Beginning birders seldom notice the shape of a bird's bill. Bills, which reflect the food birds eat, are a great aid in identification. In the drawings here, note that the bill of the cardinal is adapted for crushing heavy seeds and the bill of the crossbill for prying open the scales of pine cones. The bill of a woodpecker resembles a wood chisel. The bill of a fish-eating bird is serrated, ideal for holding on to slippery prey. The bill of a hawk is pointed and edged for rending flesh. An insect-eater uses its slender pointed bill to pry insects from tight places. A nectar feeder has a bill that excels for pumping flower nectar into its digestive tract.

BROAD-TAILED HUMMINGBIRD

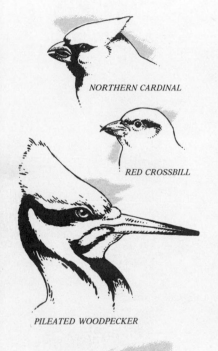

NORTHERN CARDINAL

RED CROSSBILL

PILEATED WOODPECKER

Legs, feet, and claws. These environmentally evolved appendages tell much about their owners. Feeding in deep water is more comfortable for a bird if its stomach is kept out of cold water. On the other hand, the short legs of the swifts enable them to cling close to their vertical perches. Feet sometimes are difficult to see even with binoculars, since they may be hidden beneath plumage, but they are well engineered for their work. Webbing between toes is a design for swimmers. Lobed toes, as in grebes and phalaropes, are also useful in swimming. Woodpeckers find their strong claws useful for clamping tight to the sides of trees while digging for adult insects and grubs. The feet of perching birds are so designed that when these birds clasp a perch, the weight on their inner soles serves to lock toes around a perch. In fact, such birds must exert themselves to open their toes before flying off again. Examine the other toe designs shown in the drawings to see how they are useful to birds in running, climbing, swimming, seizing prey, and other activities.

FERRUGINOUS HAWK

COMMON NIGHTHAWK

RED-BREASTED MERGANSER

24

Wings and tails. These are discussed under FLIGHT (see page 40). You will find it useful to try to determine from the silhouettes given there how various types of birds fly or go about their chores.

Eyes and ears. The eyes of birds tell something about their owners. The illustrations show that night birds generally have relatively large eyes, and those dwelling in dusky forests have eyes of medium size. Birds that inhabit brightly lit areas have rather small eyes. Almost all bird eyes are protected by a third eyelid, which flicks across the surface of the eye, cleaning out dust and other debris. This is a necessity for flying creatures. The ears of owls are as remarkable as their eyes. One ear is quite a bit larger than the other, which helps them establish the exact location of a rustling or squeaking mouse.

Shape. Differences in the external and internal anatomy of birds, although sometimes minute, provide the means of classifying them into groups and species. On page 152 we introduce you to bird classification. However, even gross features such as those we have already discussed—shape of bill, position of legs, kind of claws, shape of wings and tail, even appearance of eyes—begin to suggest overall shapes characteristic of certain groups of birds. Thus, learning silhouettes—for example, the silhouettes of ducks—will help you narrow down an identification to a species. To take another example, the posture of a bird that is perching, which depends in part on the placement of its legs in its body, will often tell you whether the bird is a hawk, pigeon, or grouse.

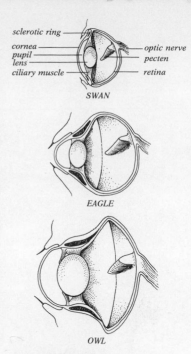

SWAN

EAGLE

OWL

VERTICAL SECTIONS THROUGH THE EYES

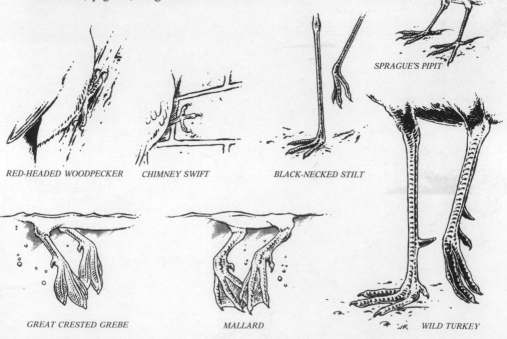

RED-HEADED WOODPECKER

CHIMNEY SWIFT

BLACK-NECKED STILT

SPRAGUE'S PIPIT

GREAT CRESTED GREBE

MALLARD

WILD TURKEY

JAN 29–FEB 4

THE
INNER BIRD

ACTIVITIES. In light snow or on a mud flat (softened, if you are in the north, by the heat of the winter sun), search for bird tracks. You may mistake them for other animal tracks. If you are lucky enough to see birds making tracks, as may be the case when you approach a flat warily or are watching birds on the strands of an ocean beach, you will have no trouble identifying them. Make a sketch, using accurate measurements, or take a photograph containing an object of known size placed next to the track. Consult Olaus J. Murie's *Field Guide to Animal Tracks* (2nd ed., 1975), which contains some bird tracks and shows how to make proper measurements.

THE INNER BIRD. No two bird species are exactly alike in anatomy, and the more distant their relation, the greater the differences between species. By systematically comparing anatomical similarities as well as differences, ornithologists can construct a family tree, which would indicate, for example, that penguins, a flightless species, probably descended from petrel-like birds known for their remarkable flying ability rather than from the flightless emus.

The basic anatomical design, however, is nearly the same for all birds, and in many respects this master design is the same as that for humans. The differences are attributable to the different ways in which humans and birds have lived over evolutionary time. For example, a bird skeleton shows the same basic bones a human possesses, altered in detail to enable the bird to fly and live its life as a bird in all other respects. Its organs and muscles are much like those of humans, but also modified. For example, in evolving toward efficient flight, the bird's digestive system has changed. To reduce weight, teeth are absent. The muscular gizzard, filled with ingested gravel, contracts to grind food into digestible and easily passed particles. The gizzard thus takes over the function of teeth and is located more centrally to improve flight stability. Another example: A bird has a larynx like that of humans, but it is simple and small and plays no part in the production of sound. The sound-maker in birds is the syrinx; located nearer the center of the body, it is yet another adaptation that helps give the bird stability in flight.

INTERNAL ANATOMY. *The inner organs of the Ruffed Grouse are similar to those of all birds.*

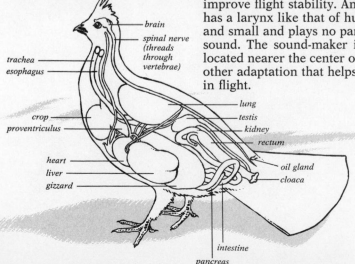

26

COMINGS AND GOINGS. Certain birds rare in most parts of the United States and Canada are nevertheless relatively common in specific regions. Local birders can usually tell you where to look for these prizes. In winter, for example, on a visit to the lower Rio Grande Valley in southern Texas, with little effort you will be able to spot the Mottled Duck, Black-bellied Whistling-Duck, Zone-tailed Hawk, and Gray Hawk. Along the Mexican border, you will easily add 50 to 60 species to your life list. If you can, plan a winter trip to the warmer regions of the southern United States.

Year-round northern limits: ▬▬ *Mottled Duck*
▬ ▬ ▬ *Black-bellied Whistling-Duck*
▬▬ *Zone-tailed Hawk*
≡≡≡ *Gray Hawk*

NOTES

Skeleton. The skeleton is the framework supporting the rest of the bird. From its design you can learn something about how a bird lives. The bones of most other animals must be strong, and since weight is not of paramount importance, they are usually heavy. Bird bones, by contrast, must be both light and strong as an adaptation for flight.

Light bones evolved in two main ways, through fusion and through hollowing. In fusion two or more bones become one, requiring less sinew to move. Compare the arm and leg bones of a human and a flying bird. In the birds, not only are bones of both structures fused, but certain bones are missing, especially in the wrist and ankle. Cutting a long wing bone lengthwise ex-

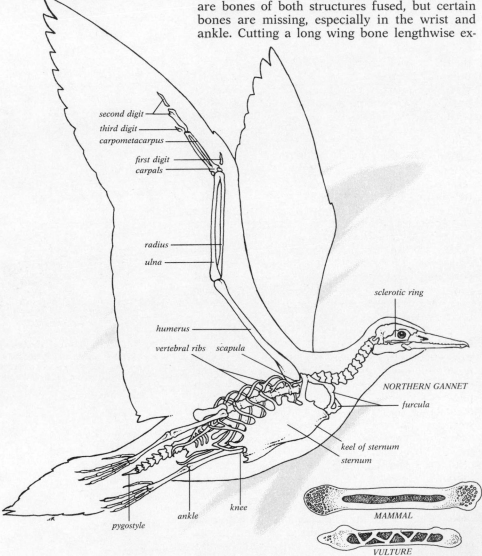

second digit
third digit
carpometacarpus
first digit
carpals
radius
ulna
sclerotic ring
humerus
vertebral ribs   scapula
NORTHERN GANNET
furcula
keel of sternum
sternum
pygostyle
ankle
knee
MAMMAL
VULTURE

LIGHT BONES. *A longitudinal section of a metacarpal bone of a mammal (above) and a vulture (below). In mammals the metacarpals are the bones between the wrist and the fingers; in birds they are the altered outer bones of the wing. The bird metacarpals are both lightened and strengthened by thinner walls and the development of struts.*

poses its reinforcing ridges, which are arranged on the inner surface of the hollow bone like struts in an airplane wing. Hollowing results in bones weighing less than solid or marrow-filled bones. Hollow bones may also be useful for air storage, but only the long bones of the wing and legs are hollow. Solid bones are found where strength is needed and weight is not an impediment to flight.

The ribs of a bird are flat and light, and the uncinate process, a flat extension to the rear of each rib, overlaps each following rib to strengthen the rib cage. Because bird necks have 13 to 25 vertebrae, they are more flexible than the necks of mammals. (Most mammals, including people and giraffes, have only seven neck vertebrae.) In falcons, pigeons, and others, two to five vertebrae of the upper back are fused, adding strength to support flight muscles. Then come several unfused vertebrae between the upper back and the lower back, or synsacrum, comprising 20 to 30 fused vertebrae that add support for leg muscles. There are a few free vertebrae between the synsacrum and the final tail bone, or pygostyle, which is a fusion of many vertebrae, as in the tail of *Archaeopteryx*. The pygostyle supports the muscles and tail feathers of modern birds. After feasting on a turkey, chicken, or duck, you might try to identify the bones and match strength with function.

The shoulder of a bird is designed to improve flight. The scapula, or shoulder bone, is much reduced, but the two clavicles are fused into a furcula—you know it as the wishbone—and a coracoid. The coracoid is a much thickened and reinforced bone joining the sternum (breastbone) and humerus and carrying the muscle power through tendons to the wings.

Muscles. Attached to the skeleton are hundreds of muscles that move feathers, legs, wings, and tail, providing power for all movement. Especially important for most birds are the muscles that furnish power for flight. The skeleton has evolved so that these large, powerful muscles are attached to the sternum, thus keeping the center of gravity near the center of the body. The power to operate limbs moves through an efficient, relatively light system of tendons and what might be called pulleys. The flight muscles, familiarly known as the white meat in turkeys and chickens, are situated on each side of the keel of the sternum. The depth of this keel indicates the size of the flight muscles. Birds with shallow keels or without keels are weak fliers or are flightless, like tinamous, kiwis, ostriches, and rheas. The keel of a hummingbird, by contrast, is proportionately quite deep. The muscles that move the legs of a bird are on the thighbone, again relatively close to the center of the body of the bird. Sinews transfer the movements to the lower legs and toes.

keel

sternum

HUMMINGBIRD

A STRONG FLYER. *Note that the keel of the sternum is deep in a hummingbird, indicating that its flight muscles are very developed for its size and that the bird is a strong flyer.*

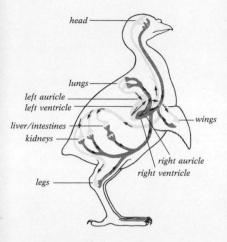

head

lungs

left auricle
left ventricle

liver/intestines
kidneys

wings

right auricle
right ventricle

legs

CIRCULATORY SYSTEM. *The blood of a bird is driven through its arteries and veins by a four-chambered heart resembling our own. Only the main blood vessels are shown: arteries in gray and veins in blue.*

Circulatory system. Like mammals but unlike most reptiles, birds have a closed circulatory system with a four-chambered heart. The system is defined as closed in that venous blood is kept separate from oxygenated arterial blood. Birds evolved a closed system because of the demand for an efficient oxygen supply for muscles during flight.

Birds are warm-blooded creatures, which means that they maintain a uniform body temperature. Most birds have a steady body temperature above 104° F. A lark or sparrow may have a temperature of about 112° F, a waxwing about 110° F, and a gull about 105° F. The high temperatures of birds are related to their flight needs. For example, their blood, which must carry a great deal of oxygen and therefore contains a large proportion of oxygen-carrying red blood cells, must circulate rapidly. The heart must beat much faster than the heart of a mammal, for example, almost 500 beats a minute in chickadees, compared with about 72 for humans. The rapidly beating heart and the intensive use of flight muscles require a high metabolic rate, aided by high body temperature. Exercise may double the metabolic rate, and the hotter the weather, the faster the heartbeat. All this is related to the need for an adequate supply of oxygen to the muscles and maintenance of body temperature.

But birds cannot let their temperatures go too high. Like humans, they must maintain a steady body temperature. Birds breathe rapidly to reduce temperature, since they have no sweat glands to produce the perspiration that in other animals evaporates and reduces temperature. A Budgerigar, for example, in air temperatures above 100° F breathes more than 300 times a minute, with bill held open, to reduce its body temperature. The air sacs in the bones and tissues of birds also help control body heat by acting as reservoirs for the excess products of respiration, such as moisture and gases that eventually are eliminated normally.

Digestive system. Another flight adjustment birds have made is development of a digestive system with the same principal organs as those in humans, but arranged so that the center of gravity is closer to the center of the body. We have already mentioned the absence of teeth and the development of the gizzard. The esophagus in humans is a simple tube from mouth to stomach, but in birds it is a compartmented structure. In most birds, the esophagus serves as a gullet that enlarges into a food storage device when food is plentiful. For food storage, chickenlike birds, doves, and parrots have evolved a crop, or strong-walled sac. This is useful for species that feed their young by regurgitation. Birds have two stomachs. The glandular proventriculus adds enzymes and other digestive juices to food in passage. The stomach also adds enzymes and other digestive juices. Birds have a liver, kidneys, and intestines, all of which function the same way as in mammals. The intestines end in a chamber called the cloaca, into which empty the products of the kidneys and intestines as well as those of the oviduct and male ducts.

Brain. Birds have relatively small brains, but that fact does not mean their nervous systems are simple. Flying is an intricate process that is controlled by a very sensitive nervous system. Except for the brains of mammals, the brains of birds are proportionately larger than those of other animals.

The brain and nervous system of a bird are well designed for its way of life, which requires the ability to make many intricate movements rapidly. Its cerebellum is the control center for some reflexes and most bird behavior, and its nerves convey such sensations as pain, touch, and sound.

Ears and hearing. Flight requires an excellent sense of balance. The ears of a bird are the center of balance as well as hearing, and no birds have external ears, which would obstruct flight. The so-called ears of owls are only decorative feathers that fold out of the way during flight.

The structure of bird ears and the means of transmitting sound to the brain are similar to those of mammals, but the acuity of hearing differs. Most birds are capable of hearing higher notes than people can hear. In fact, many small songbirds, such as the House Sparrow and canary, cannot hear low notes well. This is important for birders on field trips, who know that if talking is essential, it must be done softly. Owls, on the other hand, have extremely acute hearing, especially in the lower ranges of sound. An interesting note: The hearing of birds may be said to be more developed than that of humans, since young birds can assimilate and repeat the complex songs of their species note for note and can probably distinguish the songs of other birds. As you know, humans cannot do so with ease.

KEEN HEARING. *The Great Horned Owl has an excellent sense of hearing despite the fact that its ears are hidden beneath the feathers beside the eyes. The feathers, controlled by special muscles, rotate away from the ears, exposing the openings to the ears. One ear is larger than the other, enabling better perception of where a sound is coming from.*

operculum
(covers ear opening
when bird is
at rest)

feather tufts (not ears)

opening to ear

operculum

FEB 5–11

BULLOCK'S ORIOLE

BALTIMORE ORIOLE

VARIATION IN BIRDS

ACTIVITIES. So you think all American Robins look alike? Watch them carefully, especially during migrations. Those that nest farther north tend to be slightly larger and darker than those nesting somewhat south. Robins that breed in Newfoundland are much blacker than those that breed in the Carolinas or even in Massachusetts. In fact, ornithologists have designated the Newfoundland bird a separate subspecies, *Turdus migratorius nigrideus.* (*Nigr-* is a Latin stem meaning "black.") Other migrating birds also show differences you may be able to spot at your feeder. When you go from one part of the country to another, remember that birds of the same species sometimes show considerable variation. Where such geographic variations exist, ornithologists describe the differing populations as subspecies or races.

Differences may be environmentally controlled and not a factor in speciation, at least at the start. Birds of a species breeding in southern areas thus tend to be darker and smaller than their northern conspecifics.

BIRDS OF A FEATHER? *The migratory Horned Lark, which ranges throughout the Holarctic region, and the nonmigratory Desert Lark of Arabia are of similar size and habits. The Horned Lark needs longer, more sharply pointed wings for its long migrations. The more sedentary Desert Lark does better with shorter, broader wings.*

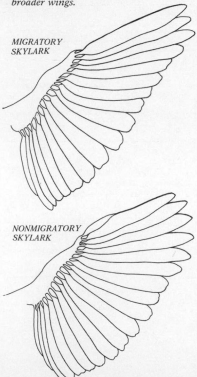

MIGRATORY SKYLARK

NONMIGRATORY SKYLARK

VARIATION IN BIRDS. Pronounced variations in color, shape, or song may be seen within members of a species, leading people to believe mistakenly that they are observing different species. For example, a birder can tell the Baltimore and Bullock's orioles apart at a glance. Yet along a wide belt where the two meet, there are intergrades with heads only partially black, so the two populations interbreed freely and therefore are subspecies of a single species.

Now consider the Common Crow and the Fish Crow, which mingle freely along our southeastern coast. Though they look much alike, the Fish Crow is smaller, has a distinctive call, and is found more often along shores than inland. The two are classified as separate species because they apparently do not interbreed.

In North America the Song Sparrow is divided into more than 30 subspecies, most separated physically from one another by geographic barriers. Most of the subspecies interbreed because they live near one another or they meet during migrations or when carried by storms into areas inhabited by other subspecies. Thus, even though the Song Sparrows of Arizona, Alaska, and New England are readily separable from one another by their markings and songs, ornithologists, consider these birds a classic example of variation within a species.

A population enclave need not be created by a geographic barrier. Among certain widespread species, for example, individuals in the northern part of the range may migrate, but not those in the south. As a result, variation can develop, with those in the south sometimes having smaller wings than those in the north.

An alert birder will notice that the Blue Jays of Florida are somewhat smaller and paler than those of the Northeast. Fox Sparrows of the West are darker and less reddish brown than Fox Sparrows of the East. Rufous-sided Towhees of the West have white spots on their backs that are lacking in the eastern species. Dark-eyed Juncos and many other species also vary from east to west.

COMINGS AND GOINGS. The Great Horned, Snowy, and Long-eared owls are now nesting or incubating eggs in parts of their breeding ranges. The Snowy Owl breeds only in the far north but in winter moves irregularly far southward. The Great Horned Owl, one of the earliest nesters in the United States and Canada, is known to incubate eggs in December, even in the northern United States. Listen for the calls and songs of the Great Horned and Long-eared owls if you wish to locate the nests of these magnificent birds. In the northeastern states, the knowledgeable birder has an additional clue to the presence of the nest of a Great Horned Owl: This owl often feeds on skunks.

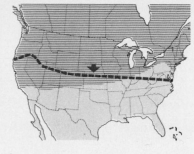

Year-round ranges: ▬▬▬*Southern limits in winter of Snowy Owl*
　　　　　　　　　　Great Horned Owl
　　　　　　　　　≡*Long-eared Owl*

NOTES

33

FEB 12–18

VISION IN BIRDS

ACTIVITIES. Long winter evenings provide opportunities to become acquainted with publications for bird watchers. One is the *Bird Watcher's Digest*, which you can subscribe to by writing to P.O. Box 110, Marietta, OH 45750. Another is *Wing Tips*, P.O. Box 226, Lansing, NY 14882. These publications are directed at the average birder. *Birding News Survey*, Avian Publications, Inc., P.O. Box 310, Elizabethtown, KY 42701, is also useful for beginning birders. Save back issues as they accumulate, because they contain dates you will want for reference.

BIRD EYES. *Though birds without turning their heads probably cannot see a full 360° at once, their eyes are placed so they can focus straight ahead (above left) and to the rear (above right). They see less clearly to the rear. The diagrams below show the lines of vision of a swallow (top) and a duck (bottom).*

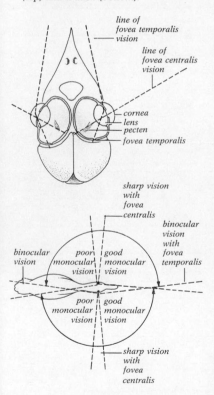

The two eyes of a bird weigh more than its brain, and the eye of an ostrich is bigger than that of any other land vertebrate.

VISION IN BIRDS. A Red-tailed Hawk probably has seven to eight times the visual acuity of a human being. A creature must have remarkable eyes to do what birds do—move rapidly, dodge through brambles and trees, land precisely on twigs and branches, see under water, hunt in the dark, and search for food on the ground from thousands of feet in the air. Though the power of sight varies from species to species, birds generally see better than humans. This is because their retinas are more densely packed with sensory cells—rods and cones—than are the retinas of other animals. Man has about 200,000 per square millimeter, the House Sparrow 400,000 or more.

Birds active at night have large eyes, which help gather light. Birds active in daytime have smaller eyes relative to body size, but the eyes may be placed so that they can simultaneously see the same distance ahead and behind. Other bird eyes are placed close together, so such birds have binocular vision all the time. And many others are placed so that the birds can see in opposite directions simultaneously but have binocular vision straight ahead.

It is believed all birds see color, possibly more different colors than humans see. Some have color preferences: Chickadees and nuthatches coming for food held in people's hands usually land first on the hands of those dressed in red.

Birds have two focal centers in each eye. The fovea centralis is used when one eye is focused on a nearby object. (What the other eye is doing is unproven, but it may be watching for possible dangers.) The fovea temporalis, situated toward the rear of the inner surface of the eye, is used for binocular vision when both eyes are focused in a forward direction. Binocular vision enables a bird to calculate distance to a perch and distance from a threat. As we said earlier, birds also have an extra eyelid, the nictitating membrane, which keeps the surface of the eye free of dust. The pecten, an organ of pigmented membrane present in each eye, is believed to be a source of nutrients for the eye.

COMINGS AND GOINGS. **East.** Among the Sea Ducks, eiders and scoters range in winter along the Atlantic and Pacific coasts of the United States and Canada, with the eiders in the east reaching a bit farther south than the others. Offshore in great flocks from November through February they bob and sway on the heaving ocean, and birders wishing to observe them must generally go to sea themselves. Sometimes, however, especially for birders who use telescopes, the flocks can be spotted from shoreline bluffs. Scoters also frequent freshwater estuaries, even the Great Lakes.

Southern limits in winter: ➤➤➤*Common Eider* ➤➤➤*King Eider* ▬▬▬*White-winged Scoter* ▬ ▬ ▬*Black Scoter* ▬ ▬ ▬*Surf Scoter*

NOTES At Green Valley, Feb 13, 1991: 70 binocs.
In arroyo-wash - House finch, curve bill th, phainopepla,
cardinal, pyrroloxia, Says phoebe, quail, hummingbird
sp?, raven, whitewing dove.

FEATHERS

ACTIVITIES. You can be witness to a molt without loss of feathers occurring right in front of your eyes. House Sparrows, Snow Buntings, longspurs, and many other species during their autumn molts grow contour feathers long enough to provide extra insulation. Since the tips of these feathers are paler and less conspicuous than the remainder of the feathers, the birds also gain extra camouflage for the winter. But now their plumage is abrading and the tip of each feather is wearing away, exposing the brighter, more contrasting colors of the plumage beneath. Watch the birds at your feeder from close up and you will also notice that your wintering American Robins become brighter as the grayish tips of their breast feathers wear off with passage of winter.

No one has counted the feathers of all bird species, but Alexander Wetmore, a famous ornithologist, once counted the feathers on some birds: hummingbird, 940; Brown Thrasher, 1960; and Plymouth Rock Chicken, 8325.

FEATHERS. A feather is beautiful, but more than that, it is a marvel of engineering. Not only is it vital for flight, but with some simple variations, the feather makes it possible for a bird to swim and dive. Its insulative quality enables birds to live in most places from pole to pole, surviving in frigid water as well as in the hottest deserts. As we pointed out in our description of *Archaeopteryx*, no other animal has feathers, and no bird exists without feathers.

Kinds of feathers. The forms that feathers take are based on their structures and functions. *Down* feathers, which are soft and pliable and lack hooked barbules, insulate the bird (all feathers have insulative value), helping to keep it warm or cool. *Vaned* feathers shape the contour of the bird in flight, furnishing a smooth surface for air to flow over the streamline of the bird. *Flight* feathers are specialized vaned feathers with rachises (shafts) that are off center to varying degrees. *Plume* feathers, another specialization, come in many shapes and sizes. *Bristle* feathers, the eyelashes of all birds and the hairlike covering of the bodies of penguins, are also specialized feathers or perhaps just the rachises of feathers.

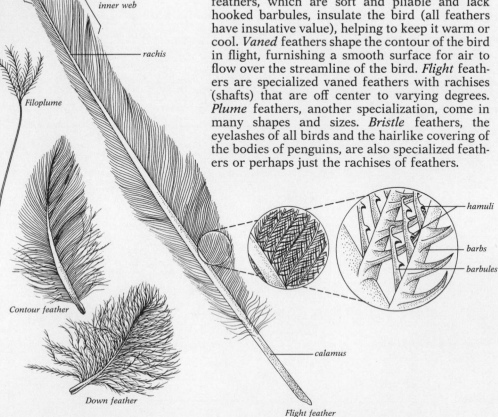

outer web
vane
inner web
rachis
Filoplume
hamuli
barbs
barbules
Contour feather
calamus
Down feather
Flight feather

COMINGS AND GOINGS. Central.

Longspurs winter on the windy grasslands of the south central United States. Birders can see, in addition to the far-ranging Lapland Longspurs, sizable flocks of Chestnut-collared, McCown's, and Smith's longspurs in their somewhat restricted winter ranges. Since longspurs breed farther north in open grassland and tundra from the north central United States to northern Canada, most American birders can watch them more easily in winter than in other seasons. Do not, however, rule out a late spring or summer trip north, since breeding longspurs then are in their brightest plumage and easier to identify.

Winter ranges: Chestnut-collared Longspur
       McCown's Longspur
       Smith's longspur

NOTES Green Valley - Patagonia Bird Refuge

Black-headed grosbeak, Bridled titmouse, yellow-rumped warbler, Flicker, Kestrel, Lazuli bunting, Black Phoebe, Bewick's wren, Song sparrow, Raven, Red-Tail Hawk - ? Woodpecker, Wilson warbler, Mourning dove, - 14

Feathers are light and surprisingly strong, contributing to the success of muscle-powered flight, which is all the more astonishing when you consider that birds fly in extreme cold and heat; in rain, snow, and wind; at very high altitudes; and, in a sense, under water.

To perform properly, feathers must be kept in good condition and replaced periodically. Cleaning is accomplished by bathing and preening, at which time the bird often separates and recloses the barbs and barbules. Due to wear, feathers must be replaced periodically in the course of molting, which takes place at least once a year in most birds. In some birds even a single worn or lost feather can be replaced. In water birds, such as ducks, geese, and swans, feathers are kept in good condition and protected by oil against water-logging. The oil is secreted by a gland at the base of the upper tail and applied to plumage with the bill.

Colorful feathers. The color of any object is light reflected from the surface of the object. A feather reflects light because of pigment scattered through its structure, because of its pearl-like surface, or because of a combination of both factors. Melanins supply browns, blacks, grays, and some pinks. Carotenoids supply yellows, reds, and oranges. Porphyrins supply reds, greens, and browns. Birds thus produce nearly all pigments except blue.

Blues, whites, and iridescence are produced structurally over a dark background by tiny pits, lines, or layers on the surface of a feather in the way that layers of oil on water reflect a variety of colors. Most greens are produced by structural blue overlying a yellow pigment. In fact, all the colors of the palette are produced by feathers.

Distribution of feathers. Hair grows more or less evenly over every part of the body of a mammal, but feathers grow in tracts, that is, in special sections of the skin, in all birds but the Ostrich, rheas,

Some birds have pigments in the oils of their preening glands at the base of the tail. The pink breast sometimes seen on Black-headed Gulls is caused by preening with such an oil.

FEATHER TRACTS. *There are no bald birds! But almost all birds are partly bald because feathers do not grow everywhere on the body of a bird. They grow from tracts that are sufficiently distributed over the body to hide bald spots as the plumage spreads out. Here are shown the dorsal tracts. On the ventral side of the body, the counterpart of the spinal tract splits into a tract on each side of the breast bone.*

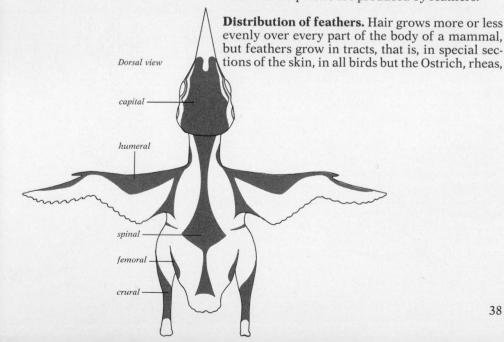

Dorsal view

capital

humeral

spinal

femoral

crural

emus, penguins, and toucans, and from the tracts spread out to cover the entire bird. They grow from follicles, starting somewhat like a bud that grows and develops. When a feather is fully grown, it loses its nutritional connection with the body and, like hair, becomes dead tissue.

Molt and feather loss. Feathers become worn and soiled and, in most species, are replaced completely once each year by the winter, or basic, plumage. Birds also undergo molts in which only part of the plumage is molted, to be replaced with alternative plumages in both winter and spring. Changes of pattern and coloration occur, moreover, without molting. An example of this is the wearing out of the colored tips of contour feathers, which are usually acquired by the basic molt, exposing the differently colored parts of the feathers beneath. For example, in the Snow Bunting, the pale brownish tips of feathers wear off during winter, and the bird becomes black and white by summer. European Starlings and American Robins exhibit less noticeable changes in plumage because of wear.

Individual feathers lost through accident may be replaced quickly, sometimes by feathers that stand out because they have the color of a previous or succeeding molt. The annual biology of the species, which is related to its need for survival, governs the periodicity of molts. So one molt may begin before the preceding one is complete.

Since flight feathers are crucial for survival, they are replaced in most species as needed in a regular order and a balanced way. For example, corresponding feathers from each wing are replaced together, and tail feathers are replaced one at a time from each side. When the flight feathers of a bird are molting, most birds become secretive because they are vulnerable due to reduced flying ability. Many geese and ducks molt all their primary feathers at one time and are unable to fly for two or three weeks after the summer breeding season ends. They stay on the water to escape from their predators by swimming and diving. Male ducks molt from their brightly colored breeding plumages into protective, dull eclipse plumage, which gives them extra protection during this dangerous period.

How fast the complete plumage is replaced is geared to the life history of a species. Species that face long migrations after their breeding seasons may replace every feather within about 35 days. The Blackcap, a European warbler that migrates to equatorial Africa, does this. Others, like the redpolls, which have very short migrations, take 50 days. Each species has its own pattern of molting, that is, the order in which it loses and regrows its feathers. It follows this pattern each year unless interrupted by sickness or starvation.

The bright red feathers in the wings of turacos (Musophagidae) of Africa, mistakenly called plantain-eaters, are soluble in weak ammonia. When acid is added, as in acid rain, the reddish color becomes fluorescent, as does yellow pigment in certain parrots.

FEATHER WEAR. *A contour feather of a Snow Bunting showing wear from October to June. As the pale brown tip wears off, the plumage of the bunting changes color from brownish in winter to black and white in summer.*

October

January

March

June

Winter

Summer

39

FLIGHT

ACTIVITIES. At dusk during winter you often can see flocks of birds heading toward their overnight stops. From high in a city building, for example, you can see radiating lines of starlings, blackbirds, cowbirds, and others flying to their favorite bivouacs. Trace the flights to the end—perhaps to the underside of a large bridge or to trees in a park—where you will find roosts filled with thousands of birds settling down for the night. In the country find a high spot from which to watch field birds flying to their overnight rest. It may be a single large tree, brush, or a group of several trees, often containing hundreds of birds. They quiet down eventually to sleep and rest.

FLIGHT. The way a bird flies helps birders make identifications. Does the bird fly in a more or less straight line while continually flapping its wings? Or does it flap its wings and then glide with wings outstretched or held closer to its body? Does it flap its wings until it gains altitude and then soar on rising currents of air? These and other types of flight not only help you identify a species but also indicate how the species spends its time, especially how it searches for food.

Mechanics of flight. Bird flight is achieved by more than the raising and lowering of outstretched wings. Such action would merely move a bird downward each time wings were raised and upward on each downbeat; the bird would go nowhere. In actuality, a bird can control each wing and each flight feather independently. On the upstroke, all the flight feathers are rotated along the axis of the shaft, as with the slats of an open venetian blind, so that the air passes easily between them. On the downstroke, the feathers are rotated to a closed position, cutting off the flow of air and forcing a step up in altitude.

VENETIAN BLIND EFFECT. A bird raises and lowers its wings by means of a pulleylike arrangement of sinews that run over smooth bone and are powered by breast muscles. The very light but strong and flexible flight feathers work on the principle of venetian blinds. They close on the downstroke and open on the upstroke. Sinews and muscles can rotate each flight feather individually or in unison.

Wing moving downward | *Wing moving upward*

BLACK-CAPPED CHICKADEE FLYING
Arrows show apparent movement of air against or through feathers.

COMINGS AND GOINGS. That large black bird you see is just a crow—or is it? In the United States and Canada, there are four species of crows and two species of ravens, all hard to tell apart. Ravens do have larger and thicker bills than crows have, but bill size is hard to see from afar. The true differentiating factors are their calls and, to some extent, their habitats. In the Rocky Mountains and westward, the Common Raven is seen more often than the American Crow. The Common Raven is rare in the East and is seen only in mountains. Look closely at the so-called crows in your area, and listen carefully. You may have more than you think.

Year-round ranges: American Crow |||||||| Northwestern Crow
   Fish Crow   Mexican Crow

NOTES

SWIFT

PIGEON

ROBIN

OWL

FALCON

WHIP-POOR-WILL

FLIGHT SILHOUETTES. *If you learn to recognize the shapes of typical birds in flight, you have a clue to their specific identities. Though swifts and falcons, for example, look superficially alike, the different shapes of their tails will identify the groups they belong to. To identify a species, find the right group in your field guides.*

LANDING AND TAKING OFF. *When settling on water, diving ducks, such as this Tufted Duck, typically slow their speed by bracing their wings upward against the air and lowering their feet into the water as brakes. They take off by pattering across the water until they gain enough speed to lift off. Puddle ducks, by contrast, can spring directly into the air.*

The tail feathers, called rectrices, are also under fine control. Spread wide, rotated to the closed position, and turned abruptly down, the rectrices function as brakes. Curved to either side, they become rudders. Rotated and spread apart, they reduce drag and so increase speed of flight.

The smaller body feathers, called contour feathers, cover nearly the entire body, adding the streamlining so dear to the hearts of aircraft designers. This explains why birds perch facing into the wind, maintaining their contour feathers unruffled. In addition, by preening these feathers, they prevent ruffling. No birds fly backward, since that would ruffle their feathers. The hummingbird does move backward through the air, but it twists its body so that the air does not disturb its contour feathers.

The silhouette of a bird in flight may tell much about its feeding and flying habits. Small birds with short, almost square wings and a long tail can dodge through thick vegetation to evade predators. Birds such as pigeons, with sharp-pointed wings and a long, broad tail, can fly swiftly and maneuver well. A long tail and short, broad wings, enable the birdhawks (Cooper's, Sharp-shinned, Goshawk) to pursue prey through dense forests. Owls use their broad wings and tails for silent nocturnal pursuit of their prey. Sea birds such as gannets dive into water for fish and then use wings and tail for power and control while submerged to pursue a catch. Penguins, of course, now use their wings only for underwater swimming.

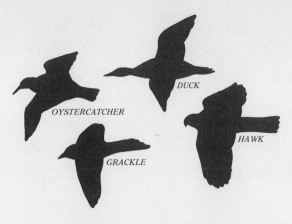

OYSTERCATCHER

DUCK

HAWK

GRACKLE

Flapping flight. The three major methods of bird flight—flapping, soaring, and gliding—are used at times by most birds. Hovering is a special kind of flapping flight in which hummingbirds outperform all other birds. Few birds flap their wings constantly in flight, but many, especially the smaller species, depend largely on flapping. Most of the others depend on flapping primarily to get airborne. Flapping requires almost constant expenditure of energy, so birds, especially small ones, that flap usually require rest periodically. In migration, flappers usually fly less than 200 miles a day and, particularly in bad weather, frequently spend a day or more resting and feeding along the way.

Hovering. Though masters at hovering, hummingbirds are not the only birds able to hover in one place. Petrels, storm-petrels, gulls, hawks, larks, blackbirds, and many others can hover, at least for short times. Hovering can be accomplished by beating the wings in circles, as hummingbirds do. Other birds hang in one spot, as if on a sky hook, by positioning their wings and tails so as to balance the forces of flight.

HOVERING *enables a flying bird to remain essentially in one spot while it searches for food. Hummingbirds are most adept at this maneuver, which makes possible efficient siphoning of nectar from flowers. A method of perching might have evolved that would have made it possible to perch on the flower as the bird sipped, but hovering on the wing enables it to fly quickly from one flower to the next, stopping at each, or to fly away from a predator with little lost time. Hawks, particularly falcons, frequently use hovering flight, as do swallows, gulls, terns, petrels, kingfishers, flycatchers, and others.*

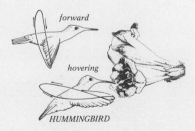

forward

hovering

HUMMINGBIRD

THERMAL SOARING. *The heat of the sun on an open area of land or on the surface of the sea causes the air to rise, creating a thermal current on which hawks and other soaring birds can rise in a circular pattern. A wind may carry this thermal current off until it separates from the source, leaving the doughnut-shaped crown drifting with the wind and carrying a few soaring birds with it. A steady wind blowing against the face of a ridge will be deflected upward, giving soaring hawks and other birds a lift.*

Soaring. Birds that depend mainly on soaring flight, for example, vultures and buteos (broad-winged hawks), are at a disadvantage in high winds, and some of them move far south to avoid the strong winds of winter. To help themselves stay aloft, soaring birds search out rising thermal currents or mountain ridges from which winds are deflected upward. On warm, sunny days birders can spot many soarers, such as anhingas, cranes, falcons, harriers, Northern Goshawks, Swainson's Hawks, Red-tailed Hawks, and Ferruginous Hawks. The sun-heated columns of air carry them to where their keen eyes can spy a meal on the ground far below.

wind drift

Gliding, or dynamic soaring. Albatrosses and petrels are expert at dynamic soaring, flying into and with the prevailing winds and depending on gravity as well as on the wind to gain energy for flight. Their long, narrow wings are wonderfully designed to carry them through the wind belts, the trade winds and westerlies. Because they need fairly strong winds for efficient gliding, only the doldrums slow them down. These are the world-encircling belts on each side of the Torrid Zone, characterized by weak and erratic winds. A cross section of the wings of these birds is similar to that of a lift-enhancing airplane wing, convex on top and slightly concave below. The albatrosses are able to soar even into the wind and are known to keep pace with and even overtake a steamship traveling at 30 knots or more. They may fall off close to the surface of the sea and drop behind, only to zoom up and begin the whole process once more. Close to home are the gulls, fully capable of dynamic soaring. You can watch their aerial artistry along the continental shores. To observe the best in dynamic soaring, however, try a voyage across the South Pacific and watch the albatrosses.

DYNAMIC SOARING. *Albatrosses, petrels, seagulls, and similar birds fly and soar into the wind, using the dynamics or forces of the wind to gain altitude. When the birds reach the desired height, they turn and coast to lower altitudes, gathering speed from gravitational pull for their next turn into the wind. They thus are able to cruise along miles of coasts, trail behind ships, or fly over long stretches of open sea without depleting their muscle power.*

Wing movement. In flapping flight, the wing tip traces a figure eight, with the lower loop rather small and the upper loop much larger and bent backward. Using moving pictures taken of various birds with tiny lights attached to the tips of their outermost wing feathers, ornithologists can see precisely how a bird moves its wings to achieve forward flight. It loops its wings upward and forward. It then moves the wing downward and backward before moving the wing in a small loop preparatory to another upward and forward looping stroke. This process is not unlike that used by a human swimmer doing the butterfly stroke. The best way to describe bird flight, then, is to say that birds swim through the air, but with wing beats so rapid that unaided human eyes can seldom follow the movements. The male Ruby-throated Hummingbird flaps its wings about 70 times a second, the House Sparrow about 13, the Rock Dove only 8. To land on water or land, birds slow their flight as they make their approach. They use their wings and tails as brakes, holding them almost vertical, and they extend their legs—light but strong shock absorbers—to seize a perch or alight on water.

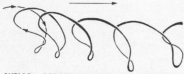

WING MOVEMENTS IN FLIGHT. *When viewed from the side while a bird is in flight, the tips of the longest flight feathers trace a figure eight. This is verified by motion pictures taken of a bird with a light fastened to one flight feather.*

THE BIRD WING. *The basic skeleton is the same as that of a human arm. Only shape, size, and function differ. The feathers, unlike hairs, are fastened firmly to the bones and are precisely controlled by muscles.*

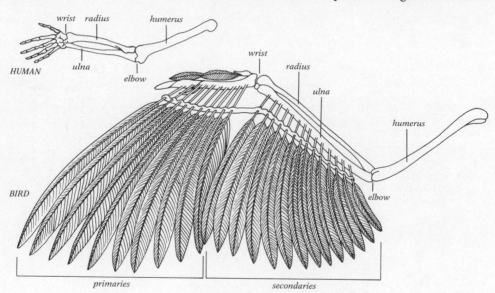

Flight feathers. The vaned flight feathers are flexible but remarkably strong, suitable for working in air and adaptable to the forces of high winds or vigorous flight. There are three major kinds of flight feathers: (1) primary and secondary wing feathers, variously modified for special roles in flight; (2) tail feathers, also modified for special functions during flight; and (3) contour feathers, with their rachises (shafts) centered from side to side, serving only a passive streamlining role in flight. The shape and position of the vanes, coloration, and size enable ornithologists to identify each flight feather by species.

46

Flight adaptations. Remarkable physiological and anatomical adaptations have enabled birds to achieve muscle-powered flight. The main adaptions—reduction of weight, increase of power-to-weight ratio, and placement of the center of weight close to the center of the body—improved the efficiency of flight by reducing energy requirements. Birds have also evolved light, long, strut-reinforced bones as well as air sacs, which also provide a reserve supply of oxygen. For example, the dry skeleton of a 25-pound Brown Pelican weighs only 24 ounces, a ratio of about 1:17, and this ratio is possibly about average for birds.

As weight was reduced, power available for flight was increased. Metabolism was speeded up by increasing body temperature and pulse rate. Insulation provided by feathers reduced energy loss through heat dissipation. Moreover, birds specialized their diet, eating high-energy concentrated foods. By contrast, other animals, such as horses and cows, subsist on such bulky foods as hay and grass. The digestive system of a bird is rapid and efficient, and it excretes uric acid as a jellylike substance rather than a urine, which

LEONARDO DA VINCI designed a flying machine, patterning it after a pigeon he dissected. It might have worked if he had had a light, powerful engine. Birds still are teaching people much about flying.

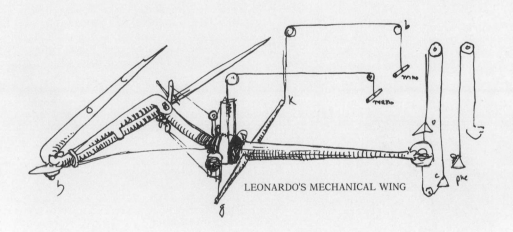

LEONARDO'S MECHANICAL WING

means that much body water is retained, and the need to drink is reduced. Water weighs a great deal, so not having to take on excessive water by drinking is an important flight adaptation. The circulatory system of a bird is adapted to provide high energy during flight, operating rapidly at high pressure. The breathing pattern of a bird, synchronized with the wing beats, is efficient.

Even the reproduction system of birds has been adapted to increase flight efficiency. For example, reproduction by means of eggs is less restrictive for a flying animal than bearing live young, especially as birth draws near.

Aeronautical engineers use many of the refinements birds developed ages ago, such as pointed and swept-back wings for speed, slotted wings for drag reduction, landing flaps for slow descent and increased landing ability, and shaped tail assemblies for directional control.

MAR 4–10

MIGRATION

ACTIVITIES. Begin listening now for the first bird songs. Do not be misled by mere calls. Your field guide will help you differentiate them. A song is the sign of the beginning of the breeding cycle. Males are staking out their territory and paying more attention to females. In your diary note the date on which you first hear the song of a species, and compare the dates from year to year. It is a good idea to record the weather as well. Is it a cold day in late winter or a warming day in early spring? There are books that give the approximate dates on which species may arrive in your region, but only you and other birders can determine the precise dates for your locality.

By training a telescope on the moon during bird migrations, you will see portions of the vast flocks of night-flying birds crossing its disk, enabling you to determine the direction of flight and estimate the size of the flocks.

FLIGHT SPEED OF BIRDS

MPH	SPECIES
26	Brown Pelican
28	Great Blue Heron
22–34	Green-backed Heron
44.3	Canada Goose
40–58	Mallard
21	Turkey Vulture
22	Red-tailed Hawk
30	Bald Eagle
62	Peregrine Falcon
22–25	American Kestrel
48	Bobwhite
60	Ring-necked Pheasant
55	Wild Turkey
28–55	Killdeer
21–36	Herring Gull
15–29	Common Tern
30±	Mourning Dove
45	Ruby-throated Hummingbird
36	Belted Kingfisher
20–25	Northern Flicker
15–23	Eastern Kingbird
23	Barn Swallow
20	Purple Martin
20	Blue Jay
19–35	Magpie
25	American Crow
20–32	American Robin
19–44	European Starling
22–28	Red-winged Blackbird
12–32	Northern Oriole
20–30	Common Grackle
18	Dark-eyed Junco
15–20	Song Sparrow
24–35	House Sparrow

RUNNING SPEED OF BIRDS

15.5	Gambel's Quail
10–20	Greater Roadrunner
(31)	(By comparison: Emu from Australia)

MIGRATION. Early humans noted that the reappearance of certain birds marked the advent of spring, and their disappearance in autumn was a sign of approaching winter. People in northern latitudes or distant parts of the world used different marker species. Those who live on the West Coast realize spring has arrived when swallows return, and easterners keep a lookout for American Robins. Eskimos, living in the far north, use the return of the Snow Bunting as a sign of spring.

By the time people began keeping written records, they had gathered considerable evidence about the dates of bird comings and goings, but they knew little else. Superstition and fantasy, not scientific information, formed the basis for explaining migrations. Lack of geographic knowledge, as well as the habit of accepting as fact all pronouncements of authorities, accounted for fantastic explanations of the sudden disappearance and reappearance of birds. That large birds, such as hawks and eagles, were strong and could fly farther than small species seemed obvious to them. Surely, then, one might also believe that small birds hitched rides on the backs of larger ones. The ancient Greeks, among others, noted that in autumn masses of swallows flew constantly over ponds and lakes. Suddenly, overnight, the swallows disappeared. Where else but into the muddy lake bottoms to spend the winter? Not even Aristotle bothered to search a lake bottom to discover whether the swallows were there. But he also never thought to count the teeth in his wife's mouth to test the belief that women had fewer teeth than men. An understanding of bird migrations had to await the age of exploration, which brought knowledge about the birds of all continents. By the 18th century, naturalists began to keep records and to correspond with naturalists in other countries.

What is migration? Migration is the seasonal movement of animals in search of food or mating partners and the eventual return of the animals to the starting place.

COMINGS AND GOINGS. Birding during winter months can be especially rewarding as well as fun. Try visiting one of the National Wildlife Refuges situated along the ocean coasts. Many of them are scenically beautiful and provide comfortable spots for watching the myriads of sea and water birds that spend winters south of their breeding grounds. Great Cormorants, for example, can be seen from Newfoundland to Florida, and the spectacular Northern Gannet from New England to Mexico. Write to the refuge you wish to visit and ask for a list of the birds than can be seen there in winter.

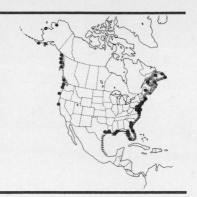

Winter ranges: ●●●●● *Coastal wildlife refuges*
 ▬ *Great Cormorant*
 ▤ *Northern Gannet*

NOTES March 7, 91-   March 8, Catalina st Pk
Florida can   Red-tail-   Redtail H. Raven
    Rbycrown k. *   Falcon
    Coopers h. *   N Flicker
    Hermit t *   Ladderback wood.p.
    Bewick's   Gila woodpecker
    Verdin   G. Towhee, Brn Towhee
    Blk. Grosbk *   Abert towhee
    Brn. Towhee   Wt C. Sparrow; chipping sp;
    Solitaire *   Lark sp.; Rufous crowned sp.
Madera   Say Phoebe, W. Flycatcher
    Bridled titm.*   Verm. Flycatcher
    Junco   Bewick's Wren
    House F   Junco; swallow
    Nuthatch   Mocking Bird
    Accorn Wood p.   Verdin, Curbill Thr.
    Magnif Hum   Gambel Q
    Broadbilled Hum.   Mn. Dove
    Grey Brst Jay   *   White wing Dove
    /119   Starling
                                     Yell Rp Warbler
                                     Gt Blue Heron
                              32? Pyraloxia   Vesper sp.
                                   House Finch Cactus Wr.

*March 9 – Madera Canyon
— at Florida Wash
U. flycatcher
+ black-chinned sparrow
at Madera —
good birding nothing new
but good look at Bewick's wren
+ found lower trail —*

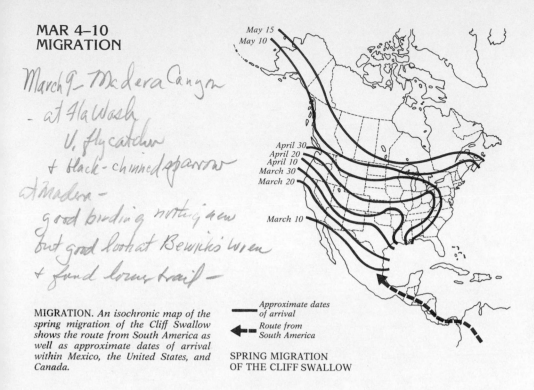

MIGRATION. *An isochronic map of the spring migration of the Cliff Swallow shows the route from South America as well as approximate dates of arrival within Mexico, the United States, and Canada.*

―――― Approximate dates of arrival

◀╸╸╸ Route from South America

SPRING MIGRATION
OF THE CLIFF SWALLOW

ALTITUDINAL MIGRATION. *The higher the latitude or altitude, the cooler the climate is apt to be, and the vegetation varies accordingly. In winter many birds need only move to lower altitudes to find the climate, food, and cover they need for survival. On slopes that face south, they need not move as far as on slopes that face north.*

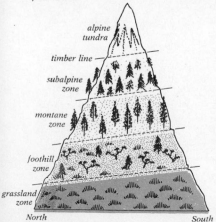

Some species of birds migrate over great distances to achieve these goals, but many do not. For example, in altitudinal migration, such species as chickadees, ptarmigan, and jays will move down the slope of a mountain range at the approach of winter to find protected and warmer areas in a valley below. This may be a journey of only a few thousand feet. Some aquatic species, such as ducks, move southward in short hops from areas where the waters are becoming frozen over to places affording open water and plenty of food. They apparently feel no urge to migrate farther south. And a few species, among them the Purple Finch, migrate only occasionally from their breeding areas to winter quarters.

Exciting birding is in store for you during migrations, when you will surely see astonishingly large flocks of birds flying overhead or congregating in woods or open fields. You will enjoy the bright breeding plumages of spring birds and be able to test your skill as a birder by identifying dull-colored birds in autumn, but the most important advantage of birding during a migration is the opportunity it affords to see new birds passing through, birds that otherwise are rare near your home.

A mighty urge. Instinct impels birds to move out and press on to distant places, and the resolve they show is astonishing. Consider *speed.* Small songbirds fly at 20 to 40 mph, ducks at 40 to 60 mph.

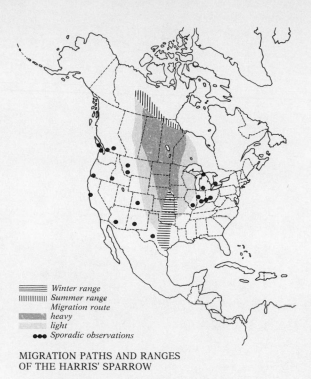

≡≡≡ Winter range
‖‖‖‖‖ Summer range
Migration route
heavy
light
●●● Sporadic observations

**MIGRATION PATHS AND RANGES
OF THE HARRIS' SPARROW**

RANGES. *This map of breeding and wintering ranges of the Harris' Sparrow shows its migration through the central part of the United States. Some of these birds may wander east or west of their more usual route. The birds that wander are referred to as* accidentals.

HOW HIGH THEY FLY

Modern radar and observations made by airline pilots have given us up-to-date, relatively reliable information on how high birds fly. The following information is taken from European sources:

**HEIGHT
(in feet)**

23,000	Small birds, perhaps dunlin or knot, migrating from Scandinavia to Great Britain, detected as radar echoes.
20,000	Godwits and curlews observed migrating south from Everest.
16,000	Migrants from Scandinavia in autumn reported occasionally.
10,000	Thrushes frequently reported departing from Scandinavia in autumn.
7,000	Kestrel and Pink-footed Geese seen by pilots over England.
6,000	Swifts can rise this high to spend the night roosting aloft; migrating lapwings reported crossing the North Sea at 3,000 to 6,000 feet.
5,000	Most songbirds migrate below this height.
4,000	Small songbirds seen flying at night from Holland to Great Britain.
3,000	Day-migrants, such as starlings and chaffinches, seen moving from Holland to Great Britain.
500	Birds spend most of their lives below this height.

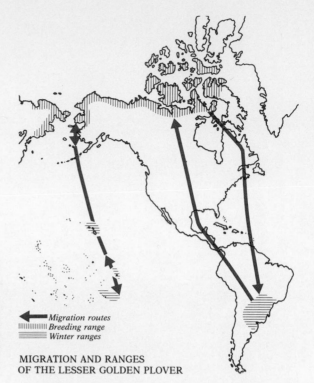

PLOVER MIGRATION. *The population of the Lesser Golden Plover breeds in western Alaska and winters in the Hawaiian Islands and islands of eastern Polynesia. Birds breeding in northern North America winter in central eastern South America. Though some individuals may stray, they are usually seen in spring migration in central North America and in the fall along the eastern coast of North America.*

← Migration routes
Breeding range
Winter ranges

MIGRATION AND RANGES
OF THE LESSER GOLDEN PLOVER

High-flying plovers and sandpipers have reached 100 mph. Many birds fly 30 to 300 miles a day, and the Peregrine Falcon has been known to cover 1350 miles in 24 hours. Consider *distance*. The Arctic Tern zigzags south over the Atlantic Ocean, flying about 11,000 miles spring and autumn. The Ruby-throated Hummingbird, weighing less than a sixth of an ounce, may fly 200 to 300 miles over water during its migration. Though most birds fly at between 1000 and 5000 feet altitude, some fly at 21,000 feet, and an airliner is reported to have flown into a snow goose at about 30,000 feet. On impact, the goose became embedded in the leading edge of the wing.

The drive to get on with the journey is overpowering. Geese breeding in the American Arctic often start their migration on foot. They cannot fly because they are still molting, but the journey must begin before winter storms end the short summer.

Is this trip necessary? The origins of migration are lost in time. Scientists have no way of determining whether fossil birds migrated—that fossils of a single species are found in many latitudes does not prove that birds migrated—and so far

"What do you mean, let's go South? This IS South!"

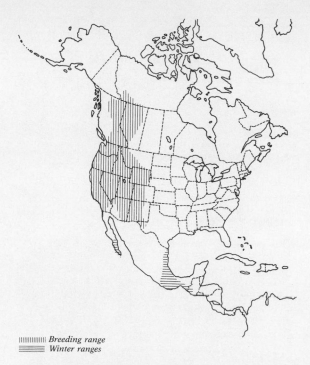

IIIIIIIIIIIII *Breeding range*
≡≡≡≡≡ *Winter ranges*

RANGES OF THE WESTERN TANAGER

RANGE OF WESTERN TANAGER. *This species breeds in the west and winters in Mexico and Guatemala. It is thought that the mountain ranges prevent them from wandering eastward during migrations.*

scientists can only speculate about why migration ever began.

The great Ice Ages, which began 600,000 years ago or more, may have started the cycle by forcing birds southward in search of food. Then, as the glaciers melted, back came the birds. But this theory does not explain annual migration unless it was triggered by seasons during the Ice Age. There are factors that belie even this hypothesis. Some birds in the Southern Hemisphere migrate southward toward the Antarctic during summer.

But surely the instinct to migrate is strong, appearing firmly rooted in innate behavior. Young birds of many species set out on the long trip without experienced adults to show them the way. It must be noted that instinct is not foolproof. Immature birds frequently become lost, with western species showing up in the East, and eastern species in the West. This is great for bird watchers, who can hope to spot new birds, but the eccentric behavior can only confound a scientist attempting to explain migration.

The availability of food and of resting places must play some part in migration if it does not explain the reason for it. Slowly drifting continents may have changed ancient pathways, thus causing the confusion as to origin and flight directions that exists today. It is no doubt comforting, at least for scientists, to know that there still remains a profound ornithological mystery awaiting solution.

MAR 11–17

SHOREBIRD MIGRATION

ACTIVITIES. Your wintering visitors have begun to move north. If you have kept daily records of sightings, you can determine the date on which you last saw a particular species. Accurate records of arrival and departure dates of species are not complete, so your notes may be valuable to ornithology one day, especially if you keep careful records year after year. Once your winter species have left, you can decide whether to keep your feeder going all through the approaching summer. Year-round birds in your area and new arrivals from the south will not need the food you put out, but it is as much fun to watch birds in summer as in winter. If you decide not to be a summer host, clean and store your feeder until autumn.

SHOREBIRD MIGRATION. In spring and in autumn along freshwater and saltwater shores, the birder can see migrating flocks of hundreds, even thousands, of shorebirds. They feed in masses on the ground or along the water's edge. They wheel in the air, showing spectacular flashes of wings and bodies. Even where bodies of water are far apart, the shores of ponds, lakes, and rivers attract shorebirds. Over 100 species of birds, mostly water birds or shorebirds, have been reported from the Bear River Refuge in northern Utah, where the Bear River enters the Great Salt Lake. In such places, birders congregate eagerly, carrying camp stools, binoculars, and telescopes to watch in comfort.

Beginning birders often believe, erroneously as it turns out, that to watch shore birds it is necessary to visit the marine coasts. In fact few North American shorebirds are restricted to marine coasts. Notwithstanding, the average American or Canadian is surprised to find sea gulls at localities hundreds of miles from the sea. The range maps in your field guides show you that some gulls, terns, and other shorebirds not only nest far inland, near freshwater lakes and marshes, but migrate great distances overland, even over extensive deserts, as long as there is sufficient food along the route.

What are shorebirds? *Shorebird* is not a precise taxonomic term, nor is *water bird* or *aquatic bird.* When referring to shorebird migration, birders mean such birds as stilts, avocets, oystercatchers, yellowlegs, godwits, curlews, sandpipers, plovers, and turnstones, which in migration move along saltwater and freshwater coasts and shores. Many of these shorebirds are found in other places even during migration. Water birds, such as ducks, geese, swans, shearwaters, petrels, storm-petrels, boobies, cormorants, auks, and skimmers, also migrate along shores and coasts or, in some cases, across open ocean.

Many shorebird species have webbing between their toes, helping them to swim when the need arises. The phalaropes, with wide lobes on their toes, are particularly adept swimmers and often are seen bobbing like corks in the water. When forced to light on lakes or oceans, most shorebirds are able to swim, feed, and take off again, but only in emergencies. Nearly all shorebirds like wetlands throughout the year, but some, especially during the breeding season, are found well away from typical shores, preferring the tiny edges of mountain rivulets and tarns. The Upland Plover is commonly seen well away from open water, on fence posts in farmers' fields.

COMINGS AND GOINGS. East.

In spring, just after the ice has melted, birders should be on the lookout at streamside. The first flying insects, usually stone flies, make their initial appearance of the season. They have reached the adult stage underwater and can now climb onto emergent stones and dead vegetation to shed their winter clothing and to take wing. Now also appears the alert Eastern Phoebe, all 5¼ inches of it, gray and white, ready to begin its regimen of insect eating. Eastern Phoebes begin their migration from the southeastern United States before March 1 and by May 1 reach the limit of their breeding territory in northern Canada.

Breeding range of Eastern Phoebe

(Could get) means I have seen it there.

NOTES "Could-get" for Madera & Florida Canyon, and Florida Wash!

Gray-breasted jay	yellow-rumped warbler
Ruby-crowned Kinglet	Red-tail
Bridled titmouse	Cooper's
Purple Finch?	Kestrel
Acorn Woodpecker	C. Raven
Ladder-backed woodpecker	Hermit thrush
Common flicker	Say's Phoebe
Magnificent hummer	Trogon!
Black-chinned hummer	Green Tailed towhee
W.b. nuthatch	Dark-eyed Junco
Painted redstart	Yellow-eyed Junco
Brown towhee	Townsend's Sol
Hepatic Tanager	Canyon Wren (heard)
Least Goldfinch	Turkey Vulture
Bewich's Wren	34
Black throated sparrow	
Vermilion Flycatcher	
Phainopepla	
Pyrrhuloxia	
Black Phoebe	

Migration patterns. Autumn migrations generally are long and leisurely, lasting in Canada and the United States from mid-July to late October. You can spot a few shorebirds as early as July when they have been unsuccessful in nesting. Usually, however, shorebirds fly in big flocks, normally made up of a single species but occasionally showing some mixing.

In spring the return trip is at about the same pace, beginning in the United States about mid-March and ending for some in Canada about mid-June. Birders can watch the parade of birds from a rocky, sandy, or muddy shore anytime during April or May, even into June. If you miss a species during one season, try the next. Shorebirds that normally travel north inland from a coast may in autumn travel south along the coast.

Shorebirds fly high over the continent, some at altitudes of about 10,000 feet. Late migrants may not leave Greenland or Alaska until September, but for the most part shorebirds in the Northern Hemisphere breed inland, nesting from mid-May to July. They winter mostly along marine coasts from southwestern Alaska and eastern Canada all the way through the West Indies to Tierra del Fuego, at the tip of South America. Over 40 species may be found wintering along our Atlantic and Pacific shores, including American Avocet, both oystercatchers, Black-necked Stilt, Piping, Snowy and Semipalmated plovers, Marbled Godwit, Long-billed Curlew, Willet, both dowitchers, turnstones, Rock Sandpiper, Sanderling, and many terns and gulls. Our shores obviously are worth braving in winter for a chance at sighting shorebirds.

Identifying shorebirds. Shorebirds have distinctive shapes, coloring, bills, and patterns of behavior. Learn first to separate sandpipers from plovers. Sandpipers have pointed bills with no swelling at or near the tip. Plovers usually have a somewhat chunkier appearance.

A birder often makes a tentative identification based on behavior. For example, unlike the sandpiper, with its rapid, pattering gait, a plover generally walks along the shore a bit more casually. Even the larger sandpipers are only slightly slower than their small, quick relatives, moving a little more deliberately as they search out larger crustaceans from the littoral, the shore zone between high and low watermarks. The smallest sandpipers, referred to as peeps, run about the beach quickly like mechanical toys in search of tiny organisms in the sand, mud, or gravel as the waves go in and out. All sandpipers take startled flight from disturbances, flying rapidly out over the water, then wheeling together to return to shore on quivering wings, perhaps only 50 to 100 feet from where they took off.

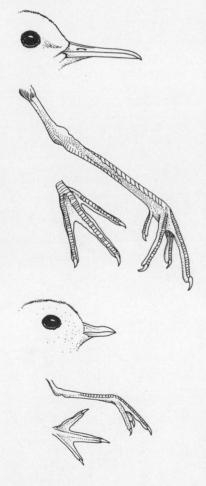

SANDPIPERS AND PLOVERS. *Learn to differentiate these two kinds of shorebirds by noting the differences in their bills, legs, and feet. The Upland Sandpiper (top) is compared here with the Semipalmated Plover.*

Oystercatchers, avocets, stilts, curlews, whimbrels, godwits, and others with very long bills or decurved bills are easily separated, not only because of their bills but also because they generally are larger and feed apart from other shorebirds. The larger shorebirds fly ponderously, even lumberingly, as befits their greater size.

A good tip for identifying shorebirds: The colors of bills, legs, and feet are nearly as important as the color of the plumage.

When birds are in autumn plumage, the differences in their field identification marks can be minute, but even though you can expect to make mistakes, you will enjoy trying to identify the different species. Visiting the shore with experienced birders is useful because they can point out obscure marks that may escape your notice.

How to find shorebirds. Consult the maps in your field guide to locate the migration pathways of shorebirds. Then locate the ponds, lakes, and larger rivers in your area that have sandbars or mud flats, and do not turn up your nose at the idea of watching from a site adjacent to a sewage disposal plant. The odor will probably not live up its billing, and birding there can be great.

Take a ride on an oceangoing fishing boat during the migration season, or join an excursion for bird watchers. You may see shearwaters, petrels, storm-petrels, and other oceanic species. These aquatic birds (see page 168) sometimes migrate close to the edges of an ocean, where you may see them from land, especially with a spotting telescope.

FLYING LONG-BILLED CURLEWS

AMERICAN OYSTERCATCHER

BLACK-NECKED STILT

AMERICAN AVOCET

PECTORAL SANDPIPER

MARBLED GODWIT

LONG-BILLED CURLEW

GREAT BLUE HERON

MAR 18–24

COURTSHIP

ACTIVITIES. Now is the time to observe rituals of bird courtship. Although many birds are still migrating, some early migrants have already mated and may have begun to nest. To become acquainted with courtship rituals, consult the books by Stokes and Stokes cited on page 201. They illustrate courtship displays of some common birds of the United States and Canada. Learn to describe as well as recognize the displays. If you are good with a pencil, try sketching them yourself. There is a chance you will observe some previously unknown courtship behavior, so watch objectively and describe fully, avoiding the temptation to interpret in human terms.

COURTSHIP. Courtship among birds has two practical outcomes. In species not exhibiting permanent pair bonding, breeding relies on seasonal affairs, so courtship brings compatible pairs together. In species in which bonds persist from year to year, courtship marks the beginning of a breeding cycle and reinforces existing bonds.

Courtship rituals also ensure to a great extent that members of a pair are of the same species, thereby reducing the chance of hybridization. For example, the Fish Crow and American Crow are very similar in appearance and have overlapping breeding seasons and ranges. Despite the opportunity for hybridization that these two factors provide, hybrids of the two species are rare because of differences in courtship rituals and calls.

Rituals. Courtship rituals may be as simple as that of the male Northern Cardinal, which offers a choice tidbit to the chosen female, or as elaborate as that of the dance of Sandhill Cranes. As spring approaches, if you have the chance, observe the activity of a male Evening Grosbeak at your feeder. The same bird that during winter may have chased females away from the food now is polite when prospective mates appear for a meal.

A ritual often is performed mainly to attract the attention of the female to sexual needs of the moment rather than to establish a lasting pair bond. Whatever the intent, the male Song Sparrow is vigorous and direct. Its ritual consists of deliberately colliding in flight with a perhaps unsuspecting female.

DANCE OF THE SANDHILL CRANES. *Just after dawn, as soon as two or three groups arrive, a curious dance commences. Several cranes raise their heads high and walk around and around. Suddenly the heads lower to the ground, and the birds become great bouncing balls. Hopping high in the air, sometimes with wings raised, they cross and recross each other's paths. The speed and wildness increase, as does the hopping over each other. The birds become a blur and the croaking becomes a noise. Occasionally the whole flock of 200 or so breaks into a short spell of crazy skipping and hopping. By nine o'clock all are tired and the flock begins to break up.*

—*Adapted from notes by Stephen S. Visher, reprinted in*
Life Histories of North American Marsh Birds *by Arthur C. Bent*

COMINGS AND GOINGS.

East. Some winter vacationers, but not birders, overlook southern Texas. In the Lower Rio Grande Valley, and nowhere else in the United States, 25 interesting bird species are sometimes seen and heard easily. Their names? Least Grebe. Jabiru. Black-bellied Whistling-Duck. Hook-billed Kite. Gray Hawk. White-tailed Hawk. Plain Chachalaca. Northern Jacana. Red-billed Pigeon. Ruddy Ground-Dove. White-tipped Dove. Common Pauraque. Buff-bellied Hummingbird. Ringed Kingfisher. Great Kiskadee. Green Jay. Brown Jay. Mexican Crow. Clay-colored Robin. Long-billed Thrasher. Tropical Parula. White-collared Seedeater. Altamira Oriole. Audubon's Oriole. Olive Sparrow.

▨ *Lower Rio Grande Valley*

NOTES
_____

_____

_____

_____

_____

_____

_____

_____

_____

_____

_____

_____

_____

_____

_____

_____

_____

_____

_____

_____

_____

_____

The Laysan and Black-footed albatrosses of Hawaii perform an elaborate courtship dance, fencing with bills raised high and producing loud clashing clatters. When the courtship succeeds, one partner tends the nest while the other goes out to sea, often for several days, before returning with food for the mate or young. On the return of the food bearer, there is another performance of the dance ritual, including the fencing. Only then is the food turned over, and soon the duties of the partners are exchanged. This ritual strengthens the pair bond and ensures proper recognition. After all, an albatross does not want to feed another's mate. An albatross bond is probably lifelong, although on the death of one member of the couple, the survivor will seek another mate.

Though some birds perform courtship rituals before they are sexually mature and sometimes form early pair bonds, they cannot breed until full maturity. The Royal Albatross reaches sexual maturity in 6 to 8 years, most eagles in about 4 to 6 years, most medium-sized birds in 2 years, and small birds in about 9 months. Regardless of size, no bird reaches sexual maturity during the year in which it is hatched, at least in temperate climes.

Pair bonding. Generally, the longer a pair bond is to last, the more complex the courtship ritual. (Notable exceptions are the birds of paradise, grouse, and pheasants.) Canada Geese, which mate for life, begin their rituals during northward migrations, and there are occasional expressions of interest during winter. Most species maintain the bond throughout the nesting period, especially when there is a second nesting in the same season. If either mate dies, the remaining bird will in most cases search for and bring back a new partner. Swans are noted for lifetime fidelity. Only rarely will the surviving member of a mated pair seek a replacement.

Both sexes often form a strong attachment to their nest site, and this nest bonding has survival value for the species. When one member of a pair fails to return to the nest, the bird remaining at the nest will seek another mate to help care for the eggs or young. This occurs even in species that form long-lasting pair bonds. Bank Swallows and House Wrens, whose pair bonds often last only for one brood at a time, offer another example of the survival value of nest bonding. While a female seeks another mate to sire a second brood, the male stays on at the nest to care for the young of the first brood.

Territory. An annual feature of courtship behavior is establishment and defense of territory. The male usually arrives first at the breeding ground. While waiting for a female to arrive, it establishes a territory and defends it against all other males

SIZES OF TERRITORIES	
SPECIES	SIZE
Laughing Gull*	3.3 sq. ft.
King Penguin*	5.4 sq. ft.
American Robin	0.3 acre
Red-winged Blackbird	0.75 acre
House Wren	1 acre
American Redstart	1 acre
Song Sparrow	1 acre
Least Flycatcher	1.5 acres
Ovenbird	2.5 acres
Black-capped Chickadee	13–17 acres
Western Meadowlark	22.5 acres
Red-tailed Hawk	35+ acres
Great Horned Owl	125 acres
Bald Eagle	630 acres
Golden Eagle	c.35 sq. mi.

*Colonial nesters

of its species. Where birds of both sexes look alike, the male even defends against females until the unmasculine behavior of the females finally dissuades the male. Defense of territory is accomplished mostly through threats, songs, and posturing. It is while setting up and defending a territory that some birds, notably Northern Cardinals, will attack their reflections in windows. It is interesting to observe that few birds, generally large species such as the White Stork of Europe, fight ferociously, even die defending territory.

In the phalaropes and some other species, there is role reversal, with the male taking over activities performed by the female in most species. In some species, including many hummingbirds, the female not only establishes a territory but also builds a nest before searching for a mate.

The size of a territory varies considerably. A Golden Eagle may defend as much as 35 square miles, a Yellow-rumped Warbler several hundred square yards, and a gull or tern nesting in a colony only the territory it can reach with its bill while incubating a clutch of eggs.

TERRITORIES. *Each pair of Song Sparrows establishes its own nesting territory along a stream, which the male defends against any trespassing Song Sparrows. These nesting areas are not the same year after year but adjust somewhat to population pressures. Complete saturation would force some pairs to seek places elsewhere. As shown by banding studies, if an adult bird returns to the same nesting territory in its second year, it will continue to return in the future if possible.*

Eighteen territories

SONG SPARROW

Twenty-one territories

61

Courtship behavior. No two bird species, even those belonging to the same genus, have identical behavioral patterns, so the variety of courtship rituals is almost infinite. An ingredient common to many courtship performances is chasing: Males chase other males away from the territory, and males chase females until the females catch them. It is fun to record such activities, noting the date and time, whether the chase is close to the ground or some distance above it, how close the birds come to one another, and other events or maneuvers. The courtship aerobatics of the hummingbirds are remarkable. A male will fly before a perched female in arcs, horizontal figure eights, vertical figure eights, circles, ovals, and other patterns.

Grouse, ptarmigan, prairie chickens, and other gallinaceous birds are truly macho. They strut, puff, boom, and drum. The Ruffed Grouse tom spreads its tail to fullest extent and struts before the hen, always keeping its tail toward the

COURTSHIP BEHAVIOR. *Lovesickness may explain the strange behavior of birds, especially in spring. The postures and actions of these birds show various rituals typical of courtship.*

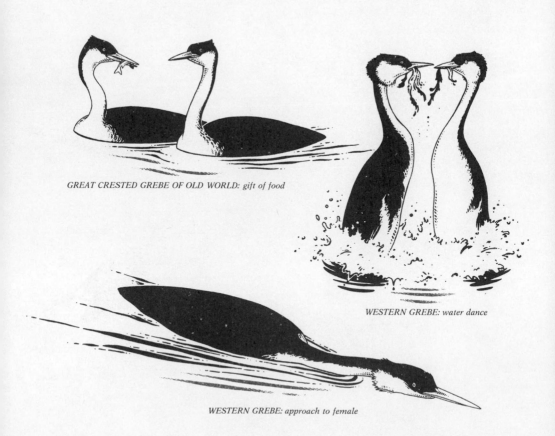

GREAT CRESTED GREBE OF OLD WORLD: gift of food

WESTERN GREBE: water dance

WESTERN GREBE: approach to female

female. Both the Greater and Lesser prairie chickens form leks, or assembly areas, in prairie clearings. Here the males strut and show off their colorful throat patches of bare skin ballooned to many times normal size. The hens do not enter the lek. They apparently are content to hover about the perimeter until they choose a mate.

Birds also indulge in courtship displays on water. The Fulvous Whistling Duck gives the impression of walking on water after mating. It treads rapidly on the surface of the water, forcing its body erect, spreading the wing that faces its mate, puffing its breast, and holding its bill downward on its breast. The Western Grebe also dances on the surface of the water but moves rapidly in a straight line, body erect, neck up, head curved down, and bill directed to the front.

There are so many different kinds of courting displays that there is much for the amateur and professional to learn. Keep notebook handy and pencils sharp.

GREATER PRAIRIE CHICKEN: display on lek

MOURNING DOVES: billing with opposite sex

KILLDEER: collar display to indicate dominance over other killdeers

SPOTTED SANDPIPER: drooping wings, ready to defend itself

KILLDEER: scraping with feet in aggression

MAR 25–31

NESTS

ACTIVITIES. Save that old sweater even though it is so worn that it cannot be patched. Unravel some of it and hang the yarn in your yard where birds will welcome it as nesting material. Stuff fragments of an old sweater in a suet rack and watch the birds move in on it. After a rainstorm, notice how robins, Barn Swallows, phoebes, and other birds gather mud from the edges of puddles. Birds that use mud for nest building must sometimes travel far for their supply. You may be able to help out. Use a hose to create a few mud puddles in your garden. You will attract many birds, especially if the weather has been dry. Based on the numbers of singing males or food-carrying adults you observe, estimate how many nests were built in your yard. In late autumn, check to see how many you missed.

Madera Canyon
March 23 — Saw the Painted
Redstart today.

NESTS. Once the leaves have fallen in autumn, you may be surprised at how many nests appear in the trees of your garden or along your favorite walk in a city park. Never suspecting they would be there, you may conclude correctly that nests are deliberately hidden from prying eyes during the nesting season. One of us, when a small boy, was challenged by his father to find all the nests in the family's backyard. The boy found several by ducking under bushes and peering up through the branches of trees. But father showed son as many more nests that he had missed. This was all the more astonishing to the boy because his father had not even gone searching—he watched as the birds flew back and forth across the yard and soon knew the locations of almost all the nests.

A word of warning: Try not to give away the location of a nest by approaching too close. A predator, whether a cat, dog, or raccoon, may follow your scent trail to a nest.

Not all birds build nests. Some lay eggs on rock or bare ground, others in nests appropriated from other species, and still others in nests where eggs of another species have already been laid. In the last case, the birds become foster parents, rearing the strange nestlings along with their own.

A tern, while incubating eggs in its ternery located back from a beach, moves pebbles and shells about until the sand under its eggs is somewhat hollow. Eventually it looks as though a nest had been built in advance for laying eggs. In fact, a nest need not be built at all, since a nest is any place where an animal places its eggs or young.

There are floating nests, nests dug in trees, nests placed on the ground, nests burrowed into the ground, nests built of mud, nests built on heaped-up soil and vegetation in shallow water, and nests placed almost anywhere except in mid-air—nests that hang from tips of branches almost achieve that gravity-defying feat. Some nests, such as those of the Bald Eagle, are used over and over, with new material added each year. Other nests, intricately designed and strongly built, may nevertheless be used only once.

NEST SIZES. The Ruby-throated Hummingbird builds a nest with inside measurements of about an inch across by an inch deep. As you might expect, some hummingbirds build the smallest nests, but other small birds build surprisingly large nests. The largest nests, which are built by eagles and storks, can be as much as five feet across by six feet deep.

COMINGS AND GOINGS. East.

A particularly beloved bird, especially among people who live in the eastern half of the United States and Canada, is the Eastern Bluebird, celebrated in song and verse. When the first insects of a new season emerge in spring, Eastern Bluebirds begin their movement north, and by the beginning of April some may already have reached their summer homes. Paradoxically, however, these birds may be seen in winter more often and in larger numbers than in spring and summer. This is because nesting pairs scatter along hedgerows and fences, but winter birds congregate in flocks of a dozen or more and are not uncommon even in the more northerly parts of their winter range.

April

March

Eastern Bluebird: ≡≡≡ Winter range
            Breeding range

NOTES "Could-get" list for Green Valley.

Turkey Vulture   Gambel Quail

Red-tailed Hawk   C. Flicker

Cooper's hawk   /24

Kestrel.

Curve-billed Thrasher

Cactus Wren

House finch

House Sparrow

Mourning Dove

White wing Dove

C. Raven

Starling

Yellow-rumped warbler

white crowned sparrow

Cardinal

Pyrrhuloxia

Phainopepla

Townsend Solitaire

Black-chinned Hummingbird

Roadrunner

Bush-tit   20

Verdin /24

GOLDEN EAGLE

OSPREY

Nest building. Many designs and types of material are used in building nests. Most birds confine themselves to what is provided by nature. This may include spider webbing, animal hair, saliva, grass, twigs, branches, mud, and down from thistles, milkweed, and other plants. Birds have even snatched hair from the heads of dozing people, and some birds may be attracted by objects made by humans. String or yarn left about the backyard by bird watchers is eagerly snatched up by some species. Bald Eagles have been known to add such exotic objects as electric light bulbs gathered from trash heaps, and a House Wren once built its nest of the rough windings cut by a metal lathe.

The design of a nest and the location chosen for it depend on the species. You can, in fact, buy guides that show you how to identify a nest not just by the material used and the inner and outer dimensions but also by height from the ground, distance along a branch from the tree trunk, and other characteristics. Some birds will nest only in certain kinds of grasses or trees. Once learned, most nests are easy to recognize. Nearly everyone, for example, can recognize the mud-and-grass nest of the American Robin, which may be placed in shrubs, on tree branches or crotches, or on ledges. The Barn Swallow nests not only in barns but also on cliffs, in caves, in culverts, and on the underpinnings of bridges. The skillfully woven, pendant nest of the Northern Oriole swings near the tip of the slender branches of an American Elm, maple, willow, birch, alder, cottonwood, eucalyptus, or similar tall, spreading tree. The western race, formerly Bullock's Oriole, builds a less pendant nest, which it frequently places in clumps of mistletoe in cottonwood or mesquite, sometimes as low as 6 feet aboveground but also as high as 50 feet.

The Black-billed Magpie builds a large, usually domed structure of thorny branches. One such arrangement was found to be 48 inches long by 40 inches wide by 48 inches deep; another nest was 7 feet deep. The base of the nest built inside such a structure is made of mud or cow dung,

LEACH'S STORM-PETREL

COMMON LOON

reinforced with vegetation, and lined with rootlets, fine grass, and hair of a cow or horse. Magpie nests may be clustered along a stream or canyon, but seldom are more than 10 found together. The nests are usually built in low thornbushes, but some may be built in tall trees, though less than 25 feet from the ground. The magpies often use their old nests as shelter during winter storms.

Hole nesters often reveal their identity by the height of the hole above ground as well as by size or shape of hole. The Hairy Woodpecker makes a round hole, the Pileated Woodpecker a large, squarish hole. The shape of the chips left on the ground below is another clue. The Pileated Woodpecker leaves squarish, oblong chips.

Most nests are designed so that rainwater will leak out, though some nests, for example, the hardened mud nest of the American Robin, will flood in heavy rain, drowning the nestlings. Adult birds often will spread their wings over the nest to help protect eggs or nestlings against the elements.

NORTHERN ORIOLE

RED-HEADED WOODPECKER

CHIMNEY SWIFT

BARN SWALLOW

ELF OWL

AMERICAN ROBIN

Family sharing. In most species, male and female cooperate in building a nest, though the male often works less effectively. In fact, the work done by the male is sometimes scorned by the more demanding female. A male House Wren, after finding a suitably located fence post or nesting box, will busily fill it with twigs and branchlets, even working at more than one nest site while awaiting arrival of the female. But it is the female that decides which nest site is right. She may empty the nest and rebuild it or add a lining if she likes her mate's work.

First-year birds may not build nests as well as more experienced birds, but they soon become master builders. The procedure can, however, be a frustrating business. It is excruciating to watch a wren or other small bird attempting to carry a long twig broadside into the entry hole of a nesting box. Or consider a bird whose nest is knocked repeatedly to the ground by a construction crew, or a bird that may have chosen a ledge too narrow to hold the completed structure. It doggedly rebuilds over and over again until a brood is raised successfully or until the drive to build fades away.

And then there is the story of an American Robin that built its nest and successfully reared its family on a ledge of a caboose that traveled from Cortland, New York, to Ithaca, New York, every morning and returned every night. Could she have had a mate at each end of the run?

APR 1–7

EGGS AND INCUBATION

ACTIVITIES. Watch for signs of nesting birds, but do not approach too close to a nesting site. Avoid disturbing nesting birds in order to prevent predators from using your presence as an indication that a nest is nearby. When a singing male is about, nesting is probably going on even though the actual nest may be some distance from where the male perches. The more secretive female is harder to spot in her own approaches to a nest, but you will often see both male and female carrying nesting material to the selected home site. Make a note of where you think the nest is, but stay away from it until autumn, when bare trees will expose it to view.

EGGS AND INCUBATION.

Many animals, for example, snakes, turtles, and amphibians, produce eggs that hatch outside the body of the mother, though certain species of snakes and amphibians give birth to live young. But no birds are born alive; all hatch from eggs. Some hatchlings, called *altricial,* are naked and helpless at hatching, requiring extended feeding and protection by their parents before they can survive on their own. Other hatchlings, called *precocial,* are covered with down at hatching. Their eyes are open and they can move about. Many are able to find their own food and scurry away from danger. Baby ducks can swim from the moment of hatching but will drown if they stay in the water too long—a parent bird drives them out of the water before their plumage becomes soaked.

These differences evolved because of the modes of living developed by remote ancestors. Species that lived in open areas, such as prairie or tundra, needed camouflage to survive. While nesting they required near invisibility, and the faster that young could scurry for safety and fend for themselves, the greater their chances for survival. In precocial birds, eggs are relatively large and take more time to develop in the female, since the young must be physically well developed at birth. Altricial young, by contrast, from hatching to past fledging are fed and protected by their parents. Nests generally are placed in hidden or secure places, and development from hatching to fledging is the most rapid of any in the world of vertebrates. This is why young altricial birds are fed so frequently.

EGG SIZES. *The smallest bird egg, that of a hummingbird, weighs about a fiftieth of an ounce. The largest, that of an Ostrich, weighs about three and a third pounds. The egg of the extinct Madagascar Elephant Bird weighed as much as 20 pounds.*

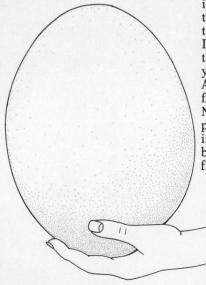

OSTRICH EGG

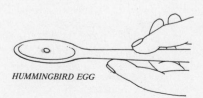

HUMMINGBIRD EGG

68

COMINGS AND GOINGS. East.

Dawn and dusk in the eastern United States and Canada—from the beginning of April in the South and the beginning of May from the Great Lakes to southern New England—are noteworthy for the sound of the Wood Thrush, a three-star attraction along with sounds of the more widespread Gray-cheeked, Hermit, and Swainson's thrushes. The song of the Hermit Thrush is thought by many to be the most beautiful bird song of all. But the thrushes are birds of deep woods and forest. The Wood Thrush, more willing to share its song with people, offers concerts in backyards and city parks, cheering early-morning and late-afternoon birders even in New York City's Central Park.

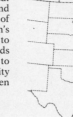

May 1

April 1

Breeding range of Wood Thrush ▬▬ Early spring limit
▬▬▬ Late spring limit

NOTES March 29 -
G.U. - Quail · Pyrrhuloxia
Curve-bill   white-wing done
Phainopepla   morning done
Starling.
Madera: Hermit thrush   shrike
Ruby-crowned Kinglet
Rufous-sided towhee
House wren   w. b. nut hatch
Sparrow - w c. ?
Cardinal   27
Dark-eyed Junco
Yellow-eyed "
Bridled Titmouse
House Finch
Pine Siskin
Scotts Oriole
Acorn Woodpecker
Magnificent hummer
Broad-billed "
Black chinned "
Verdin
Turkey Vulture

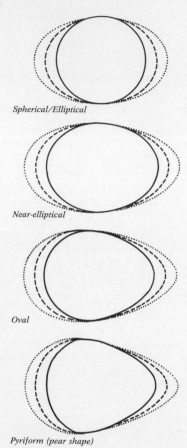

Spherical/Elliptical

Near-elliptical

Oval

Pyriform (pear shape)

BASIC EGG SHAPES. *All bird eggs can be described in terms of these basic shapes. A chicken egg, for example, is near-elliptical, but remember that eggs of even the same species can vary in shape.*

The egg. An egg provides safety for the embryo. The shell is a strong structure of calcium carbonate salts hardened by calcite crystals and strengthened by connecting protein fibers. Nevertheless, it is sufficiently porous so the developing chick can breathe and the waste gases from respiration can be released. The shell is a kind of incubator. It helps stabilize interior temperature and protects against disease, bad weather, and small animals.

Bird shells must be thick enough to support the weight of the incubating adult, so it is not surprising that an Ostrich ready to emerge may take two days to break out. If a shell is malformed or too thin, the chick has little chance of survival. In falcons, for example, DDT in food results in thin eggshells, which break easily. This can abort a nesting season, since the long incubation period of falcons precludes a second attempt in a season.

No bird lays a perfectly spherical egg, though some owls come close. The shape, texture, and color of eggs vary from species to species, so an egg often can be identified with the help of a field guide. Egg markings are classified according to patterns: wreathed (specks or dots around the larger end), capped (markings covering the larger end), overlaid (one color over another), scrawled (like scrawled writing), streaked, marbled, dotted, spotted, blotched, and splashed.

An egg forms in the oviduct of the female, through which the egg moves like an automobile on an assembly line. The process begins when the ovary discharges the ovum into the upper end of the oviduct, where it is fertilized. The ovum—we know it as the egg yolk—moves down the oviduct, where are added two membranes and the albumen, or egg white. In the uterus, at the end of the process, are added the shell and coloring. Everything added after fertilization furnishes food or protection for the developing embryo. For ducks, geese, chickens, and most small birds, the trip from ovary to nest takes 24 hours. For the Ostrich, owls, hummingbirds, and others, it takes 38 to 48 hours. For some cuckoos, it takes 62 hours. Emus and penguins require 3 days, and condors and kiwis 5 days. These assembly-line schedules govern the interval between eggs, since the oviduct can hold only one egg at a time.

All yolks are within the red-yellow part of the spectrum, some bright red, some dark maroon. During World War II, a British taste panel rated the eggs of all birds as palatable. On a scale of 1 to 10, the chicken egg was rated 8.7. Above this were placed the eggs of the Common Cassowary, Whimbrel, Wandering Albatross, Common Peafowl, and the Willow Ptarmigan—birds probably not found in your backyard. The Black Tit, a relative of our chickadees, got the lowest rating. In our view a duck egg makes excellent eating and, because of its large yolk, is more nutritious than a chicken egg.

Incubation. A human baby develops from a tiny fertilized egg in the mother's womb until it is ready to be delivered to the world for care and feeding. A chick develops inside the eggshell, growing into space formerly occupied by the bulk of the albumen. When the chick has filled the egg, it is time to leave. Growth inside the shell requires energy in the form of incubating heat. Incubating adults develop brood patches—patches of inflamed bare skin on their abdomens—that improve heat transfer from parent to egg or young.

As we have said, incubation time depends on whether a species is precocial or altricial. Yet, while egg size is not directly related to length of incubation, it may generally be said that the larger the egg, the longer the incubation. Some species begin incubating eggs only after the last egg of a clutch has been laid, so all the eggs hatch at about the same time. Other birds, including most precocial birds, begin incubating when the first egg is laid, so the adults are still incubating while the earliest hatched young scramble about the nest for food. The shortest incubation period, 10½ days, is that of a few small perching birds, cowbirds for example, and the longest period among birds in the United States is that of the Black-footed Albatross of Hawaii, 67 days. Adult birds typically incubate about 60 to 80 percent of the time, and the incubating temperature of most species is 95°F.

Not all birds incubate, but all birds provide some parental care. For example, the moundbuilders of New Guinea and Australia bury their eggs in decaying mounds of vegetation. The adults tend the mound continually, helping to regulate its internal temperature by rearranging the vegetation so as to add to or reduce the heat produced by decay and to care for the young as they emerge.

The adaptability of birds, living as they do in all parts of the world, and their continuity over time have depended on the success of the egg. Samuel Butler summed it up this way: "A hen is only an egg's way of making another egg."

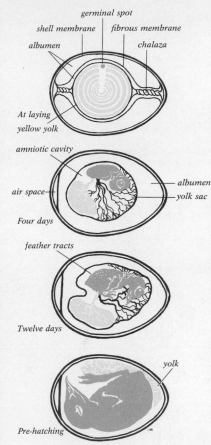

INCUBATION. *The drawings show development of a chick within an egg from laying to almost hatching. The white of the egg, or albumen, which is the basic source of food, is consumed as the chick fills the shell. The chalaza, a slight thickening of the albumen, keeps the yolk centered within the shell as the egg is moved during incubation.*

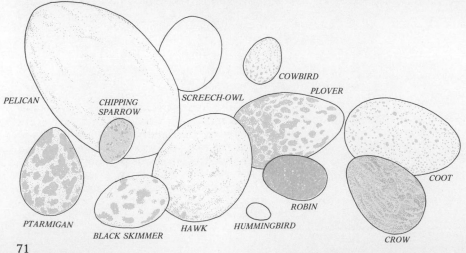

APR 8–14

"Real birds don't eat milo!" Sandy

DIET

ACTIVITIES. Most birders respect and love the entire natural world. They enjoy watching not only birds but other forms of wildlife as well. By now spring wildflowers have been blooming in many parts of the country, and birders know that the appearance of these flowers, species by species, signals that certain birds are about to arrive from the south. You will find it helpful to note in your diary the wildflowers that are in bloom in your neighborhood when the first spring migrant birds appear. But flowers are not the only harbingers of bird arrivals. The fresh growth of buds of various conifers also announces the imminent arrival of some bird species.

SOME FLESHY FRUITS
FAVORED BY BIRDS

NUMBER OF SPECIES EATING	FRUIT
114	Raspberry etc.
101	Elderberry
79	Dogwood
71	Sumac
66	Grape
64	Cherry, Plum
62	Bayberry
52	Mulberry
48	Pokeberry
42	Strawberry
39	Virginia Creeper
38	Holly
38	Greenbrier
38	Hackberry
38	Juneberry
36	Sour Gum
36	Juniper, Red Cedar
30	Currant, Gooseberry
30	Red Haw
30	Huckleberry
26	Black Haw
22	Snowberry
17	Spicebush
17	Rose
16	Buckthorn
15	Honeysuckle
15	Sassafras
14	Mountain Ash
14	Wild Sarsaparilla
13	Chokeberry
13	Buffaloberry
12	Supplejack
12	Bearberry
10	Barberry
10	Pepperberry
10	Mexican Mulberry
10	Partridgeberry

DIET. Birds do get sick—even get bird malaria —but they generally thrive. The assumption, therefore, is that their diets are balanced and include suitable vitamins. Modern zookeepers have known that captive pets often lose their bright color. One keeper fastened on diet as the possible cause and found that when flamingos were fed a more natural diet, including tiny unshelled crustaceans, they got back and kept their bright pink plumage. Caged canaries also lose natural color. When fed special foods at the start of their molt, for example, paprika mixed with olive oil and hard-boiled egg as well as food closer to what they eat in the wild, canaries soon develop a brighter yellow plumage.

The conical bills of some birds enable them to find and eat seeds quickly and easily, but ornithologists know through field observation and studies of stomach contents that seed-eating birds need more than seeds in order to thrive. Sparrows and finches will eat insects from time to time. Raptors (birds of prey) may add vegetables to their diet inadvertently while consuming herbivores, since they eat some parts of the intestinal tracts of their prey.

Animals able to eat the greatest variety of foods have the best chance of surviving the rigors of a year and, in an evolutionary sense, of thousands of years. The specialist feeder, restricting itself to a single food, dies when that food disappears as a result of drought, pestilence, or flood. The generalist feeder is the fittest. A lesson for all of us: A nestling eats whatever its parents offer— no spurning a proffered dish. Rejection of food leads to starvation and death.

CONSIDER WHAT A BIRD SPECIES EATS *before you try to feed a nestling or an injured adult. The next time a child brings a baby American Robin in from the yard, do not give it bread soaked in milk. A Robin eats worms, so give it dog food, which offers better nutrition than bread soaked in milk. A crow eats nearly everything, so offer an injured crow whatever occurs to you, say scraps of vegetables and meat from your table. The important thing is that it eat. Above all, never give a bird whiskey—spirits will kill it.*

COMINGS AND GOINGS. East. The Swallow-tailed and Mississippi kites, known for their aerobatics above the treetops, arrive early in April for nesting in southern United States. The Mississippi Kite reaches the mid-Mississippi Valley a month later. The Swallow-tailed Kite—long, forked tail and black flight feathers against stark white plumage—is unmistakable. This kite is extending its range north, so watch the records in *American Birds*. The kites remain in their breeding ranges throughout summer, but spring is so lovely that you ought to consider taking a trip south in April, from there moving north with the birds. You will find the journey memorable.

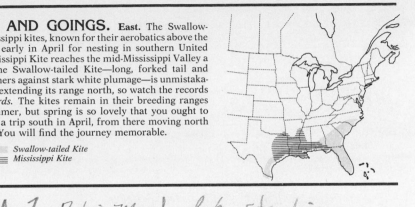

Northern limits: ▨ Swallow-tailed Kite
　　　　　　　　 ▤ Mississippi Kite

NOTES Ap.1: Robin, Meadowlark, Starling, G-Scaup, Red-head, Mallard, C. Goose, Canvasback, Godwall, Pintail, Ruddy, Shoveler, S.H. Crane, Gt Blue Heron, Yellowleg, Killdeer, Cormorant, C. Gull, Tern, H. Lark, Crow, / 23 (Pablo Lane, etc.) Coot, Ring-billed Duck   23

/ LateMar - April - Patagonia Lake

What a day! 53 birds

New: Lone-tailed hawk
　　　 Swamp sparrow
　　　　 Marsh wren
　　　　　 Black Vulture
Earlier at Arivaca:
　　　　 Cassin sparrow
Black bel-Westling Duck

BIRD BEHAVIOR

ACTIVITIES. Birds have biological clocks that govern their daily activities. Since biological clocks are affected by the sun, and the sun rises at significantly different times as the weeks pass, time activities from sunrise each day. The astronomical tables in newspapers give the precise time of sunrise and sunset every day. For birds of each species, record when they start and stop singing, when they feed at your feeder, when they are quiet, and when they perform other activities, such as preening and sunning. Be aware that special conditions sometimes trigger bird activity. For example, thrushes, mockingbirds, and other birds sing at night, especially when the moon is full.

HEAD SCRATCHING. *Each bird species scratches its head in one of two ways, either by reaching over or by reaching under its wing. A Great Black-backed Gull, for example, always reaches under its wing.*

BIRD BEHAVIOR. Ethology is the study of behavior. Its methodology is that of describing behavior precisely, including date, time, place, and pertinent information about the environment. Study of such descriptions may lead to formulation of hypotheses about the origin and reasons for a behavioral trait. Among the questions ethologists ask is whether one species, an entire family, or all birds have a given trait. They also want to identify the event causing the behavior. An apparently simple action by a bird, for example, scratching its head with its foot because of an itch caused by a parasite, is more complex than one might think. Some birds always stretch the scratching leg over the wing; others move it under. Why? No one knows. Most behavioral traits, regardless of how they originate, are beneficial to the survival of a species.

What to watch for. A bird feeder makes a fine headquarters for observing how birds respond to their environment. For instance, how do the various species respond when a dog, cat, or hawk suddenly approaches? How do they approach the feeder? Do many birds of a single species approach at one time, or does only one bird approach? Which species seems to rule the feeder? Do all other species, or only some, leave the feeder when a member of the dominant species arrives? Do they leave the area, or do they wait nearby until the kingpin leaves? Soon you will recognize threat displays, which occur when a bird of one species chases another of the same species out of its way, and you will recognize submission behavior, in which a threatened bird cowers and moves out of the way.

Make note of which species walk along the ground and which hop. Do they do so habitually? Observe that some birds are left-footed, always moving that foot first when beginning to walk. Many seed-eating birds grasp a large seed in one foot while breaking it open with the beak, so observe carefully to determine how various species at your feeder do this.

COMINGS AND GOINGS. When bird species leave their wintering areas for their breeding grounds, alert birders will be on the lookout for replacements from the south. Unless you keep careful records, however, you will not know, for example, that the Tree Sparrow you saw on your feeder on April 2 was the last wintering or migrating member of its species. In late April or early May, you will see your first tanagers, the Scarlet Tanager in the east and the Western Tanager in the West, but by then no Tree Sparrows are about. So the disappearance of Tree Sparrows is a valuable clue that new arrivals are on their way.

Southern Limit about April 1: ▬▬▬ *Tree Sparrow*
Northern Limits about May 1: ▬▬▬ *Scarlet Tanager*
▬▪▬ *Western Tanager*

NOTES

Some behavioral patterns, such as flight patterns, give clues to the identities of birds. For instance, the flight of the American Goldfinch is uniformly undulating. (Since other finches also fly in a similar fashion, be on guard to avoid a misidentification.) A flock of Pine Siskins may be separated from other finches, especially from the goldfinches with which they often fly, by a side-to-side movement that produces a sort of weaving flight. Another kind of undulating flight is shown by most woodpeckers. They flap their wings, then dart ahead a few feet with wings folded to their sides, at which time they may lose some altitude. The net effect is a rising and falling flight pattern. Patterns of hopping, walking, and flying are important to learn as a means of identifying birds as well as for increasing your knowledge of bird behavior. Keep notes about what you see, and consult your field guide for useful tips.

FLIGHT PATTERNS. *Almost instinctive recognition of flight patterns is part of jizz.*

TURKEY VULTURE

MALLARD

BARN SWALLOW

KESTREL

AMERICAN ROBIN

AMERICAN GOLDFINCH

HOUSE WREN

RUFFED GROUSE

Communicating by behavior. Nearly all bird behavior is a form of communication, helping members of a species to recognize one another and hold together in pursuit of survival.

One common form of behavior is so-called body language. In tilted perching, for example, a perching bird tilts its body to one side or the other, perhaps to show evasion of a threat. A drooping of one or both wings at the approach of an invader into the territory of a bird may indicate a threat or willingness to defend. In another form of threat, the head is thrust forward, usually with mouth open. A bill thrust upward is usually part of an attempt to dominate a mate or rival. Tail flicking is commonly a signal of possible danger. Breast feathers spread and fluffed indicate excitement, and the greater the spreading and fluffing, the greater the excitement. Wings spread while bill and head are directed upward indicate displeasure at the proximity of rivals or of other birds at the feeder. Note that when one bird lands near another, it raises its crest—even birds with no crests try to do this. Head bobbing indicates alarm, but neck stretching is usually limited to the dominant birds in a flock. These and other behavioral traits vary from species to species.

BODY LANGUAGE OF BIRDS. *The positions shown are general, but they are almost the same for every species.*

WHITE-BREASTED NUTHATCH: *wing spread (against possible competitors)*

WHITE-BREASTED NUTHATCH: *head bobbing (when faced by opposite sex)*

FIELD SPARROW: *head forward (ready to defend)*

FIELD SPARROW: *wing droop pose (aggressive, ready to defend)*

FIELD SPARROW: *crest rise ("I'm number one when near other members of my flock.")*

NORTHERN CARDINAL: *lopsided pose (part of courtship)*

NORTHERN CARDINAL: *up and down tail flick (alarm)*

YELLOW WAGTAILS: *spreading breast feathers (at boundary of territory)*

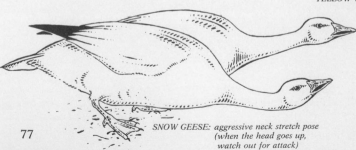

SNOW GEESE: *aggressive neck stretch pose (when the head goes up, watch out for attack)*

Variation in voice, another aspect of bird behavior, is a form of communication between mated birds or between rivals. One example of variation is a change in the rhythm of a call or the use of only part of the bird's song. While out walking, listen for voice variations of familiar birds, and try to search out the cause. Crows vary the rhythm and vigor of their caws to indicate various emotions or to communicate information to the rest of their flock. Try to classify the calls you hear. Are they mild alarm signals? Strong alarms? Or merely sounds to hold a flock together?

Each species has its repertoire of voices. You can learn to recognize the purpose behind each variation, which is probably the same for all species, just as you can learn the different calls and their variations within each species. Many birders can identify numerous species just from their calls and songs.

Keeping records. You will find it useful and enjoyable to keep a notebook for recording observations of bird behavior. The subject is so complex that you might concentrate first only on species commonly seen around your house. Set aside a section in your notebook for each species so you can find it easily. By keeping records, you will soon become an expert on certain species.

Record the date and time of day as well as temperature and other weather conditions. Some bird behavior changes in certain seasons, mostly in connection with breeding activities: establishment of territory, courtship, mating, nest building, and caring for the young. Most other forms of behavior occur throughout the year. You may watch for manifestations of aggression, fear, pleasure, and anger at any time, and it is this opportunity to observe bird behavior that provides one of the continuing joys of birding.

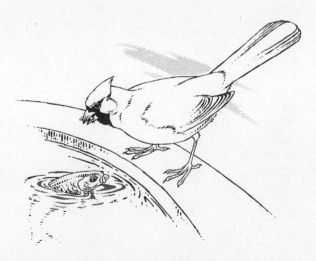

FEEDING BEHAVIOR. *This Northern Cardinal was observed in North Carolina in the act of feeding a fish. Ornithologists believe that the gaping mouth of a nestling triggers the adult bird to stuff food down the throat of the young bird. Could the gaping mouth of the fish have fooled the Northern Cardinal?*

BEHAVIOR CALENDAR

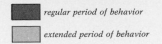
White-breasted Nuthatch

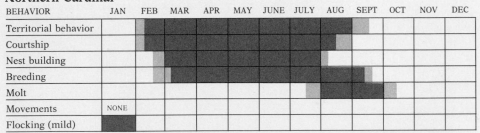

BEHAVIOR	JAN	FEB	MAR	APR	MAY	JUNE	JULY	AUG	SEPT	OCT	NOV	DEC
Territorial behavior												
Courtship												
Nest building												
Breeding												
Molt												
Movements	NONE											
Flocking	NONE											

Northern Cardinal

BEHAVIOR	JAN	FEB	MAR	APR	MAY	JUNE	JULY	AUG	SEPT	OCT	NOV	DEC
Territorial behavior												
Courtship												
Nest building												
Breeding												
Molt												
Movements	NONE											
Flocking (mild)												

Photocopy these blanks for your notebook.

BEHAVIOR	JAN	FEB	MAR	APR	MAY	JUNE	JULY	AUG	SEPT	OCT	NOV	DEC
Territorial behavior												
Courtship												
Nest building												
Breeding												
Molt												
Movements												
Flocking												

BEHAVIOR	JAN	FEB	MAR	APR	MAY	JUNE	JULY	AUG	SEPT	OCT	NOV	DEC
Territorial behavior												
Courtship												
Nest building												
Breeding												
Molt												
Movements												
Flocking												

APR 22–28

SWIMMING AND DIVING

ACTIVITIES. Search a marsh or bog for water birds, but expect to get your feet wet or muddy. Experienced birders eschew leather boots for such trips, since water and mud are the enemies of such foot gear. Instead, they wear old sneakers, long socks, and old pants or jeans. With trouser legs tucked into socks and held in place by bicycle clips, birders are ready for serious wading. They know wading is often the best means of approaching water birds, which are adept at keeping still and hiding in emergent vegetation. But ducks, rails, and herons are often easier to see if they are frightened into moving. A drifting canoe or rowboat also makes for excellent bird watching. No matter which method you use, be sure to take along plenty of insect repellent.

DIVING. *The Brown Pelican, which is found along the Atlantic, Gulf, and Pacific coasts, searches for food as it flies slowly as much as 30 feet above water. When it spots a fish, it will dive into the water, making such a splash that the observer wonders whether it has been smashed to smithereens.*

SWIMMING AND DIVING. No other class of vertebrates has adapted as successfully as birds to all three environments—air, land, and water. Most birds are remarkable flyers, some astonishingly fast runners, and a few are able swimmers, both on the surface and below water. Consider the penguin, the most aquatic of birds. It cannot fly, but it uses its wings to propel itself like a submarine, attaining underwater speeds of 20 mph. The most common adaptation of swimming birds, however, is the conversion of feet to paddles by the development of webbing between toes (see pages 24 and 25), such as you see on ducks, or of lobes on the toes, as you may see on coots and grebes. Lobes seem to work as well as webbing. The large oil glands of many water birds are another important adaptation for life on and in water. The oil spread on feathers by preening prevents waterlogging, which would otherwise make the birds too heavy for easy takeoff and flying.

Loons and grebes are examples of swimming and diving birds that can increase their specific gravity by expelling air from their plumage, lungs, and air sacs, making it easier for them to sink below the surface of the water. Other birds can increase their available supply of oxygen by quickly producing additional red blood corpuscles, which permit them to stay underwater longer. The loon can stay under for as long as 3 minutes. Longer dives have been reported, but probably erroneously, since the loon's rapid surfacing for air between dives can easily be missed.

In diving, some birds submerge directly from the surface of the water, but others plunge from heights of 100 feet or more. The Common Loon and Old Squaw Duck have been trapped in fishnets at depths of 180 to 200 feet.

UNDERWATER WALKERS. *The American Dipper, a year-round resident of Alaska, Canada, and the western United States dives into mountain streams to walk underwater along the bottom by clinging to rocks. There it feeds on the larvae of aquatic insects and other invertebrates while the air temperature may be −40°F.*

COMINGS AND GOINGS. East.

From December in the South to May in the North, the American Woodcock puts on outstanding evening performances of its courtship display. The male is puff-breasted, strutting around its mate, which remains motionless on the ground. With wings creating soft whistling sounds, the male takes to the air and circles ever higher. Suddenly the male zigzags downward, emitting soft, three-syllable musical calls. Then it volplanes steeply toward its mate. The whistling continues during the descent, ending often with a plopping sound produced when wings extend to function as air brakes. Do not miss this fascinating display. And be prepared to stay until after midnight.

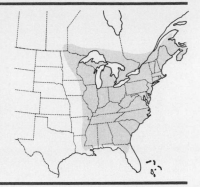

Breeding range of American Woodcock

NOTES New birds in 97: Bell's Vireo, bushtit, ash-tht Fly, whiskered screech owl; blue-tht hummingbird.

CALLS
AND SONGS

ACTIVITIES. Now is the time to pay careful attention to the calls and songs of new arrivals and year-round residents. Many male birds are singing as though they fear songs may go out of style. Try playing your records or tapes of bird songs near an open window, and watch the reactions of birds in your yard. You might also try your hand at recording calls and songs. If you have trouble remembering particular calls and songs, invent words or symbols to represent the sounds. One of us hears the Olive-sided Flycatcher singing, "Hic! Three beers." You will increase your birding fun by using your ears as well as your eyes.

BROKEN SONGS. *Though many birds issue calls all through the year, they sing only during the mating and nesting seasons. As winter days lengthen and the temperature rises, you can hear birds in your backyard begin to sing. At first you will just hear broken songs, tentative snatches of what will soon be heard. As spring advances, the songs become increasingly complete until, one fine day, the birds produce their entire, vigorous repertoire. These early-season broken songs may be a part of the behavioral communication of the species.*

SOUND BOXES. *The larynx in mammals is located near the mouth. The syrinx in birds is located near the center of the body, which is an adaptation for flight. The beautiful songs of songbirds are achieved by a complex system of syringeal muscles, producing sounds a larynx cannot duplicate.*

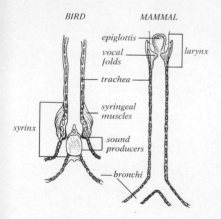

BIRD   MAMMAL

epiglottis
vocal folds   larynx
trachea
syringeal muscles
syrinx
sound producers
bronchi

CALLS AND SONGS. Birds make various types of sounds. Some, like the squawks made by Green Herons, are unpleasant to our ears. Other sounds, like the laughter of Common Loons, send primal shivers down our spines. Still others, like the murmurings and mutterings of Northern Ravens, remind us of nothing so much as politicians grumbling in a smoke-filled room. And then there are sounds like the songs of the Hermit Thrush, so liquid and musical we travel miles to find a spot where we can listen and enjoy every note. These anthropomorphic characterizations are entirely divorced from what bird calls and songs mean to birds themselves.

For the most part, ornithologists do not know in detail exactly what birds are communicating through their calls and songs. Calls appear chiefly to be forms of communication: "Hey, where is everybody?" "Where's Junior?" "Danger! Let's get out of here!" Songs, contrary to popular belief, are not intended primarily to attract females, although they also have that effect. Rather, they are challenges to other males of the same species to stay away from preempted territory.

How sounds are made. Birds have larynxes, but their calls and songs are produced in the syrinx, which is farther down the pharynx and closer to the center of the body. Songbirds (oscines) within the order of perching birds (Passeriformes) have a syrinx that can produce complex songs—as well as the relatively simple caw of the crow—but all their songs are more complex than the songs of the American Tyrant Flycatchers (suboscines). The nonsongbirds, which comprise all the other orders, have more simple syrinxes, therefore much less complex vocalizations.

The anatomic structure of the syrinx enables birds to produce notes higher on the musical scale than those humans can produce. Birds with high tremolo whistles and other very high notes may not be heard by the average human ear, and many people as they age become less capable of hearing the higher notes.

COMINGS AND GOINGS. West. About April 1

Long-billed Curlews begin to move northward from their coastal wintering ranges to their inland breeding ground. They fly in rough, compact V formations. They once bred farther into the rich prairie lands to the east and were common migrants along the Atlantic and Gulf coasts. Widespread hunting reduced their numbers in the East, but wintering birds can still be found along the southern Atlantic coast of Georgia and both Florida coasts. Long-billed Curlews nest among the tall grasses of the high plains, preferring the sloping edges of a river valley. Despite the great size of these birds, they are difficult to spot in tall grass.

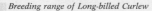
Breeding range of Long-billed Curlew

NOTES Saw (1) Townsend's solitaire in Laramie on Apr. 30th 1990 We see a migration of these in the spring - like the robins - in addition to the few over-winter presidents that we see on campus.

Trip to Pahlo - Hutton May 4 - w/ Ken Dianne Wiem

Swainson's Hawk	Greenwing Teal
Meadowlark	Cinnamon Teal
Sage Thrasher	Cal. Gull
Redwing Blackbird	Gt Blue Heron
Yellow headed Blackbird	Shoveler
Avocet	Kildeer (21)
Mallard	Tern
Canvasback	Barn Swallow
L. Scaup	Gadwall
W. Grebe	Merganser
Ring neck Duck	Horned Lark (27)
Blue wing Teal	Cormorant
Canada Goose	Raven
Coot	Pied Bill Grebe
Redhead	Common Loon /(31)
Pintail	McCown's Longspur

Sage Thrasher

Some birds make sounds in other ways. They may twang stiff feathers in their wings, snap their bills, gurgle in their throats, hiss, duel with their bills, clap or boom with their wings while on the ground or in the air, or even create what can only be called oomping sounds from their throats or esophagi. All these sounds are related to courtship, nesting rituals, feeding, alarms, threat actions, and other circumstances of the moment—in other words, they communicate something. Consider the drumming of a woodpecker, produced by its bill hammering on a resonant stump or tree limb, and the drumming of a grouse, produced while the bird clutches its perch tightly and flaps its wings vigorously, producing a sound similar to that made by flapping stiff paper or cardboard in the air. Both of these are announcements of staked-out territory.

Aids in identification. Calls and songs are distinctive and are used by birders to identify bird species. Careful listening will teach you the calls and songs of the birds in your yard and neighborhood. You might consider buying tapes or records that give calls and songs of some of the species listed in field guides. When you listen to the tapes and when you hear a new song in the field, make your own squiggles or coin your own words or expressions as a means of transcribing the sounds. Keep-

NONVOCAL SOUNDS

SPECIES	SOUND	FUNCTION
grebes, some species	bill fencing	courtship
American Bittern	swallows air and releases it, making pumping sound	perhaps territorial
waterbirds, many species	whistling noise from air through wings in flight, also foot splashing	courtship
Ruffed Grouse	drumming sound made by wings beating rapidly over breast	courtship, although heard year-round
American Woodcock	soft twittering caused by passage of air through three modified outer primaries of male in upward flight	territorial, courtship
Common Snipe	tremulous bleating sound made by air passing over wings and causing vibration of stiffened outer pair of tail feathers	territorial, courtship
most owls	bill snapping	threat, defense
Rufous and Allen's hummingbirds	wing whine or buzz; Allen's, by tail bobbing, makes ripping sound at climax of courtship flight	courtship
most woodpeckers	drumming sound made with bill on sounding boards while feeding or courting	incidental, courtship

ing records of what you hear will help you remember the calls and songs. Incidentally, when you are in the field, be sure to note where you heard the unfamiliar sound: dense forest, scrub or brush, edge of a field, or near a stream, pond, or marsh. If you hear a song coming from a tree, note how high in the tree the bird is. These records are far more useful in getting help from an expert than merely trying to imitate the song. There are, for example, so many calls that sound like *bri-git bri-git* that even an experienced birder cannot help you identify a new bird unless you are a great imitator or know the habitat in which you heard it.

Sonograms. Sonograms, graphs representing sound, appear in many modern field guides. They are more accurate than musical notations, which cannot cover all the notes and pitches sung by birds. In field guides, sonograms show only 2.5 seconds of each call or song even though many bird songs are much longer. To use sonograms best, birders should study the sonogram of a song they know well, noting the kilohertz (kHz) measurement indicating pitch, which is marked on the perpendicular line to the left. A song of high pitch will have a higher kilohertz number than a song of low pitch. With practice, birders will be able to use sonograms in the field to aid in identifying birds they cannot see.

Sharpening your ears. On your walks, take pains to listen to all the sounds of nature. Some insects, frogs, toads, and mammals make birdlike noises, but soon you will be able to distinguish them, especially when you are with an experienced naturalist. You might take a tape deck with you to record for yourself the songs you hear during your walks. It is fun to identify a bird you have not seen well by comparing your recording with one you have bought, especially when you are aware that ornithologists have not yet recorded all the variations in calls of all species.

One of our friends, who has failing sight but good hearing, lies in bed mornings with his window wide open so he can listen to the birds. Not only can he identify the common local birds, but he also recognizes the songs of newly arrived migrants. He often telephones to tell us of birds to look for when we take our morning walks. One of us had a grandmother who was stone deaf but took pleasure in watching singing birds perched outside her window. In her mind's ear, she could recall the songs by watching the movements of their beaks. At night, even the beginner can identify owls and other night birds sounding off. Mockingbirds, which often are vocally active on bright moonlit nights, will learn night sounds and then imitate them for your benefit during the day.

SONOGRAMS OF SONG OF CHIPPING SPARROW

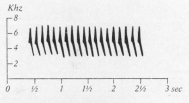

VARIETY WITHIN UNIFORMITY: *Just as the color and size of a species may vary considerably, so may its songs. A Song Sparrow in California produces a song that an eastern birder can recognize, but it is not quite the same after all. The fact is that the differences are sometimes difficult to pin down, because the components of the song are complex. For example, try recording the song of a Song Sparrow on a variable speed tape recorder and play it back at a much slower speed than you used in recording. You will hear an astonishing number of notes, overtones, and nuances, all delivered in less than 3 seconds.*

MAY 6–12

BIRD IDENTIFICATION

ACTIVITIES. Learn to use weather forecasts in planning your birding. If a high-pressure front is approaching your region, you can anticipate a great number of migrating birds in flight. This is because the good weather implied by high-pressure fronts is also good flying weather. When a low-pressure front is on its way, the approaching storm may cause birds on long trips to settle down and wait it out. The migrating birds pile up along an approaching low front, sometimes in large numbers, in order to avoid bad flying weather. Birding on days when every bush and tree seems filled with migrants is, of course, especially rewarding. You will hardly have time to identify one bird before another pops up before your eyes.

BIRD IDENTIFICATION. When you consult a field guide for the first time, do not be overwhelmed by the variety of birds it includes. As in all endeavors, it is best to go from the known to the unknown, so which birds do you know now? Probably the House Sparrow, American Robin, sea gull—you may know several species—swan, Mallard, Wild Turkey, flamingo, tern, Rock Dove (domestic pigeon), hummingbirds, swallow (Barn Swallow in particular), crow or raven, and Northern Cardinal. Perhaps you know many more.

Any new species you see can be placed somewhere among those you know with respect to size, body and wing shape, leg and bill size and shape, and habitat. Ornithologists have sorted birds by their similarities, as shown in the silhouettes here, and it will be best for you to learn these a few at a time. Begin with the birds in your own locality. Bird clubs usually publish time-saving lists of local birds. If you cannot find a list, mark your local birds in your field guide, and be sure to note the first time you see any bird on the checklist at the back of this diary. In the space for notes at the beginning of each week, you may wish to note where and under what conditions you see a new bird. As you become familiar with each bird in your yard, for example, mark it and begin to concentrate on other species while not ignoring the ones you know. For each new species, note the shape, color, size, bill length and shape, leg shape and size, wing shape and size, and prominent markings, such as wing bars or patches and head markings. Then look in your field guide.

COMMON LOON

HORNED GREBE

GREAT BLUE HERON

SANDHILL CRANE

BROWN PELICAN

RED-TAILED HAWK

GYRFALCON

TURKEY VULTURE

BALD EAGLE

COMINGS AND GOINGS. East.

When spring stretches its warmth northward, in sparse woodlands and brushy areas loud, clear notes can be heard plaintively addressed to females as yet unattached. The calls are almost certainly those of young male Northern Bobwhites. The hens may respond with an *a-loi-a-hee,* but the lonely young males probably listen in vain. Alas, most of the season's brides have already made their choices. Bobwhites have a large vocabulary, and birders who live in the country may already be able to identify calls other than the familiar *bobwhite.* Finding a covey of quails, one of the common names of bobwhites, is not easy. They are adept at finding cover to escape danger.

Year-round range of Northern Bobwhite

NOTES Hermit Thrush at feeder in Laramie on May 12.

We saw Swainson's hawks mating, both on Pablo lane on May 4, and again in outskirts of Littleton, on May 5.

I saw what may have been a Peregrine falcon between Laramie & Ft Collins on May 5.

RING-NECKED
PHEASANT

RUFFED GROUSE

WILD TURKEY

SPOTTED
SANDPIPER

SEMIPALMATED
PLOVER

LONG-TAILED JAEGER

MOURNING DOVE   ROCK DOVE

SAW-WHET OWL

BELTED KINGFISHER

LEWIS' WOODPECKER

Organization of field guides. Field guides are usually arranged in taxonomic order; that is, they begin generally with birds thought to be the most primitive on the evolutionary scale. Order by order, and family by family within orders, the pictures and descriptions of the birds parade through the pages. Most groups of birds can ususally be identified by a general silhouette, so if you learn silhouettes you will be able to find the parts of a guide containing the groups in which fall birds that are new to you.

Some of the silhouettes reflect behavioral traits. For example, some swimmers and divers float higher in the water than others—cormorants can sink low enough to swim with only their heads above the surface. You can make a preliminary identification of some aquatic species by noting in what manner and for how far the bird must move along the surface of the water before getting up enough speed to become airborne. Many birds can be identified, at least to order or family, by their flight silhouettes. (See pages 42, 43, 57, and 76.) Even though some bird families have similar silhouettes, for example, American warblers and vireos, you will soon be able to tell one from the other. Moreover, knowing about habitats and about other behavioral differences will help you place birds in their correct families despite their similar silhouettes.

Some field guides provide the sonograms of bird calls and songs, which were described earlier. Remember that songs vary not only from bird to bird but sometimes also for the same bird, and a field guide cannot illustrate all variations. Fortunately, most birds you hear more often than see—the owls are a good example—have loud and often distinctive voices. Since some of these birds are nocturnal, birders may have difficulty attaching the sound to the right bird. In fact, the sound may not come from a bird at all. For this reason, not all calls and songs of even common night birds have been catalogued properly, and songs you record may have to be identified by experts. Some confusion also exists with daytime birds. As yet there has not been proper identification of all the noises made in dense marsh vegetation by unseen rails and other creatures.

When you have placed an unknown species in its proper category—let's say you have identified it as a warbler—you may go through the pictures in the field guide and still not identify the species. It is time to read the field guide, a practice beginning birders may neglect. There is not space enough in a guide to illustrate the plumage variations of every species. The authors of field guides therefore provide descriptions giving full information. Remember that the date on which you sight a bird may signal that you have seen an autumn migrant or even an immature bird, which is not illustrated but may be described. Another important point to keep in mind is that the coloration shown in the guide may not match the actual color phase of a bird going through its molt.

Field marks. Field marks, which we also discussed on pages 22–23, are spots, patches, bars, and other color markings, including black and white, that differentiate a species. Field marks may also include behavioral traits that enable a birder to identify a species. Field guides describe or otherwise indicate telltale markings and habits. Some are easy to see, but others are not.

Throughout the year, females of many species do not have prominent field marks. Even males in other than breeding plumages may present difficulties. Though the guides illustrate the females, you may find that they provide little help on how to differentiate females in the field. They may suggest that you identify females by the males accompanying them. Having several guides with you on a trip may be a help. When possible during our own field trips, we carry three or more of the most recent and popular guides and may keep a more detailed reference work in the car.

You may find it helpful to write your own field marks for females and juveniles on the pictures. Be careful. Test your field marks in the field or in a museum that exhibits a bird collection. For example, many female warblers have nearly oval white patches on the underside of their tails, but of these only the female Palm Warblers have yellow undertail coverts. You may also find it useful to record in your guide any identifying habits you observe.

Some breeders become so familiar with certain groups or species of birds that they do not immediately recall the field marks or behavioral patterns that enabled them to identify the birds. This type of recognition is known as jizz. Jizz is not unlike the ability to identify friends at a great distance without being able to say how you do so.

By watching birds in the field and at your feeder, you will develop some jizz for them. But remember that birds are beautiful, and even if you have developed your own jizz, birds deserve more than a glance. Even the most common bird is always interesting, and the point of bird watching is to have fun. Being the first or the quickest to identify a bird, even a particular favorite, is not as important as increasing your fun by learning to identify more and more birds through careful observation.

GRAY FLYCATCHER

BARN SWALLOW

AMERICAN CROW

BLUE JAY

TUFTED TITMOUSE

HOUSE WREN

WHITE-BREASTED NUTHATCH

CRISSAL THRASHER   HERMIT THRUSH

SOLITARY VIREO

PROTHONOTARY WARBLER

SCARLET TANAGER

EVENING GROSBEAK

HOUSE FINCH

RED-WINGED BLACKBIRD

Confusing species. Some species are often confused by birders. You should pay careful attention to the following birds. Do not hesitate to consult birding friends, especially if you see any of the following species out of range or season. The birds are listed in field-guide order:

SPECIES EASILY CONFUSED

loons	Yellow-billed Loon and Common Loon
shearwaters	Sooty Shearwater and Short-tailed Shearwater Audubon's Shearwater and Manx Shearwater
storm-petrels	Leach's Storm-Petrel and Wilson's Storm-Petrel
tropicbirds	Red-billed Tropicbird and White-tailed Tropicbird
geese	Snow Goose and Ross's Goose
ducks	American Black Duck and female Mallard
scaups	Greater Scaup and Lesser Scaup
vultures	Turkey Vulture and Black Vulture
hawks	Cooper's Hawk and Sharp-shinned Hawk
coot	American Coot and Pied-billed Grebe
plovers	Black-bellied Plover and Lesser Golden Plover in winter Piping Plover and Snowy Plover
yellowlegs	Lesser Yellowlegs and Greater Yellowlegs
sandpipers	Common Sandpiper and Spotted Sandpiper in winter; sandpipers, including small peeps, are difficult to identify except under ideal conditions
dowitchers	Long-billed Dowitcher and Short-billed Dowitcher
jaegers	Parasitic Jaeger, Pomarine Jaeger, and Long-tailed Jaeger (especially when molting)
terns	Arctic Tern, Common Tern, and Roseate Tern
gulls	Glaucous Gull and Glaucous-winged Herring Gull, Thayer's Gull, California Gull, and Ring-billed Gull immatures of Laughing Gull and Franklin's Gull
murres	Common Murre and Thick-billed Murre
doves	Common Ground Dove, Inca Dove, and White-tipped Dove
owls	Great Horned Owl and Long-eared Owl Barred Owl and Great Gray Owl Boreal Owl and Northern Saw-whet Owl Northern Pygmy Owl and Ferruginous Pygmy Owl
whip-poor-will	Whip-poor-will and Common Poorwill
nighthawks	Common Nighthawk and Lesser Nighthawk
swifts	Black Swift, Chimney Swift, and Vaux's Swift
hummingbirds	(especially females) Ruby-throated Hummingbird, Broad-tailed Hummingbird, and Anna's Hummingbird Black-chinned Hummingbird and Costa's Hummingbird Rufous Hummingbird and Allen's Hummingbird
woodpeckers	Nuttall's Woodpecker and Ladder-backed Woodpecker Downy Woodpecker and Hairy Woodpecker
kingbirds	Western Kingbird and Cassin's Kingbird Tropical Kingbird and Couch's Kingbird

CONFUSING BIRDS. *Hairy (left) and Downy (right) woodpeckers, showing differences in size, length of bill, and black spots on outer tail feathers of the Downy.*

flycatchers	Great Crested Flycatcher, Brown-crested Flycatcher, and Ash-throated Flycatcher Acadian Flycatcher, Willow Flycatcher, Alder Flycatcher, and Least Flycatcher Hammond's Flycatcher and Dusky Flycatcher
wood pewees	Western Wood Pewee, Eastern Wood Pewee, and Greater Wood Pewee
swallows	Violet-green Swallow and Tree Swallow Bank Swallow and Northern Rough-winged Swallow
jays	Gray-breasted Jay and Pinyon Jay
ravens	Common Raven, Chihuahuan Raven, American Crow, Fish Crow, and Northwestern Crow
chickadees	Black-capped Chickadee, Carolina Chickadee, and Mexican Chickadee
titmice	Tufted Titmouse and Plain Titmouse
nuthatches	Brown-headed Nuthatch and Pygmy Nuthatch
wrens	House Wren and Winter Wren
thrashers	Brown Thrasher and Long-billed Thrasher
thrushes	Swainson's Thrush and Gray-cheeked Thrush
gnatcatchers	Black-capped Gnatcatcher and Black-tailed Gnatcatcher
pipits	Water Pipit and Sprague's Pipit
shrikes	Northern Shrike and Loggerhead Shrike
warblers	Be careful with all species in autumn migration; Virginia's Warbler and Colima Warbler Yellow-throated Warbler and Grace's Warbler McGillvray's Warbler, Mourning Warbler, and Connecticut Warbler Northern Waterthrush and Louisiana Waterthrush (which are warblers)
meadowlarks	Eastern Meadowlark and Western Meadowlark
blackbirds	Rusty Blackbird and Brewer's Blackbird
grackles	Boat-tailed Grackle and Great-tailed Grackle
cowbirds	Brown-headed Cowbird and Bronzed Cowbird
tanagers	Summer Tanager and Hepatic Tanager
grosbeaks	Blue Grosbeak and Indigo Bunting
finches	Purple Finch, Cassin's Finch, and House Finch
redpolls	Hoary Redpoll and Common Redpoll
sparrows	Sharp-tailed Sparrow and Seaside Sparrow Black-throated Sparrow and Sage Sparrow Cassin's Sparrow, Botteri's Sparrow, and Bachman's Sparrow Tree Sparrow and Chipping Sparrow Clay-colored Sparrow and Brewer's Sparrow

MAY 13–19

BREEDING BIRD SURVEYS

ACTIVITIES. A map of your favorite birding spots drawn to scale, such as 1 inch = 1 foot, is a help in birding. The map should show trails, streams, ponds, buildings, and the like. In suburban areas a real estate agent may provide such maps, and you can have them enlarged if necessary. By using the triangulation method with the map, you may be able to locate a singing male bird and then its nest. Hold the map so that the trail you are on is parallel with the same trail on the map. Place a ruler on the map in the direction of the singing bird and draw a line on the map from your position toward where you hear the bird singing. Walk about a hundred yards farther along the trail and repeat. Where the lines intersect will be about where the singer was located.

When are birds classified as breeding? On your walks, especially in May and June, you will see many birds that appear to be breeding. You may wish to list them as possibly, probably, or certainly breeding. A species may be classified as possibly breeding if the male is observed singing in the same place every day for a week or more, if the male performs courtship displays in front of a female, or if either sex carries nesting material to a nesting place. It is probably breeding if the birds are seen carrying food for young or if actual breeding activity is seen. It is certainly breeding if the nest, eggs, and young are seen. The ultimate proof comes when fledged young are seen at the nest to which birds have previously carried food.

BREEDING BIRD SURVEYS. Birders hope every state soon will complete a breeding survey, reporting the status of all its species. Which are increasing, which decreasing? Which have recently moved into the state? Which are endangered or threatened? Surveys provide accurate data about such important information as breeding schedules, locations of nests, and trees or shrubs favored by different species. It will take years for all the information from all states to be computerized and analyzed.

Ornithologists want birders to check certain areas frequently, especially those from which species are missing and those in which rare or first-time species are reported. Breeding atlases and other kinds of surveys and censuses are beginning to show that irreversible damage has significantly reduced the populations of some of our birds.

An atlas containing a census of breeding birds provides accurate and detailed information, requiring fieldwork over a large area and repeated trips by expert birders looking for species that may have been missed. But even beginners can assist in atlas fieldwork by reporting all nests they discover to their local bird club, which will pass the report on to the census committee.

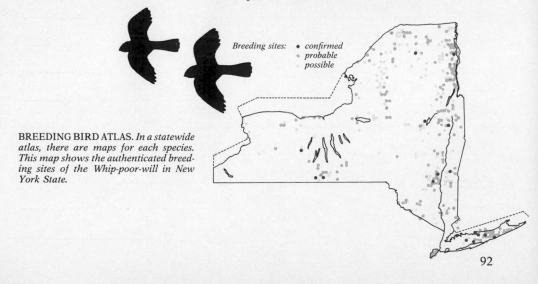

Breeding sites: ● confirmed
        ● probable
        possible

BREEDING BIRD ATLAS. *In a statewide atlas, there are maps for each species. This map shows the authenticated breeding sites of the Whip-poor-will in New York State.*

COMINGS AND GOINGS. West. A well-named

bird is the Sage Grouse, for it is among the thickets of sage that the largest populations of Sage Grouse are found, and there it is that the males form their leks and conduct their mating rituals. You will find the rituals interesting to watch. Ask members of local bird clubs for advice on how to locate a lek (see page 63). When you find a lek, you must make an effort to be on the spot between 3 and 4 A.M. to observe the arrival of the macho males, who begin to strut and inflate their throat sacs. The hens, who will mate with the winners, cluster along the perimeter of the arena, an area as large as four or five acres. By 8:30 or 9 A.M. the birds are gone from the lek.

Year-round range of Sage Grouse

NOTES

MAY 20–26

SPRING CENSUS

ACTIVITIES. Many birders will be taking part in a spring bird census during this week. If you cannot participate in a club's census, set out on your own on the agreed date, preferably with a friend who can help verify your observations. If you happen to be traveling in the United States or Canada, even in a foreign country, make the count and report your findings to your local club or to *American Birds* on your return. Your sightings will not be added to your club's report, but you will have had the experience of participating in a count. By the way, if you find a rare bird far from its home, report your observation to the nearest bird club or to the editor of *American Birds*.

Join the effort. Most bird clubs welcome all birders to their count days. There must be two or more birders on each team, because reports by only one person are not acceptable by records committees. If you chance to be out alone, report all birds you see as quickly as possible so that any rarities can be checked by expert birders. You should attend a meeting of the club prior to the census to learn the rules and arrange to join a team. Members can tell you where there is good birding in your area. Bird clubs, besides keeping monthly records of birds their members see, store the records of censuses made in previous years. These records help alert you to birds you can expect to find.

SPRING CENSUS. Bird clubs in the United States and Canada, as well as in other nations, have established the practice of taking an annual census of wild birds during spring, when the largest number of species can be anticipated in any locality. It was called the Century Run when the aim was to report at least 100 species. Now the aim is to count every species no matter how few or how many in number, and many clubs also try to estimate the number of birds seen of all species.

Count days usually occur in May, early in the month in the South and late in the month in the North. In parts of Canada and Alaska the count may take place in early June. Counts last through a 24-hour period from midnight to midnight. Birders organize teams, each team covering one segment of the total area covered by the club. Some birders who equip themselves with sleeping bags to count night birds skip the daylight hours, but the truly hardy count throughout the 24 hours.

The skill of the birders has a great deal to do with how many birds are counted and how reliable the identifications are. Much useful information has already been gathered. For example, it appears that warblers that winter in the uppermost stories of tropical rain forests in Central and South America but breed in the United States and Canada are markedly reduced in number, probably because of the wholesale destruction of rain forests. Knowing whether the populations of species are increasing or decreasing throughout their ranges is essential for wildlife management. Through cooperation and international exchange of knowledge, scientists may be able to save some birds and animals from extinction.

In your own area, study reports through the years and note any changes. Plant succession will cause some birds to leave a local area and be replaced by other species. For example, as a forest grows and matures, it attracts different species than those it attracted earlier, and comparisons of previous reports with the latest will point out possible changes and indicate other changes you may anticipate in future bird populations.

COMINGS AND GOINGS. Central. In 1985 the

Whooping Crane numbered more than 100 individuals, including those breeding in captivity. Nearly wiped out by hunters, by 1954 the birds numbered only 28 adults in the Aransas National Wildlife Refuge in Texas, where the entire population winters. In the wild, the Whooping Crane breeds at Wood Buffalo National Park in northern Alberta, Grays Lake National Wildlife Refuge in Idaho, and possibly in the the remote pothole area of northern Saskatchewan. All birders hope they can soon watch these great and graceful birds soar overhead on their annual northward migration.

Spring migration of Whooping Crane ▬▬ *To Grays Lake NWR*
from Aransas NWR ◄▬▬ *To Wood Buffalo NP*
▬·▬ *Formerly to Mackenzie*

NOTES May 22 - Savannah sparrow at Mortensen Lake; Goldfinch at our home in Laramie.

May 23/95 - ♂ Western Tanager at home in Laramie - saw ♀ on walk "around the hill"

95

MAY 27–JUNE 2

BUXTON - CAPE POINT AREA
HATTERAS ISLAND VISITOR CENTER OPEN

ACTIVITY	M	T	W	T	F
Morning Bird Walk (1½ hr)		7:30a			7:30a
*Fish with a Ranger (2 hr)	8:00a		8:00a		

GROUP BIRDING

ACTIVITIES. One reason for learning the names of your local trees and shrubs is to enable you to point out to fellow birders where certain birds are perching: "There's a Hermit Warbler high in that Ponderosa Pine." "A Pine Warbler is at middle height in the lone White Oak." Bird watchers should always pay attention to all kinds of vegetation in which birds keep house and feed. This knowledge is a great help in finding and identifying birds. You come to know in advance of exploring a field, forest, or marsh the species you are likely to encounter. There are field guides to the trees and shrubs of all areas of the United States and Canada that will help you make these identifications.

THE BIRD WATCHER FRATERNITY. *There are 30,000,000 Americans and Canadians who go bird watching—second in number to those who garden and greater than those who hunt or fish, and it is estimated that 62,500,000 people feed wild birds. Over 600,000 field guides are reported to be sold annually, grossing almost $18,000,000 in 1985. It is also reported that birders spend $54,700,000 for bird feeders; $25,000,000 for bird baths; and $20,200,000 for bird houses. The National Audubon Society estimates that birders annually spend about $34,700,000 for cameras; $739,400,000 for film; $79,300,000 for binoculars and other optical equipment; and $98,500,000 for special clothing. Birding is now a billion dollar industry (and a powerful voting bloc).*

GROUP BIRDING. People of many backgrounds enjoy outdoor nature activities, and each year more and more people take up birding as regular recreation. You will probably find birding more enjoyable when you share the pleasure with others, and sometimes even a well-behaved dog can increase your fun. Our pet fox terrier learned we were searching for birds whenever we took our walks and would point birds she saw.

The principal objective of birders in the field is to see and hear birds. A secondary aim is to help newcomers or to show local birds to visiting birders. Finally, there is the enjoyment of nature.

Many organizations schedule bird trips to certain places at carefully selected times, usually in anticipation of seeing special species. If you wish to join such an outing, ask the leader before including children or pets, because the terrain may be unsuitable for them. Also, if you are a stranger to the locality, you may not realize that a trip may entail cross-country hiking on rough trails.

Experienced birders joining a field trip for the first time in an area should tell the group something about their backgrounds. But even some ornithologists who spend their time primarily on their research specialties may not be expert field birders or know local areas well. So, for all birders on their first trips in an area, it is best to be quiet and learn from others. If you have the opportunity to attend a state, regional, or national meeting of birders or ornithologists, do not complain about accommodations your hosts have arranged for you—they may be the best available—or about birding places to which your hosts may take you. In Australia, we attended an international meeting in which one person complained when our group was taken to see a common North American bird. In fact, the purpose was to elicit opinions from people who knew the bird well.

Some people—not us—differentiate birders from bird watchers, defining birders as those who enjoy field trips to look for birds, and bird watchers as those who keep detailed records, even write for journals.

One autumn a birder described a large sparrowlike visitor in her yard as yellow, green, and red plaid—not a bad description for a male Scarlet Tanager in its autumn plumage.

COMINGS AND GOINGS. East.

The beautiful Bachman's Warbler now is probably extinct. Its breeding range has been reduced to small scattered areas over the southeastern United States, and its range in Cuba, where it wintered, has been taken over by sugar plantations. There is enough good breeding territory left in southern states, but summers are not enough. All bird watchers are concerned that the winter quarters of many warblers and other birds are being destroyed by lumbermen and plantation owners all over the New World, especially in Latin America. If you manage to see a live Bachman's Warbler, you are indeed fortunate.

• *Possible breeding areas of Bachman's Warbler*

NOTES

_____

_____

_____

_____

_____

_____

_____

_____

_____

_____

_____

_____

_____

_____

_____

_____

_____

_____

_____

_____

_____

_____

_____

Some people seem unable to get any-where on time. They almost always hold things up. Before group field trips, we have asked friends to pick up the late arrivals and found that we then had even more people arriving late. The only solution was to print instructions on bright red paper and leave them at our rendez-vous to inform latecomers of where they could catch up with the group.

Field courtesy. Unfortunately, not all birders are sufficiently considerate of others. By following rules of courtesy when in the field with other people, you will increase your fun and that of all the others.

1. Do not shout or run about. Commotion often chases birds away.

2. Do not try to be the first birder to identify a species under observation. Hurried identifications are wrong more often than right.

3. Do not crowd up or block others from seeing.

4. Do not step in front of anyone using binoculars, a telescope, or a camera. When people stop to watch a bird, stop with them to prevent scaring away their find.

5. Do not monopolize a spot after seeing a bird; give others a chance to see it. After the other birders have moved on, watch again for as long as you wish.

6. Even though you may already be familiar with a bird being observed, others may not. Be patient with those who want to learn more.

7. When traveling with a group, keep to the group schedule unless you spot a real rarity or unless others agree to spend additional time at a particular place.

8. Do not monopolize equipment belonging to someone else.

9. Be quiet while other birders are attempting to listen to a bird song.

10. When moving through brush, do not hold back branches for those following. Overly solicitous birders usually manage to let go of a branch at precisely the worst moment.

11. Be helpful to beginners.

12. Do not try to set a rapid pace. If a group must move ahead more slowly than you like, drop back and search for birds the group may have missed.

13. If you see other members of a group staring fixedly at a spot, do not ask what they are looking at. If they are observing a worthwhile species, they will tell you.

14. Obey all posted signs. Being a bird watcher conveys no special privileges. Obtain permission before entering private property. Property owners may tell you where to look for special birds on their land.

15. Do not litter, remove plants, disturb animals, or walk off pathways without permission from the owner.

"Now that's carrying bird-watching a bit too far!"

Rules of the road. If you are birding by car, and your car is one of a group, follow these rules:

1. Establish rules for each driver in the caravan, such as no blowing of horns except in emergencies. Flick headlights on and off or from dim to bright to signal a bird find or minor trouble.

2. Do not tailgate.

3. Remember that other people use back roads. Signal them to pass at first opportunity.

4. Other vehicles cannot pass your car if you stop in the center of the road, so pull well off.

5. If you are in a caravan, keep to the schedule set by the leader. Establish a signal that indicates that you are leaving the tour.

On one post convention bird tour, a thoughtless member delayed his group and other convention members for more than an hour while he leisurely scanned the fields for birds. On another, a careless driver returned home without notifying all his passengers, leaving a member of his party stranded.

CODE FOR THE BIRD WATCHER. *For some people, birding alone is more fun than joining a group. Here is some good advice:*

- *The welfare of the bird must be your first concern.*
- *Standing still and watching often produces best views of birds.*
- *Avoid making tracks to nests, and replace foliage if you disturb it.*
- *If a bird shows anxiety, move away. You may be keeping it off its eggs.*
- *Tread carefully near colonies of ground nesting birds and do not linger.*
- *Do not chase tired migrants.*
- *Before entering private land, obtain permission*

—From the Royal Society for the Protection of Birds

JUNE 3–9

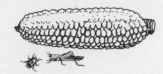

NATURAL FOODS

ACTIVITIES. The health of birds at your feeder deserves attention. A bird in the wild may not be as healthy as it looks, but it is hard to determine whether the odd behavior of a bird in your backyard or on your window tray is abnormal. Abnormal behavior is not always a sign of illness. For example, a bird can get drunk from eating fermented fruit. It will act strangely, staggering on the ground and flying into things. Sometimes birds acting strangely may have eaten poison spread intentionally or accidentally by one of your neighbors. If many birds of various species are behaving abnormally, they have probably been poisoned, and you should notify a local conservation officer.

Knowing the kinds of foods certain birds prefer will help you locate them within their ranges.

Remember: A range map does not mean that a given bird species occurs everywhere within the territory shown. You also need a vegetation map to show you where the right food grows.

Caution: A bird on the wing may show up almost anywhere, but if you see an albatross on a bird feeder in central Kansas, call National Audubon and the Smithsonian. Such sightings of accidentals increase the fascination of birding.

NATURAL FOODS. Natural food is the mainstay of all wildlife, and the base of the world's natural food supply is vegetable. No animal lived in the sea or on land until after plants were established in both environments. Over barely imaginable lengths of time, countless species of plants and animals have spread over the sea and the earth. Creatures that subsisted on only one kind of food found themselves in a death-dealing evolutionary blind alley. Those that preferred a variety of food had the best chance of survival.

So far as ornithologists know, only one species of bird in the United States and Canada is restricted to a single species of food. The Snail (Everglade) Kite has developed a bill and feet designed solely for eating the Apple Snail. Today, because of the draining of the Everglades and other marshes in Florida, in the United States this snail is restricted to a small area in south-central Florida. As a result, the Snail Kite is similarly restricted. While the Snail Kite is also found in Cuba and Mexico and south to Uruguay and northern Argentina, the habitat of the Apple Snail may eventually be destroyed even in this large area, forcing the Snail Kite into extinction. By contrast, in Florida the Limpkin, which also feeds on the same snail, eats many other foods as well and therefore is thriving. Birds have their food preferences, but if a favored food is temporarily short, they switch to the next most preferred item.

Mobility makes for variety. The power of flight makes birds especially mobile. When they find a food supply reduced, they usually emigrate. Since emigration may force birds to new areas containing different food, they must become accustomed to it or die. Furthermore, birds that remain throughout the year in the temperate zone, that is in most of the United States and Canada, must change their diet with the seasons. Occasional droughts, interspersed with seasons that are wetter than normal, also affect the growth of plants. This changes the composition of the natural food supply, and resident birds adapt or perish.

COMINGS AND GOINGS.

Chimney Swifts and White-throated Swifts arrive at their breeding ranges in the United States and Canada from late March to early May. These swifts are adept home builders. Chimney Swifts have learned to use their gluelike saliva to attach their nests to the inside surfaces of house chimneys rather than to hollow trees and rock cavities. White-throated Swifts usually nest on cliffs and canyon faces, where they glue their nests to the surfaces or in cracks. White-throated Swifts have also built their nests in fissures in buildings, for example, in the cracks of California's Mission of San Juan Capistrano. Swifts are among the fastest flying birds, and their aerobatics are fun to watch.

Breeding ranges: *Chimney Swift*
                       White-throated Swift

NOTES

_____

_____

_____

_____

_____

_____

_____

_____

_____

_____

_____

_____

_____

_____

_____

_____

_____

_____

_____

_____

_____

_____

_____

AN OMNIVOROUS EATER. *The American Crow is an example of a bird that eats a wide variety of natural foods. More than 650 different items have been recorded in its diet, about 30 percent animal matter, 70 percent vegetable matter. This variety of diet is one reason for the success and wide distribution of the American Crow. It is abundant in the eastern United States and Canada and common coast to coast.*

We have seen beautiful desert gardens planted with attractive cacti, Datura, Phacelia, Penstemon, Delphinium, paloverde trees, Paradise Poinciana, and agaves. A small shaded pool usually will attract to such a garden even greater numbers of birds, such as thrashers, wrens, Verdins, Bushtits, Northern Cardinals, and Pyrrhuloxias. Think of the bonuses: no mowing of lawns, no water wasted on alien plants, and excellent visibility of your bird visitors.

A simple but effective addition to a desert garden is a plastic container pierced with tiny holes and hung above a birdbath. The water you fill it with will drip slowly into the bath, where desert birds will welcome it. They are accustomed to warm water.

In addition to normal migration, birds frequently make temporary moves into areas where the supply of food is more plentiful than in their usual ranges. Ornithologists use the word *irruption* to designate such a population shift, which may last only a few weeks. For example, the Snowy Owl and the Rough-legged Hawk appear in large numbers in the northern United States when there is a winter shortage of rodents farther north. Seed eaters, such as finches, crossbills, and grosbeaks, may move south when nuts, acorns, or pine seeds are in short supply up north.

Birds that temporarily extend their ranges may find a supply of the same foods they are used to at home, or they may eat new kinds of foods. The rule is the same: The more different kinds of food a bird can eat, the better its chance of long-term survival. European Starlings, gulls, crows, and jays are known to be omnivorous. Consider the Ruffed Grouse, a true gourmand: It is known to eat 414 plant and 580 animal species.

The balance of nature. The so-called balance of nature is constantly teetering in local areas or habitats. It is a balance between producers and consumers, that is, between plants and herbivores, prey and predators, animal remains and scavengers. If the populations of plants and animals do not remain fairly constant over a period of time, the balance becomes upset, and the habitats destabilize until a new balance is achieved, perhaps with a different mix of plants and animals. Since the populations of plants and animals fluctuate with changes in climate, introduction of diseases, and other factors, the presence of plants and animals normally does not change much in the short term. If one or two species disappear or become extinct, other species move in and fill the gap. If many species disappear, the balance of nature takes longer to restore itself. In short, the balance of nature is not stable over long periods.

In the long-term adjustment required when major environmental changes become relatively permanent, birds must adapt to the new conditions, move on to greener pastures, or face extinction. Staying in a place and accepting new foods means that over time there will be a body or behavioral change. The deprived species may become smaller or larger, or it may become restricted to certain parts of the environment, such as the understory in a woods or the highest branches of trees.

Abundance of food. Well-fed birds produce a goodly number of eggs, and if natural food is readily available, more nestlings are able to grow to maturity. But with a good food supply, the predators also increase, so populations remain relatively stable.

SOME PLANTS AND BIRDS THEY ATTRACT

C	Central	nrly	nearly
cst	coastal areas	NW	Northwest
E	East	S	South
int	intermontane	SE	Southeast
mts	mountains	SW	Southwest
N	North	U	ubiquitous
NC	Northcentral	W	West
NE	Northeast		

PLANTS	SPECIES	REGIONS
Algae	most ducks, American Coots, etc.	U
Blackberries	grouse, Ring-necked Pheasants, prairie-chickens, tanagers, sparrows	U
Blueberries	grouse, tanagers, thrashers, others	E & W
Bristlegrasses	Bobolinks, blackbirds, buntings, sparrows, Pyrrhuloxias	U
Brome Grasses	geese, partridge, quail, sparrows	U
Buckthorns	Crested Mynahs, Phainopeplas, Pileated Woodpeckers	U
Clovers	grouse, quails, prairie-chickens, buntings, sparrows	U
Cord Grasses	waterfowl, Seaside and Sharp-tailed sparrows	cst: E & W
Crab Grasses	doves, Wild Turkeys, juncos, longspurs, sparrows, others	U ex. n. mts
Dogwoods	Wood Ducks, pigeons, doves, grosbeaks, robins	nrly U
Doveweeds	doves, Pyrrhuloxias, sparrows	S & C
Dropseed Grasses	juncos, longspurs	nrly U
Duckweeds	American Coots, ducks, gallinules, rails	nrly U
Eelgrass	Brants, ducks, geese	cst
Grapes	grouse, Wild Turkeys, bluebirds, cardinals, Phainopeplas	U
Hackberry	Northern Mockingbirds, thrashers, robins, sapsuckers	nrly U
Hawthorns	grouse, Fox Sparrows, Cedar Waxwing, others	nrly U
Knotweeds	prairie-chickens, Rosy Finches, Grasshopper Sparrows	U
Maples	grosbeaks, Sharp-tailed Grouse, finches, nuthatches	U
Mesquite	quails, ravens, crows	SW
Naiads	ducks, geese, aquatic birds	NE, S
Needlegrasses	Buntings, longspurs, prairie sparrows	W, SW
Oaks	Wood Ducks, prairie-chickens, jays	U
Pacific Madrone	Band-tailed Pigeons, Long-tailed Chats, Varied Thrushes	W
Panicgrasses	Black Ducks, Green-winged Teals, blackbirds, sparrows	U
Pigweeds	Snow Buntings, Lawrence's Goldfinches, Song Sparrows	U
Pines	Spruce Grouse, Red Crossbills, Nutcrackers, Pinyon Jays	U
Poison Ivy and Oak	Catbirds, flickers, thrashers, Wrentits	nrly U
Pondweeds	swans, ducks, Coots, American Avocet, godwits, dowitchers	U
Prickly Pears	Curve-billed Thrashers, Cactus Wrens, woodpeckers	SW
Ragweeds	Ring-necked Pheasant, Northern Bobwhites, goldfinches, juncos	nrly U
Sagebrush	Sage Grouse, Sharp-tailed Grouse, others	W, int
Serviceberries	crows, magpies, tanagers, thrushes	nrly U
Smartweeds	swans, geese, ducks, rails, Northern Bobwhites, cardinals, sparrows	nrly U
Snowberries	Franklin's Grouse, Sharp-tailed Grouse, Pine Grosbeaks	U ex. S & SE
Sumac	Ruffed Grouse, Wild Turkeys, robins, European Starlings	U
Sunflowers	doves, longspurs, sparrows, chickadees, cardinals	U
Wild Cherries	grouse, robins, thrushes, waxwings, many others	U
Wild Celery	Canvasbacks, Redheads, many other aquatic birds	NE, SE

JUNE 10–16

> *Farmers in Jersey Call Swans Pests and Ask U.S. for Hunts*

BIRDS AS PESTS

ACTIVITIES. As nesting advances, male birds that have fallen silent may resume their singing, perhaps announcing a second or third nesting. Look for fledglings hanging around, sometimes still fed by their parents. You may even see immature birds, perhaps orioles, thrushes, and phoebes, from last year's nesting season. Watch how nestlings are cared for by adult birds, for example, protected against bad weather or predators. Ornithologists do not yet have complete information on how and when many common birds get through their breeding cycles, so keep good records of your observations. Do not neglect dates or prevailing weather as you make your objective descriptions of bird behavior.

DIET OF HOUSE SPARROW

FOOD ITEMS	YEARLY AVERAGE (PERCENT)
ANIMAL FOOD	
Weevils	0.69
Scarabaeid beetles	.98
Click beetles	.07
Ground beetles	.05
Leaf beetles	.03
Other beetles	.19
Grasshoppers, crickets, and other Orthoptera	.57
Caterpillars and moths	.23
Bugs	.06
Flies	.10
Ants, wasps, bees, and other Hymenoptera	.31
Other insects	.04
Spiders and other Arachnida	.03
Other animal matter	.04
Total	3.39
VEGETABLE FOOD	
Feed	59.57
Oats	14.37
Wheat	2.70
Corn	.43
Other grain	.58
Grass and weed seeds	16.97
Mast and wild fruit	1.39
Cultivated fruits and vegetables	.02
Other vegetable matter	.58
Total	96.61

BIRDS AS PESTS. Pests are usually defined as creatures that in some way annoy or offend humans. Animals harbor pests, such as horseflies or lice, which rarely are lethal in themselves but are annoying and can carry death-dealing disease. Lists of birds characterized as pests differ. For example, a farmer's concerns differ from those of an apartment dweller or homeowner. Again, people react individually to birds in typically different human ways. A few birds, for example, vultures, are called pests because they offend the aesthetic sense of some people; others, such as eagles and other hawks, because they engender fear; still others, such as blackbirds and sparrows, because they damage structures and crops; and some because people convince themselves that the birds are guilty on all counts.

In China, a nationwide program against sparrows and other granivorous birds reflected the belief that the birds ate grain that people wanted for themselves and were human health hazards. Rock Doves (domestic pigeons) are disease-carrying, destructive, dirty—some even say ugly—birds and thus are considered pests, but people in many lands love these birds and take pleasure in feeding them.

Though birds sometimes are pests, slaughtering them wholesale is not rational. Consider ranchers pleading hardship from depredations of the Golden Eagle on their livestock, who fire rifles from their airplanes at any eagle even if it has not caused the damage.

Birds and farmers. It is not normal for every seed planted to grow to maturity and bear fruit, so farmers know they will lose a small part of a crop. But if a swarm of crows or a flock of geese descends on a sprouting cornfield, the loss may be large, especially for small farmers. Yet the problem is not that simple. When the size of a crop is finally known, it may be impossible to determine whether the loss was caused by birds or insects. In fact, birds accused by farmers may actually have been feeding as much on insects as on corn.

COMINGS AND GOINGS. There are 319 known species of hummingbirds, a family occurring only in the New World. The largest, the Giant Hummingbird, is 8½ inches long. The smallest, probably the smallest known bird, is the Bee Hummingbird, only 2½ inches long. In the United States and Canada, there are 20 recorded species. To see the greatest display, visit Ramsey Canyon in southeastern Arizona, often called the Hummingbird Capital. In the East, only the Ruby-throated Hummingbird is known to occur regularly. In the West, the Black-chinned Hummingbird is widespread. A specially built hummingbird feeder in, say, southern California or southeastern Arizona, is a joy to watch when several species dine at once.

Breeding ranges: ▬▬Black-chinned Hummingbird
▬▬Ruby-throated Hummingbird

NOTES

What is the farmer to do? Killing all birds in a place is not the answer, even though the law permits farmers to poison or shoot bird pests on their own property during an attack on a crop. The U.S. Department of Agriculture and the Fish and Wildlife Service, along with universities and other organizations, search for effective and humane control methods. Even so, some farmers scatter pesticides and destroy birds where they cause no harm, at the same time killing beneficial birds.

Orchardists may also have bird problems. Blackbirds, orioles, robins, thrushes, and other birds may damage ripening fruit. Methods for controlling damage have not succeeded. In addition to pesticides, devices that produce noises may be set up in an orchard. Tape recorders playing distress calls of pest species may drive them away. Unfortunately, many methods of pest control are costly for small orchardists.

In people's minds, the bird that has done the most damage is the so-called chicken hawk. Many farming families keep a shotgun handy to bring down this bird. When fairly large hawks are seen overhead, chickens in barnyards scurry for cover, so it is thought the hawks are after a chicken dinner. As a result, many hawks are classified on the spot as vermin and killed with shotgun blasts. In the East, this means Red-shouldered Hawks, Broad-winged Hawks, and Red-tailed Hawks; in the West, Swainson's and Ferruginous hawks. Christmas often brings "Vermin Day": Farmers' sons, using their brand-new guns, shoot all the hawks they can spot. While rodent-eating hawks are tumbling from the skies, the true bird hawks (Sharp-shinned Hawks, Cooper's Hawks, and Northern Goshawks), almost unnoticed, hedgehop into the barnyards, escaping with fresh fowl. It has taken decades to dissuade most farmers, yet many still kill beneficial birds.

Birds and airplanes. At airports, gulls and European Starlings have been scooped into jet engines, sometimes causing fatal accidents. This has been controlled by driving the birds away, by shooting some, and by playing recordings of bird distress calls over loudspeakers. Eliminating perching places and cutting down brush and trees also help.

The U.S. Air Force had problems on Pacific islands where nesting albatrosses and petrels interfered with aircraft landings and takeoffs. To compound the problem, albatrosses have long incubation periods and times from hatching to fledging, so some birds were present throughout the year. The biggest danger was from flying birds. The problem was solved by ornithologists. When the sand dunes beside the runways were leveled off and partially covered with blacktop, updrafts were no longer created, and soaring flight by birds became difficult. The birds soon moved elsewhere.

PLAY IT AGAIN, SAM! *A tape deck in a cornfield constantly playing the distress signals of the American Crow, European Starling, or Red-winged Blackbird will frequently succeed in driving these pests away. Turn the volume way up.*

Attacking birds. Attacks by birds, seldom serious, occur most commonly near nests. Even tiny hummingbirds will fly at people near their nests but usually veer off before striking. Bigger birds, especially hawks, eagles, swans, and geese, will strike people. Swans and geese, especially when guarding a nest, can break a bone with blows of their wings, rarely of their bills. Children should be kept away from nests of these birds. Anyone who has banded nesting hawks or owls knows that these birds can inflict damage. Hawks and owls strike with their talons, not their bills, so guard against these weapons. Since even small birds may attack the eyes, be careful when you approach the home or family of a bird.

Birds that build their nests on porches can be pests. Blue Jays once nested on a low maple branch overhanging a sidewalk, from where they attacked pedestrians, especially women in bright hats. House Sparrows, House Finches, and Rock Doves may build messy nests behind window shutters, on window sills, or on other parts of a home. Killdeers have laid eggs on gravel driveways. On early mornings in spring, people may be annoyed by the hammering of a woodpecker signaling the approaching nesting season on a resonant stump or on a sounding board he has found on a house. If this happens to you, nail soft fiberboard over the spot until the drumming season is over. Most problems caused by pesky birds will go away if nature is allowed to take its course.

Few of us get close to birds, so danger of sickness is slight and easily countered by good sanitation. If you handle live or dead birds, remember that birds have no means of proper sanitation, and even a veterinarian seldom can identify sickness in birds at a glance. Bird nests may be infested with parasites and bloodsucking creatures. So if you or your children handle birds or bird nests, make sure hands are washed after each exposure. Any puncture, wound, or scratch by a bird bill or claw can become infected, so take precautions. Children are apt to cuddle a sick bird and must be careful.

BIRDS AND DISEASE

Bird diseases can be transmitted to humans only with difficulty, though people working closely with birds must be careful. The following bacterial sicknesses are known to be transmissible.

Botulism (western duck sickness)	Develops in stagnant alkaline waters containing decaying matter. Hygiene and avoidance of such waters protect humans.
Chlamydiosis (Psittacosis and Ornithosis)	Caused by bacteria carried by various birds and transmitted by particles in the air. It is most common among those who frequently handle birds, such as duck farmers, and is treated successfully by antibacterial drugs.
Dermatitis	Blistering of the feet, passed from foot to ground to foot. Shoes and hygiene are protection.
Encephalitis	A viral inflammation of the brain, referred to as equine encephalitis. Bloodsucking insects such as mosquitoes, lice, and ticks carry it from birds to horses; other carriers take it from horses to humans. It or a variety can also be carried directly from birds to humans. Inoculation of horses is thus far the most effective control.
Erysipelas	A skin disease causing fever and red blotches. It is transmitted from soil to open sores.
Histoplasmosis	This disease, resulting from inhaling fungus spores from bird and bat droppings, causes enlarged liver and spleen as well as fever and anemia. Proper cleaning of feeders protects against this sickness. Anyone who tramps through the woods should avoid trees of colonial or roosting birds.
Salmonellosis	A bacterial disease spread through food and dried animal feces, causing so-called food poisoning and diarrhea in humans. It is controlled by proper hygiene.

JUNE 17-23

BIRDS AND PESTS

ACTIVITIES. When it is hot outdoors for you, it is hot for birds as well. Observe how birds keep themselves cool in oppressive weather. Since birds have no sweat glands, they depend on other means. A bird commonly keeps cool by breathing rapidly, with bill agape, and you will often see a robin, for example, sitting on its nest and panting in this way. And although you may pity newly hatched young covered and brooded by a parent in hot weather, this is really a way of keeping the nestlings cool and shaded from the sun. In deserts and other hot regions notice how birds use the shade of plants, even cactuses, and how on hot days they avoid any activity under a noonday sun.

Appearances are deceiving. When a bird pecks a prize apple, it is considered a pest. When a bird eats an apple worm, it is a friend.

Consider the rather ugly, smelly Turkey Vulture. It is protected by law in some southern communities, where Turkey Vultures clean dead animals from streets and highways. Why then should these birds not be esteemed more than they are?

Consider also the sleek, swift Purple Martins, eagerly sought after by the many householders who place in their backyards bird apartment houses designed especially for the species. Purple Martins have become special friends because they are believed to control mosquitoes. In fact, Purple Martins are not efficient exterminators of these insects, which are best controlled by making sure that marshes, ponds, and rivers are well stocked with fish and amphibians that eat mosquito eggs and larvae. Spreading oil on the waters of a pond infested with mosquitoes not only walls off the natural enemies of the insect pest, but also increases stagnation and pollution.

Now consider the powerful and beautiful hawks and owls. People apparently have always sought to exterminate hawks and owls in the mistaken belief that they destroy songbirds. In truth, hawks and owls consume significant numbers of rodents. Ironically, by indiscriminately destroying valuable wildlife habitats, people have themselves killed off far more songbirds than could all birds of prey combined.

It all comes down to one dismal conclusion: Efforts to control pests and encourage friendly wildlife have resulted in more pests and fewer friends.

BIRDS AND PESTS. Birds are often depicted as symbols of human aspirations and institutions. The dove, for example, represents peace, and the eagle represents government. But Salt Lake City, Utah, has a unique monument to gulls. In this monument, the gull represents only itself. In 1848 gulls arrived in Utah in great flocks and ate millions of locusts that were devouring food crops of the Mormon settlers. The gulls saved the Mormons from starvation.

Nevertheless, birds generally are less than efficient pest controllers, for they cannot eat enough crickets, caterpillars, or rodents to make a dent in these pest populations. The chief benefit of birds to man is based on the complex and often unknown role played by all classes of plants and animals in maintaining the balance of nature. If birds were destroyed, the natural world as we know it would probably collapse, and humans themselves very likely would not survive.

There is as yet no place known from which birds have been completely removed, thus causing extinction of other species. However, introduction of bird species in a given area has been known to drive away other bird species. The House Sparrow and the European Starling, settling in our cities and countryside, have caused the departure of many native species. Not only are the habits of these two birds disturbing to people, but they also have the effect of attracting rodents and other pests. Biologists are aware that extinction of a bird species creates opportunities for such species as Rock Doves, House Sparrows, and European Starlings, which move into the vacated niche. The replacement usually turns out to be undesirable and harder to eradicate than the birds driven out.

Birds have benefited humans by serving as a source of food. All over the world domestic fowl are important in the human diet, and birds are still hunted and trapped as food. The Red Jungle Fowl of southern Asia was domesticated about 3000 years ago. This bird—people know it as the chicken—now is raised throughout the world for its eggs and meat.

COMINGS AND GOINGS. From late March to mid-May, kingbirds move northward through the United States and Canada. These birds are relatively common and can often be seen perching on telephone and power lines. Birders may assume that the Eastern and Western kingbirds are similar in appearance, but this is not so, as your field guides will show. There is another difference between them. The Western Kingbird has a preference for areas that are much more open and treeless. As a result, the increase in farmland in the East has had the effect of encouraging eastward movement by the Western Kingbird. Incidentally, both species feed exclusively on insects and are called bee martins by many beekeepers.

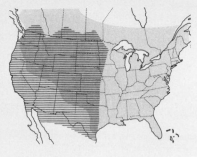

Breeding ranges: *Eastern Kingbird*
                Western Kingbird

NOTES

JUNE 17–23
BIRDS AND PESTS

The Mallard, native to most of the Northern Hemisphere, is the ancestor of almost all our domestic ducks. The American Turkey and Muscovy Duck—both misnamed—originated in America. All over the world people eat birds, from sparrows and finches in Africa, China, and Italy to herons, sandpipers, storks, and cranes elsewhere. And eggs are eaten by humans everywhere.

Finally, in addition to the importance of the scientific study of birds, there is the pleasure that birds give us. Sportsmen and bird watchers are attracted by the elusiveness, speed, power, and beauty of birds. On a spring day a few years ago, in New York City's Central Park, people hurrying about their business came to a complete stop in order to watch flocks of migrating warblers. Enthralled by the beauty of the birds, many people stayed for 10 to 15 minutes, perhaps thinking someone's pet birds had escaped.

Birds as pest controllers. In the natural world, there often is an explosion in the supply of one kind of food, for example, seeds, fruit, insects, spiders, or rodents. The windfall attracts animals that eat that food. An eruption of lemmings on the march, for example, will soon be surrounded by predators: hawks, ravens, weasels, foxes, and the like. This is an example of how the balance of nature is maintained. Pest controllers do not often arrive fast enough or in sufficient numbers to save crops, so farmers take drastic action, spraying poisons on their fields and orchards—often 17 spray-

WHAT BIRDS OF PREY EAT. *The contents of stomachs of fallen birds of prey have been examined to gain insight into whether such birds actually attack barnyard birds in significant numbers. The information in the chart that follows lists various types of food found in the stomachs of various species of birds of prey. The first column supplies the names of the species and the number of stomachs examined for each species. Subsequent columns list the number of stomachs containing each type of food.*

WHAT BIRDS OF PREY EAT

SPECIES (STOMACHS EXAMINED)	POULTRY, GAME BIRDS	OTHER BIRDS	MICE	OTHER MAMMALS	REPTILES	AMPHIBIANS	FISH	INSECTS
Sharp-shinned Hawk (159)	6	99	6					5
Cooper's Hawk (133)	34	52		11	3	1		2
Goshawk (28)	9	2		10				3
Red-tailed Hawk (562)	54	51	278	131	37		3	47
Red-shouldered Hawk (220)	3	12	104	40	20	39		92
Zone-tailed Hawk (5)					2	3	1	
Broad-winged Hawk (65)		2	15	13	11	13		30
Roughleg Hawk (49)			40	5	1			1
Golden Eagle (6)		1		2				
Bald Eagle (21)	1			5			9	
Prairie Falcon (11)	3	5						2
Duck Hawk (20)	7	9	1					2
Sparrow Hawk (320)	1	53	89	12	12			215
Barn Owl (39)	1	3	17	17				4
Long-eared Owl (107)	1	15	84	5				1
Short-eared Owl (101)		11	77	7				7
Barred Owl (109)	5	13	46	18		4	2	14
Screech Owl (255)	1	38	91	11		4	1	100
Great-horned Owl (127)	31	8	13	65			1	10

ings for an apple orchard in a typical season. So heavy is this use of poisons that when birds consume the food, they often die as a result of ingesting lethal accumulations.

Single-crop farming often compounds the problem by creating over a large region a vast supply of the food a pest likes best. Where there is a diversity of plants and animals, birds help control small outbreaks of native and alien pests for which they have acquired a taste.

Populations of birds and other enemies of crop-damaging insects and other pests, under natural conditions, are usually large enough to control pests even though some damage is done. In 1877 at Middle Creek, Nebraska, a plague of locusts—as many as 135 to the square foot—attracted quail, larks, Bobolinks, plovers, curlews, and Greater Prairie-Chickens, which soon eliminated the trouble. In 1939 in Mount Vernon, New York, a shallow temporary pond became overpopulated with tadpoles—128 were trapped in a single cup of water scooped from the pond. Bitterns, herons, grackles, Blue Jays, crows, American Robins, quail, and Killdeers lined the shore and feasted until the tadpoles were nearly gone. The U.S. Department of Agriculture has in its files many similar accounts. In 1982 Gypsy Moths plagued eastern New York, and the following two years saw an increase in the population of cuckoos, which thrive on a diet of hairy caterpillars. The cold winter and spring of 1984 finished off the depleted pests.

DIVERSITY OF DIET. *Most birds, particularly the most successful, eat a wide variety of food. This chart shows that during the breeding season the Black-billed Magpie eats more animal matter, mostly insects, than vegetable matter. Throughout the rest of the year it eats more vegetable matter, mostly wild fruit. It is rare for birds to eat enough of one kind of food to destroy a farmer's crop or to control all the pests that attack crops.*

ANIMAL MATTER
A. weevils 2.1%
B. ground beetles 3.0%
C. caterpillars 3.5%
D. bees, ants, etc. 3.1%
E. grasshoppers 14.0%
F. misc. animal matter 12.7%
G. carrion 13.8%
H. small mammals 7.6%
   Total: 59.8%

VEGETABLE MATTER
I. grain 13.4%
J. cultivated fruit 2.9%
K. wild fruit 21.1%
L. vegetable rubbish 2.8%
   Total: 40.2%

DIET OF THE ADULT MAGPIE THROUGHOUT THE YEAR

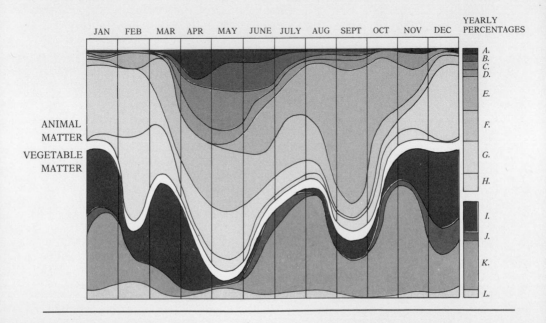

JUNE 24–30

BIRDS AND COLOR

ACTIVITIES. You are watching a Common Flicker as it lands on your lawn, showing its glaring white rump. Suddenly it seems to disappear completely. You have seen the magic of camouflage. The flicker has turned off its glaring mark and left only the well-camouflaged back and tail, which are difficult to see on browning grass. A bird hawk, Cooper's or Sharp-shinned, follows the bright rump of a Yellow-rumped Warbler until the warbler makes a sharp turn. The glowing yellow is almost completely hidden, and the hawk misses a meal. A Brown Creeper has prominent light tan patches on its wings, which allow a pursuing hawk to follow it right to the bole of a tree, where the creeper seems to melt into the bark, sidling to one side and seen no more. Collect examples of camouflage, a phenomenon used as a field mark by birders and as a safety device by birds.

Though it is not true that some species, like the American Crow, will drive an albino away from the flock, they may not welcome it because white can attract predators. Again, a yellow Northern Cardinal, despite giving the proper calls and songs, may find itself an outcast from its species. The behavior of the bird will generally lead to acceptance in a flock of the same species.

BIRDS AND COLOR. Most birds can perceive color, but whether they distinguish colors the way humans do—whether, for example, they see blue as blueness—is not known. Ornithologists do know that bird survival depends in part on the colors of birds themselves, since the coloration of each species is a product of evolution and, it is presumed, has helped give a species a competitive advantage. Coloration is no different in this regard than length of beak, lobes on toes, or shape of wing—all have evolved in particular ways so that birds can get along well or at least not suffer a disadvantage.

No matter how brightly colored a bird may be, no matter how it may stand out in its habitat, the advantages a bird gains from brightness must outweigh the disadvantages created by its heightened visibility. If brightly colored birds were to fall prey to hawks or other predators so often that their numbers became significantly reduced, natural selection would veer away from bright colors toward dull, because brightly colored birds would be removed from the breeding population.

Contrasting colors in bird plumage may attract a birder's eyes as a field mark, but if the colors fool a predator or cause it to strike the wrong part of the bird, color works to the advantage of the bird under attack. A feature for survival is the fact that predators may be drawn to the brightly colored adult male rather than to the young or to the plainer hued female. You may think that a Killdeer is faking a broken wing to lure you away from its nest, eggs, or young, but it may in fact be displaying a brightly colored wing to achieve the same result. At any rate, the act works for survival.

The variegated plumages of many species demonstrate that color is useful in camouflage. Sandpipers on a graveled beach are almost impossible to see from above, so a marauding hawk or jaeger flying over an incubating adult does not easily find a dinner. Brownish mottled sparrows remain still as a predator flies overhead and thus have their best chance of escaping destruction.

COMINGS AND GOINGS. East. Of all the birds in the continental United States, Kirtland's Warbler occupies the smallest breeding range, about 600 square miles. This endangered species, with a population of about 500, is restricted to Michigan's lower peninsula, nesting only in jack pines about 5 to 8 feet tall, which are found only in woods that have been burned over. If the woods are not burned over periodically, this warbler faces extinction despite the vast stretches of jack pine in Canada, to the north. Another warbler with a small range is the Golden-cheeked Warbler, which breeds only in the forested portion of the Edwards Plateau of south central Texas.

Breeding ranges: ■ *Kirtland's Warbler*
≣ *Golden-cheeked Warbler*

NOTES

Camouflage works because animals close their bright eyes and remain perfectly still. When birds are moving, camouflage works poorly. If you spot a young Killdeer or other camouflaged young bird, you will be amazed at how closely you can approach the fluffy mite before it moves—you may even be able to touch it. Nestlings are not mesmerized by the eyes of an approaching snake. They are following the first principle of camouflage: Do not move! Snakes, which have a poor sense of smell and hearing, may pass the nest and young without incident.

Protective coloration. Color of bird plumage often protects a bird from predators in the air or on the ground (1) by being so much like the color of the ground that the bird is difficult to see or (2) by being discontinuously distributed so that the shape of the bird is distorted in the eyes of the predator.

For example, some species have patches of white or bright colors that contrast with the colors of their wings or rump. A hawk seeing a bird as prey will follow these patches as the bird flies. When the bird lands and folds its wings, the patches disappear, and the hawk is thwarted.

Many birds and other animals are dark above and light, almost white, below. On the ground, the lighter color is shaded by the body of the bird, making it look almost as dark as the back of the bird and therefore difficult to see. Breaking up the shapes and shadows makes it difficult for enemies to recognize birds from above. Some sparrows and notably the American Bittern, caught in the open when a hawk flies overhead, assume grotesque postures, looking most unbirdlike. Ducks, plovers, and other birds crouch close to the ground as a predator approaches or flies overhead. This hides the black shadow that would clearly outline its shape, and the birds remain motionless until danger passes. Each species has evolved the best camouflage for its habitat. Thus the American Woodcock is found mostly on leaf-covered ground, and the Common Snipe inhabits marshes, where its colors and patterns serve it best.

DISRUPTIVE COLORATION. *This Semi-palmated Plover stands out like a sore thumb against the plain sand, but almost disappears when it crouches among the pebbles of its usual habitat.*

The extensive range of larks in Siberia and Mongolia includes deserts and grasslands. Larks that nest in the desert areas are pale brown, much like the sands of the desert, but the coloration of the grassland inhabitants is more like their favored habitat. Color also helps keep flocks together. When a birder flushes a large number of field birds, the birds when only a few feet off the ground join up with their own kind, an action made possible by identifying colors, marks, and actions. Birds attacked by hawks may fly from a place in dense flocks to confuse or frighten their enemies and make it difficult for them to hit a particular target in the flock. This practice must have survival value, since flocking reaction is common also to small species of insects, fish, and mammals.

Color often enhances threat behavior by making a bird appear larger or more terrifying than it is. Color, including contrasting patches of white in a dark wing, also enables a bird to make a warning flash to other members of its species in a flock.

Color and the birder. In the field, you may not have a chance to enjoy the colors of birds before they fly away. But your feeder can provide a clear view from a ringside seat. By placing a feeder at eye level with a sweep of view behind it, you can watch birds fly toward you as they approach for a landing. Again and again you can see birds come in with tails and wings spread wide, all colors showing to maximum advantage. You will observe colors flash in a way you usually cannot otherwise see. Discover, for example, how striking are the bright epaulettes of the Red-winged Blackbird seen from head-on. Notice how the face of the Black-capped Chickadee appears almost menacing from the front, so unlike its somewhat tame appearance from the side.

You may become interested in quality reproductions of paintings or photographs of birds, either as large prints or as book illustrations. The colors usually are lifelike. In addition, the artist or photographer has produced a thing of beauty depicting an object of beauty.

How about the quality of color illustrations in books, especially field guides? The inks used in field guides will fade or change. But the colors are adequate if the birder does not insist on exact matches—and the birder should also know that the color of a Northern Cardinal in California will vary from that of a Northern Cardinal in Tennessee.

THREAT BEHAVIOR. *You can watch birds on a feeder utilizing color and shape to establish dominance. For example, the Common Grackle swells its feathers and shows off its iridescence to intimidate a rival. Notice how this Black-capped Chickadee, seen head-on, seems more bold, more striking. Do other chickadees see it that way? Be careful not to read your own subjective reactions into bird behavior.*

JULY 1–7

"National Geographic Special ▼ is on!"

INTELLIGENCE AND INSTINCT

ACTIVITIES. When you describe bird behavior, be accurate and objective. Characterizing an action by a bird as instinctive or as a sign of intelligence is dangerous. Do you have reliable knowledge of what a bird has been taught? Consider this: The next time you pull your hand back from a hot stove, is your action a result of instinct or intelligence? What about birds? Although you may feel certain that a bird ate a seed because it was hungry, the action could have been a compulsive reflex. Beware, then, of interpretation and explanation. Just record what you see. For example, if there is an infestation of insect pests, such as beetles or moths, concentrate on recording the species and numbers of birds that feed on them.

LEARNED BEHAVIOR. *After milk began to be delivered in bottles to doorsteps in England, Blue Tits learned to remove the caps in order to drink the cream. This new behavior spread rapidly, leading some ornithologists to conclude that tits taught each other how to pry open the caps.*

INTELLIGENCE AND INSTINCT. Intelligence in animals may be defined as the ability to learn from experience or instruction. In that sense all birds have some intelligence, and some birds appear to have more than others. Instinct may be defined as the set of reactions an animal is born with, that is, its reflexive responses to stimuli. By observation and experiment, scientists have learned that most animal behavior, even reaction to fire, is a mixture of learned behavior and what scientists now refer to as innate, or instinctual, behavior. No one can be certain whether any example of behavior is solely learned or solely innate. Animals that learn quicker and remember longer than other animals probably exhibit higher intelligence. Animals that appear slow to learn and do not remember what they learn are considered to show primarily reflexive reactions.

When animals pull back from a fire, are they displaying solely instinctual behavior—a reflex requiring no conscious thought—or have their brains and nervous systems, learning from their earliest experiences, recognized the danger and instructed their muscle systems to pull back automatically? Children certainly learn about fire partly from experiencing pain and from then on avoid fire. So do other animals. In individual birds or in a species, some behavioral patterns become imprinted; that is, a given stimulus quickly provokes the appropriate response. This explains how Ivan Pavlov, the Russian physiologist, could train his dogs to salivate at the sound of a bell and why animals can be trained to push buttons for a reward of food. The behavior is learned, so it involves some degree of intelligence.

When a newly hatched, blind nestling opens its beak for the first food brought by its parent, is this an innate reaction, or has the nestling somehow learned it? And what was the stimulus that caused the nestling to open its beak? No one can answer these questions with certainty, especially because once a bird is out of its shell, conditions for learning exist even if ornithologists have not yet observed the process.

COMINGS AND GOINGS. Mount McKinley, called Denali by Indians, in south central Alaska, is the highest mountain in North America. Visiting it in summer can be a rewarding experience for birders. Over 100 species have been reported in Mount McKinley National Park, open from June 1 to September 30. Among the species are Harlequin Duck, Barrow's Goldeneye, Bald Eagle, Golden Eagle, Spruce Grouse, Willow Ptarmigan, Rock Ptarmigan, White-tailed Ptarmigan, Lesser Golden Plover, Surfbird, Long-tailed Jaeger, Bonaparte's Gull, Arctic Tern, Northern Hawk-Owl, Three-toed Woodpecker, Boreal Chickadee, American Dipper, Arctic Warbler, Northern Wheatear, and Varied Thrush—birds you will not come across every day.

■ *Mount McKinley National Park*

NOTES

JULY 1–7
INTELLIGENCE AND
INSTINCT

Learning may occur even inside the shell, for it is known that sound passes through to the developing chick inside. Young birds placed in soundproof chambers, where they cannot hear adult songs, have difficulty in singing properly. If eggs are incubated in the soundproof chamber, learning to sing is apparently even more difficult, which suggests that some learning of adult songs takes place in the shell. But innate behavior certainly does occur: Without any identifiable learning or stimulus from the outside, a chick begins to peck its way out of the shell at the right time. Without training, some precocial birds begin to peck for food immediately after hatching, and they also may walk about and peep.

Though psychometry is a difficult science or art, the only way in which animal intelligence can be measured is to determine how much animals learn and remember and whether they put this knowledge to work solving problems in everyday life.

TOOLS AND INTELLIGENCE. *Humans select one tool first and then another to accomplish a task. A few birds use objects as tools to help them accomplish their own tasks. A Woodpecker Finch (above) uses a cactus spine to pry insects from crevices; a Hooded Crow pulls in a fisherman's line to retrieve a fish; and an Egyptian Vulture (far right) tosses a rock at an Ostrich egg to break it open. But these may be examples of stereotyped behavior rather than intelligent choice: The vulture, for example, may throw a rock again and again at an egg already broken open and emptied.*

Stereotyped behavior. Many birders mistakenly use the word *instinct* to describe everyday activities that are stereotyped and repeated frequently, especially by all birds of the same species. Actually, what may seem to be stereotyped behavior may not really be so rigid.

Observe the behavior of birds at your feeder. Keep notes of their actions, individual by individual, species by species. Place an object strange to the birds—a water glass, a plastic toy, a glass prism—in the center of your most popular feeder, and note the reactions of each species. Do some avoid the feeder? Do they make alarm calls? Do they show aggression or fear? What are the reactions when the object is removed? Now, perhaps, you may be ready to attempt to classify their behavior as instinctive or intelligent.

The brain. Although the brain of a bird differs from that of a human and most other mammals, the major parts are the same, and to varying degrees they perform the same functions. The smooth-surfaced cerebral hemispheres are relatively large in birds. In humans these hemispheres are the thinking parts of the brain, and in birds the hemispheres may perform some of the same functions. Note the rather small olfactory lobes attached in front. Their size suggests that the sense of smell is relatively unimportant in birds, with a few exceptions such as the kiwis. On the other hand, the optic lobes, which are situated beneath the olfactory lobes, one on each side of the brain, are rather large, indicating that vision is important—birds can distinguish many colors.

The cerebellum, the wrinkled, medium-sized rear part of the brain, coordinates muscle activities. It apparently is related to special behavior and may be the seat for innate activities, such as nest building and some courtship behavior. Behind the cerebellum lies the medulla oblongata, the enlargement at the top of the spinal column, where messages that require action are deciphered. Here is where sound messages are received. Hearing is acute in birds, though some do not hear sounds as low in pitch as the human voice.

Do birds think? Birds may be taught to press buttons or levers for a reward of food. Sparrows and other birds have been taught to thread beads on a needle—after all, nest-building requires similar skills. Birds may easily be taught to respond to whistles or other sounds. Even so, birds do not think the way people do. This may be hard to accept, since it is so easy to interpret bird behavior in human terms. Remember that the nervous system of a bird is geared to a different way of life, basic to which is flight, not record keeping or writing, which appear to be important in human thinking. Yet birds are highly successful: They have survived and evolved for nearly 200 million years, and this adaptability may well enable them to outlast humans, our poisons, and powers of destruction.

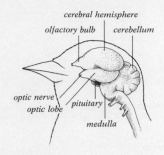

cerebral hemisphere
olfactory bulb | cerebellum
optic nerve
optic lobe | pituitary
medulla

THE BIRD BRAIN. *A foolish person is often called a birdbrain, but there is nothing foolish about the behavior of birds. In fact, like all other animals, except perhaps for humans, birds weak in the head soon die, resulting in a gradual evolutionary improvement of the brain for doing better what a bird requires for survival.*

JULY 8–14

MYTHS AND FABLES

ACTIVITIES. You will hear many statements about birds and not know whether they are fact or fable. Here are some. (1) Birds fly north and south on the same dates each year. (2) The biggest birds lay the biggest eggs. (3) Owls are the most intelligent of birds. (4) Loons and geese are the most stupid of birds. (5) All bird eggs are edible. (6) Rails and dippers can walk on pond or river beds while totally submerged. All these statements are discussed in the pages of this diary, but as your experience in bird watching grows, you will come across many more facts and a surprising number of fables. A compilation of folk beliefs about birds in your region would be a worthwhile project.

THE GOOSE TREE. *Goose Barnacles, hanging like fruit from leathery stalks, were said by medieval travelers to develop into geese.*

THE ROC. *The most famous of these huge birds are perhaps those encountered by Sinbad the Sailor.*

MYTHS AND FABLES. A myth may be regarded in part as an explanation of nature and, like modern science, concerned with facts based on what people know or deduce from what they know. Ancient people lived closer to nature than do most people today, so it is not surprising that animals, especially the highly visible and numerous birds, figured in the myths of the ancients.

Myths about birds. Small birds hatch from small eggs and so, reasoned the ancients, the bird that hatched from the 13- by 9½-inch egg of the Madagascar Elephant Bird—remnants, even whole eggs, are still found—had to be huge. Elephant Birds, now extinct, were big and could not fly, though this was not known by early travelers. Thus was born the myth of the man-carrying Roc of *The Arabian Nights*.

A very ancient myth, whose origins are apparently lost forever, has it that the swan sings just before it dies. Not even the Tundra, or Whistling, Swan can ever be said to sing, so to claim that a swan sings before its death is superstition. But Plato and Aristotle believed it, and the sweet song of the swan before death is a recurring conceit. A Greek myth has it that the soul of Apollo, god of prophecy, light, youth, music, and poetry, passed into a swan—hence the Swan of Avon (Shakespeare) and the Mantuan Swan (Virgil).

Saying that the soul of a dead person has entered a bird is one way of asserting the immortality of the soul and its eventual return to life among men. Consider Arthur of the Round Table, the once and future king, who is said to survive in the form of a bird, a chough or crow or, according to some, a puffin.

"As soon as the he-Rukh came up with us, he let fall upon us the rock he held in his pounces; but the master put about ship, so that the rock missed her by some small matter and plunged into the waves with such violence, that the ship pitched high and then sank into the trough of the sea and the bottom of the ocean appeared to us. Then the she-Rukh let fall her rock, which was bigger than that of her mate, and as Destiny had decreed, it fell on the poop of the ship and crushed it, the rudder flying into twenty pieces; whereupon the vessel foundered and all and everything on board were cast into the main."
—From The Thousand Nights and a Night, *translated by Richard F. Burton*

COMINGS AND GOINGS. West.

Mountain birding does not necessarily demand strenuous hiking. While vigorous birders can get all the exercise they want, many birders find that searching a sunny slope or small glen in the western mountain regions can be rewarding. Visiting high mountains in summer is something like traveling to northern regions. You may find birds that normally breed farther north. Or you may see birds, like the Mountain Bluebird and the Rosy Finch, that prefer to nest at high altitudes. At any rate, in western mountains, keep your eyes peeled for White-tailed Ptarmigan, Great Gray Owls, Boreal Owls, Lewis' Woodpecker, Gray Jay, crossbills, and many other interesting birds.

• National parks in western mountains

NOTES *1990*

July 11 – We left Laramie and drove to Denver. Big hailstorm. On July 12 a.m. we flew to Seattle, bussed to Vancouver, and embarked on the MS Noordam for Ketchikan, Juneau, Glacier Bay & Sitka, Alaska. *at Ketchikan* We saw a Bald Eagle at the Totem Bight Park. Also learned a little about the n.w. Indians & totems. The raven is one of their animals of interest – with bears, wolf, beaver, frog, eagle, and humans. But we saw no ravens. Then at Juneau, lots of crows. Finally, at Sitka, both crows & ravens. But no frogs. No one I talked with knew what frog the frog of the totems was based upon.

Other birds seen on the trip included: Kittiwakes, (black footed?), Glaucus-winged Gull, Puffins – sp?, Guillemots (Pigeon); some other gulls & small shore birds.

Sometimes a bird is held to be a transformation of the body, accomplished by sorcerers, as when Gottfried was turned into the swan that drew the boat of Lohengrin, Knight of the Swan. Another magical example concerns the swan maiden, half human and half supernatural, who is released from her swan's body by the talisman of her lover, only to be transformed once more into a swan when her lover disobeys the maiden. This motif appears in almost every culture.

Perhaps the oldest immortality myth concerns the phoenix, the red and golden bird that, according to Herodotus, was about the size of an eagle. In Egypt the phoenix was the symbol of the ever-rising sun. Bearing the body of its father, the phoenix appeared in the temple of the sun at Heliopolis every 500 years. In some versions the phoenix was burned on the altar by the priests, only to rise again 3 days later. In Persian legend the simurg, said to be 30 birds in one, lived 1700 years before a young simurg was hatched. To keep the species alive, only the old bird of the opposite sex was burned. In other versions the phoenix cast itself into the flames, and a young phoenix arose from the ashes. Thus the bird was a symbol of reincarnation and immortality.

It was commonly believed by early scientists that no bird above a certain size could fly. Then paleontologists in Argentina dug up Teratornis, *with a wingspan of 25 feet. (Pterosaurs, the fossil flying reptiles, had wingspans of up to 32 feet.)* Teratornis *lived from about 6.5 million years ago to about 10,000 years ago, and its territory may have included the southern United States. Although no feathers were found with* Teratornis, *its fossilized wing bones closely resemble those of modern eagles and could only have been used for active flight.*

The simurg, or simurgh, of Middle Eastern mythology was an enormous bird that survived three destructions of the world and was the all-knowing creature. It is possible that this mythological bird had its origins in observations of Elephant Bird eggs, as did the Roc. *Teratornis,* a giant vulture, lived in the New World thousands of years ago, so presumably it could not have formed the basis for myths of the Old World.

Fables about birds. All peoples developed myths that have faded from belief but may persist as fables, intended to be told to children. The Indians of the Americas were no exception. Many of their animal myths arose from religious associations, perhaps engendered by the shamans, who selected creatures having traits they attributed to the gods. Of the birds, eagles and hawks were defined most frequently, and to make them more impressive, their sizes often were exaggerated.

The Micmac Indians of eastern Canada envisioned a gigantic bird that created winds and storms by beating its wings. Such a bird also appears in Norse and Icelandic mythology and can be traced to the Adapa tales of ancient Babylon. The Andean Condor has its roles in the mythology of the Indians of the Andean region. The Golden Eagle soars through the tales of the North American Indians, including the Iroquois of New York, who also told of a giant bird, called Os-ha-da-ge-a, whose wings, big enough to darken the skies, fanned breezes and created dew and rain to revive parched earth. The giant thunderbird, responsible for lightning and thunder, appears in many Indian myths, and the Wild Turkey was honored for bringing corn to the Indians. One legend has it that the Dewbird will be killed by another bird, the lands will dry up, and all humanity will die from hunger and thirst.

In fables animals usually speak, generally to teach a moral. A good example is the fable of the hawk and the nightingale, told by Hesiod about 2700 years ago and said to be the oldest known Greek fable. The nightingale, saying he is too small to satisfy his captor, pleads with the hungry hawk to release him. The hawk replies that a small bird will appease his hunger better than a big bird not yet caught—even in ancient Greece, a bird in the hand was worth two in the bush.

Fables sometimes offer explanations of how an animal got its shape, color, or personality. In our culture the American Robin (based on the European Robin) is said to have received its color when it plucked a thorn from Christ's crown on His way to Calvary, the flowing blood turning the breast feathers permanently red. The Roller of India, while perched on a fence post, appears a dull sooty brown, but in flight its tail and wings flash a striking pattern of light blues. A fable relates that the Roller was beautifully colored from head to tail until it flew through a forest fire to warn the napping god Rama of approaching danger. The fire seared the fine plumage a sooty brown, but Rama rewarded the bird by endowing it with gorgeous blue wings and tail.

Superstitions involving birds often appear in folklore as well as in fables. In many parts of the world, a bird, especially a white one, flying inside a house is a sign of imminent death. A woodpecker tapping on a house is warning of bad news, but a wren building a nest near a house brings good luck. A crowing rooster announces that company is coming, a hooting owl that bad luck or death is on its way. Lest we think superstition is dead, in parts of the United States it is believed even now that wedding presents should not carry decorations or designs based on birds. Why? The happiness of the newlyweds will fly away!

A superstition is without truth, but myths and fables may reveal some fact and often some wisdom. So let us end with the story of the goose that laid the golden egg, as told by Aesop, the Greek fabulist of about 2500 years ago:

A certain man had a goose that laid a golden egg every day. Dissatisfied with one egg a day, and thinking he could seize the whole treasure at once, the man killed the goose, cut her open, and found no more than he would have found in any other goose.

Suitably warned, let's get on with bird watching.

In one fable, the European Robin is said to cover the dead with leaves:

Thus wandered these poor innocents,
    Till death did end their grief;
In one another's arms they died,
    As wanting due relief:
No burial this pretty pair
    Of any man receives,
Till Robin-red-breast piously
    Did cover them with leaves.

        —From "The Babes in the Wood"
        (anonymous)

THE TREE GOOSE. *Described and illustrated by Konrad von Gesner (1516–1565), based partly on descriptions from the thirteenth century, the Tree Goose was said to ripen on trees. It goes without saying that Gesner, whose work in natural history launched modern zoology, never saw the phenomenon himself. Perhaps this myth arose because no scholar had seen its breeding grounds, just as the myth that swallows hibernate in mud at the bottoms of ponds developed because no one knew where swallows went in winter.*

JULY 15–21

FIRST AID

ACTIVITIES. Vacation time is here, and you may want to include birding in your plans. Fortunately, birding can be pursued anywhere—town or country, north or south, shore or mountains, far away or close to home. In fact, even on a business trip, when you may not have much free time, there is nearly always a chance of looking for a new bird. Birders were once considered oddballs, but now that bird watching is one of the most popular sports, slipping a pair of binoculars out of an attaché case should not cause astonishment. But some planning is in order for any trip. See page 158 for tips about planning.

HOLDING BIRDS. *A bird as small as the Blackpoll Warbler shown here can be held in the bare hand, but be careful of sharp pecks. A big bird, such as this Mallard, can give a severe bite or blow with its beak, so for protection always wear gloves and heavy, long-sleeved shirts.*

FIRST AID. In most of the United States, a permit is required to keep a native wild bird captive. Among the exceptions are crows, certain blackbirds, House Sparrows, and European Starlings. If you pick up an injured wild bird, therefore, you should inform the local representative of your state fish and game department or your state conservation department. Informing the appropriate official about the injured bird and how you came to get it protects you from the accusation that you stoned or shot the bird and then claimed you found it injured. The official may also tell you how to care for the bird or suggest where you can take it for proper care. If you cannot find a helpful official, try your local bird club, where a knowledgeable member will tell you how to help the bird.

When you are the doctor. On a birding trip you will not often see an injured bird, and if you do there is little chance you can get close enough to capture it. But your interest in birds gets around. Friends and neighbors, especially small children, soon bring you birds that need help. Though there are books on bird first aid, you will usually be on your own. While someone telephones a fish and game officer, hold the bird gently on its back in one hand and examine the bird for signs of blood and broken bones. If the bird is large or struggling, devise a paper tube to fasten around its body. This will immobilize it more or less.

If a bird is found perching motionless, apparently in shock, place it in a cardboard carton. Close the cover to darken the inside and put the box in a cool, quiet place. The bird may recover in a few hours or overnight. Do not attempt, at first, to give the injured bird food or water, and do not give it an alcoholic beverage. People are warned not to drink and drive, so consider a bird's problem when it drinks and attempts to fly.

Many birds have sharp bills or talons, so wear gloves and a long-sleeved shirt while handling birds, especially large ones. But guard your eyes and do not put your face close to any bird—or any other wild animal, for that matter.

124

COMINGS AND GOINGS. East.

A striking bird year-round on coastal beaches and mud flats is the American Oystercatcher, which also occurs along the eastern and western shores of Mexico. In the eastern United States it is extending its range northward. It flies in small, boisterous flocks, calling *wheep-wheep-wheep* and demanding the attention of everyone within earshot. In spite of its high visibility, it is wary, and birders find it hard to approach. Incidentally, although it eats shellfish, crabs, worms, and many marine invertebrates, the American Oystercatcher does not eat oysters. So much for the infallibility of species names.

▬▬ *Year-round range of American Oystercatcher*

NOTES

A strong paper sack or burlap bag is useful in dealing with large birds, especially hawks and owls. Even an owl will quiet down in pitch darkness, so have a covered box handy with holes for ventilation.

Nestlings. A bird brought to you may turn out to be a nestling or fledgling and therefore easy to pick up. Such birds usually are not injured at all. Place the bird in the crotch of a tree or on a branch near where it was found. The calls of the nestling will ordinarily attract adult birds. If a young bird cannot even flutter on its own, place it in an open cardboard or berry box you can tack to a tree. The parent birds usually will be making a fuss there, so keep pets and children away and let the parents take over. They know what and when to feed their offspring.

If you feel you must take a bird inside and try to feed it, remember that most young birds feed on insects. The best home substitute is probably moist canned dog food. Roll the food into pellets and, with fingers or forceps, push a pellet well down the youngster's throat. Pigeons and doves feed their young pigeon milk, which is grain partially digested in the crops of the adults. For young doves, therefore, mix milk with pablum or similar meal to form a watery mixture, and use a medicine dropper for the feeding. Few veterinarians work with birds, so if you take an injured wild bird to a vet without telephoning first, you may be wasting your time and still have to pay a fee.

Stunned birds. A sudden thud against a windowpane or wall of your house near your bird feeders may announce that a bird has had an accident. You may find the bird unconscious on the ground nearby or perched motionless and unaware of your presence. First make sure no stray cats are about looking for a free meal. Watch the bird for

SUBSTITUTE NEST. *An empty berry box tacked to a tree makes an excellent refuge for a young bird you cannot put back into its nest.*

SETTING A BROKEN WING. *A bird, such as this finch, whose wing droops has probably broken it. Setting a bone break is best left to an expert, but there is something you can do. Try immobilizing the bird with paper or cloth strips. Do not use adhesive tape, which will stick to the feathers and add to the problem. Prevented from flying, the bird should be kept in a box or cage from which all perches and obstructions have been removed. In time the broken bone may heal. If you intend to care for an injured bird, first consult a good text, such as John Eric Cooper and J. T. Eley's First Aid and Care of Wild Birds (1979).*

a few minutes to see if it regains consciousness and flies off. If this does not happen, pick the bird up carefully and examine it, feeling first for a heartbeat and then checking for possible broken bones or signs of blood. If the bird seems whole, place it in a safe place to permit it to recover. If it does not recover in a few minutes, place it in a covered box so that the bird will be in darkness while it recovers. The bird may have suffered severe concussion and die, but you are giving it its best chance for survival.

Broken bones are best left to veterinarians and bird experts. The illustrations on this page show the simpler methods of handling damaged birds. If you know that a bird has broken bones and intend to take it to an expert, remember that the patient must be handled in such a way as to prevent movement of the broken bones. Cuts and bleeding must be handled in much the same way you would treat such injury in a human or a pet mammal. Use of compresses is the simplest procedure for stopping bleeding.

Birds loose in a house. Your home is a strange habitat for a wild bird, arousing panic and causing the bird to fly about wildly. Thumping into windows is common, because the bird is unaware of the glass and sees it as an escape route. Avoid moving toward a bird flying about in your home until you darken the room completely. Before turning off the last light, mark the position of the bird and then cover that spot with a light cloth to trap the bird. If you do not trap it, open a window or door to the outdoors so the bird can fly out of the house. Do not make wild grabs at a bird, because it may cause damage as it flies about.

You might ask curators at your local museum whether they would like to have dead birds for their collections. If they do want them, provide dates and places where you found the birds.

Many birds are killed on roads, and some may be worth saving and reporting. The birds can be wrapped in aluminum foil or put in plastic bags, then into a freezer for storage before being taken to a curator. Many specimens in museums bear DOR *on their labels, meaning "dead on road," and were probably brought in by birders. The New York State Museum has a Red-shafted Flicker, the only New York specimen known, and it is labeled* DOR.

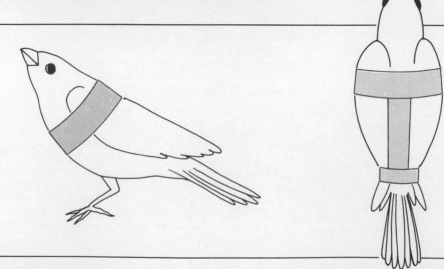

JULY 22–28

ATTRACTING BIRDS

ACTIVITIES. By listening carefully to the sounds that birds utter, you can learn to interpret what they are saying. They certainly communicate with one another. What they say is not directly understood by people, but the effect of the sounds is observable. Listen to crows. Hear them become excited; hear their caws become shriller and shriller. Even from a distance you can tell they have found a hawk in the open or an owl perched alone. We have located owls by listening to crows and heading to where they are congregating. An American Robin probably cannot communicate with a Wood Thrush or a crow, and certainly not with a hawk. But the alarm notes of robins and thrushes increase in tempo and somewhat in pitch as danger draws near them or their nests and young—and other forms of wildlife pay attention.

Birds that use man-made structures are not going to be put off if the sizes of the structures are wrong by a matter of inches, just so long as the locations are good and they are able to get in and out of the holes. In fact, a house built for an Eastern Bluebird will easily accommodate wrens, American Tree Swallows, and others—especially if the entrance hole has been made a little larger than the 1+ inches recommended for bluebirds. If youngsters build a lopsided house out of scrap wood according to their own plans, put it up. You may find birds using it in preference to a beauty for which you paid $50.

ATTRACTING BIRDS. The kinds and numbers of bird species you can attract to your garden and feeders depend mostly on the natural setting of your home. If your house is in a wooded area, you should be able to attract such woodland birds as thrushes, tanagers, and Purple Finches. Set in the midst of fields, your feeders may attract larks, pipits, cowbirds, goldfinches, and redpolls. If you live close to ponds and streams, you may attract such water birds as ducks, American Coots, and sandpipers, particularly if you scatter food along the shores or in the shallows. In the suburbs you will see species that favor open woods and brushland: nuthatches, tits, chickadees, jays, wrens, thrashers, and many others. If you know which species of birds are present in your area, you can develop a plan that will attract a large variety of birds. This requires proper placement of feeders, shelters, birdhouses, and birdbaths.

Birds will also be attracted by other inducements, such as a supply of sand (grit), nesting materials, shelter against severe storms, or a variety of foods. For example, American Robins, Barn Swallows, and a few others will appreciate an area of wet soil that offers the mud they need in nest building. Place other kinds of nesting materials where birds can reach them easily. An unraveling sweater enables birds to do their own plucking, as do tufts of hair, cotton, and vegetable fiber. Hair gleaned from currycombs in stables, lengths of string or yarn, scraps of wood shavings, and almost any fibers are welcome.

Birdhouses. After feeders and a source of water, birdhouses will probably attract more birds to your garden than most other inducements. Birdhouses may profitably be placed in suitable trees at appropriate heights, as indicated in the table on page 130. One birder placed 132 birdhouses on half an acre. Only four were occupied by the unwanted House Sparrows and European Starlings. Remember too that a dead tree left in a corner of your garden may attract a bird that has its own architectural plans.

COMINGS AND GOINGS. West. The American
Black Oystercatcher frequents the Pacific coast all the way north
to the Aleutian Islands throughout the year. One of us, perched
on a ledge along a rocky stretch of the California coast in mid-
June to watch whales and seabirds offshore, was agreeably dis-
tracted by a flock of seven of these birds flying by, all giving their
wheep-wheep-wheep calls in slightly different notes and together
producing a pleasing harmony. Birders visiting on the West
Coast should take lodgings on a Pacific bluff where, while awaiting breakfast, they can watch the abundant sea life and, with a
little luck, see the rather uncommon American Black Oystercatcher.

▬▬▬ *Year-round range of American Black Oystercatcher*

NOTES

BUILDING HOUSES FOR BIRDS

Following are dimensions and recommended locations for some birdhouses. The species are listed in field guide order.

SPECIES	HOUSE WIDTH/ DEPTH/ HEIGHT	HOLE DISTANCE ABOVE FLOOR	HOLE SIZE	HEIGHT ABOVE GROUND	LOCATION
Wood Duck	10″/10″/15″	8–12″	4″	4–20′	woods near water
American Kestrel	8″/8″/12–15″	9–12″	3″	10–30′	woods near field
Barn Owl	10″/18″/15–18″	2–4″	6″	12–18′	on wall near field
Northern Saw-whet Owl	6″/6″/10–12″	8–10″	2.5″	12–20′	thick forest
Eastern Screech-Owl	8″/10″/16–18″		3.25″	11–13′	forest or edge
Red-headed Woodpecker	6″/6″/12–15″	9–12″	2″	12–20′	open woods, edges
Golden-fronted Woodpecker	6″/6″/12–15″		2″	6–20′	open woods, edges
Red-bellied Woodpecker	6″/6″/12–15″	9–12″	2.5″	12–20′	open woods, edges
Downy Woodpecker	4″/4″/8–10″	6–8″	1.25″	6–20′	woodland
Hairy Woodpecker	6″/6″/12–15″	9–12″	1.5″	12–20′	woodland
Northern Flicker	7″/7″/16–18″	11–13″	3.25″	12–20′	forest edges
Great Crested Flycatcher	6″/6″/8″	8–10″	2″	8–20′	woodland
Purple Martin	6″/6″/10–11″	6″	2.5″	15–20′	open areas near water
Tree Swallow	5″/5″/6–8″	5–6″	1.5″	4–12′	open areas near water
Violet-green Swallow	5″/5″/6–8″	5–6″	1.5″	4–12′	open areas near water
chickadees, tits, nuthatches	4″/4″/6–8″	8–15″	1.25″	5–15′	forest edges
House, Bewick's, Carolina wrens	4″/4″/4–6″	6–8″	1.25″	5–10′	open woods or edges
Eastern, Western, Mountain bluebirds	5″/5″/5–6″	6–8″	1.5″	4–12′	open areas or forest edges

AMERICAN ROBIN

HOUSE WREN

BUILDING NEST SHELVES FOR BIRDS

Following are dimensions and locations for nest shelves.

Osprey	6′ by 6′; 1–25′ above ground
phoebes	6″ by 6″; under porch or other roof or bridge
Barn Swallow	6″ by 6″ or 5″ by 6″ ledge; in barn or open building
American Robin	6″ by 8″; in tree or against building 6–15′ above ground
Song Sparrow	6″ by 6″; in tree or shrub 1–3′ above ground
Shelves for small birds	may have a 2- to 4-inch edge on the outer side only

HOUSE WREN

HAIRY WOODPECKER

EASTERN BLUEBIRD

NORTHERN FLICKER

AMERICAN ROBIN

JULY 29–AUG 4

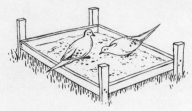

BIRD FEEDERS

ACTIVITIES. If you know shut-ins who have trouble filling their days with interesting activities, why not provide window bird feeders for them. At the same time you might provide field identification guides to stir interest in identifying birds that come to the feeders. It is also helpful to provide telephone numbers of birders willing to answer questions that may arise. Bird comings and goings can provide fresh topics for conversation each day. There are good tray feeders for upper-story windows of shut-ins, and some birds prefer feeders placed well above the ground. New birds will show up as the seasons progress, so keep the feeders going all year round, and do not forget that some summer birds like fruit sections and berries in the feeder.

COMMON
REDPOLL   PINE SISKIN

GRAY SQUIRREL

A SQUIRREL-PROOF FEEDER

BIRD FEEDERS. What is important about a feeder is not the beauty of its construction but the kind of food it contains (see pages 10–12) and how easily and safely birds can use it. A bird finds the food, checks out the scene for such dangers as cats and hawks, and then may condescend to eat.

But you will want to consider some factors that do not concern the birds themselves. Is the feeder an attractive addition to your house or garden? Can it hold enough food to last while you are away from home? In addition, you may care more than birds do about the creatures dining alongside them. You may not want to feed chipmunks, squirrels, rats, jays, or crows. If you are particular, you can design or buy feeders that more or less successfully keep out freeloaders. Squirrels seem to be the animals people want most to exclude. This usually can be accomplished by placing an inverted cone on the post that supports the feeder or by buying a hanging feeder covered with a plastic dome from which a squirrel will slide off. Remember that squirrels are able to drop onto feeders from overhanging branches or structures.

Location and design. Feeders should be placed where birds can see them, yet close to shrubs and trees so that the birds can find quick shelter. Some birds prefer to feed on the ground, among them grouse, Ring-necked Pheasants, Greater Roadrunners, doves, towhees, thrushes, many sparrows, juncos, grackles, Common Flickers, and larks. Such birds may feed from high feeders if there is no ground food for them. Other birds prefer platform feeders 5 or 6 feet off the ground, among them goldfinches, chickadees, jays, woodpeckers, Pine Siskins, blackbirds, most sparrows, and finches. Birds partial to *haute cuisine* like even higher feeders, which can be attached to a second-story windowsill: finches, jays, grosbeaks, Pine Siskins, and others. And then there are the finches, titmice, and chickadees, which delight in feeders that hang and sway. In short, to attract the greatest number and variety of birds, feeders of different types should be placed in various locations.

COMINGS AND GOINGS. West.

Two members of the thrush, or robin, family of the western United States and Canada are the Townsend's Solitaire and the Varied Thrush. The Solitaire prefers coniferous forests at high altitudes, but in winter it descends to lower slopes, canyons, and valleys. The Varied Thrush has a more restricted range in the West, although it breeds all the way into northern Alaska. It is an interesting bird, in the nonbreeding season wandering great distances beginning in late July—it is seen occasionally from Maine to Virginia and in Texas and the Gulf states. In fact, while we were writing these words in February, a Varied Thrust had been sojourning for a week one mile from us, near Albany, New York.

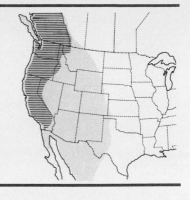

Year-round ranges: ≡Varied Thrush
Townsend's Solitaire

NOTES
_____

_____

_____

_____

_____

_____

_____

_____

_____

_____

_____

_____

_____

_____

_____

_____

_____

_____

_____

_____

_____

_____

_____

_____

_____

_____

FEEDER PREFERENCES

	GROUND FEEDERS	PLATFORM FEEDERS	HANGING FEEDERS	SUET RACKS
blackbirds	■			
buntings		■		
cardinals	■	■		
chickadees	■	■	■	■
doves	■	■		
finches	■	■	■	
flickers	■	■		■
goldfinches	■	■	■	
grackles	■	■		
grosbeaks	■	■		
jays	■	■		
juncos	■	■		
magpies	■	■		
mockingbirds	■	■		
nuthatches		■	■	■
orioles		■		■
Phainopepla		■		
Pyrrhuloxia	■	■		
quails	■			
Greater Roadrunner	■			
robins	■			■
Pine Siskin	■	■	■	
sparrows	■	■		
European Starling	■	■		■
tanagers		■		■
titmice	■	■	■	■
thrashers	■	■		■
thrushes	■	■		■
warblers	■			■
waxwings		■		
woodpeckers		■	■	■
wrens	■	■		■
Wrentit	■			■

Since nearly all seed-eating birds, when hungry enough, will use a platform feeder, that type should be your choice if you want to keep only one feeder going. A large flat board will do. Nail slats around the edges to prevent wind from blowing

MOURNING DOVES

food to the ground. Fix the board atop a post with an inverted cone beneath it, or nail it to a window-sill. In the northern United States and in Canada, a location on the south side of a house is generally best. In any case, protection against prevailing winds and a position near good escape cover are the two most important criteria in siting a feeder.

One of us puts a seed hopper big enough to need filling only once a week directly on the flat board. The other pours food onto the board each morning, enough to last until midafternoon. Both methods work well. We also scatter seeds directly on the ground and on a stump every day, locations that attract quail, grouse, doves, ducks, and others. Remember that the simplest feeder plus regularity in providing food will produce excellent results. Other basic feeder designs that you may be interested in trying are shown here.

HOUSE WREN

BLACK-CAPPED CHICKADEES

DOWNY WOODPECKER

NORTHERN FLICKER

WHITE-BREASTED NUTHATCH

BLACK-CHINNED HUMMINGBIRD

BLUE JAY

NORTHERN CARDINAL

AUG 5-11

BIRD SANCTUARIES

ACTIVITIES. Most serious bird watchers acquire large-scale maps of the areas in which they most frequently do their birding. Such maps are especially useful when birders want to leave the beaten trail and explore potentially good birding spots, such as wetlands. The U.S. Geological Survey publishes a series of topographic maps with a scale of 1:24,000 (2⅛ inches = 1 mile). These maps cover nearly all of the United States. They show ponds, lakes, roads of all classes, trails, buildings, and more. You can probably get the map for your area at an Army and Navy or sporting goods store. If you cannot, try writing to the U.S. Geological Survey, Washington, DC 20242.

Introduction of plants or animals into a sanctuary should be kept to a minimum. The new life forms may soon spread and take over large areas of a sanctuary. State nurseries may offer free trees and shrubs, but regard such gifts with suspicion—in the long run, controlling them may cost your club too much in money or labor. Government agencies that spray land for pest control also may be working against your interests. Natural controls in your sanctuary will probably do a better job.

The references listed here are helpful across the country, even those whose titles suggest usefulness in only one region. The U.S. Fish and Wildlife Service publishes bulletins for most areas, and your state may issue similar publications.

American Wildlife and Plants, *Martin, Zim, and Nelson. Lists plants used by wildlife across the United States.*

Shrubs and Trees of the Southwest Uplands, *F. H. Elmore. Use with Martin, Zim, and Nelson.*

Trees, Shrubs, and Vines for Attracting Birds, *De Graaf and Witman. A manual for the Northeast.*

Land Conservation and Preservation Techniques and Technical Assistance Notifications. *Many titles in these booklet series concern conservation, fund raising, and land acquisition. Write to the Heritage Conservation and Recreation Service, U.S. Department of the Interior, Washington, DC 20243.*

BIRD SANCTUARIES. Local bird clubs may operate a neighborhood sanctuary or join with other organizations to support one. Sanctuaries may range from a few acres to large tracts with many different habitats. Since landowners can often secure tax advantages by donating land for a wildlife sanctuary, a small local club faced with unexpected largess can be placed in the position of having to decide whether management of one or more sanctuaries is within its means and whether it can staff the sanctuaries. A sanctuary provides service to the community as an educational and recreational asset used by schools, scouts, garden clubs, nursing homes, birders, and naturalists. And members of the community may help in the maintenance of a sanctuary, which includes keeping trails clean, building steps and bridges, donating supplies, and raising funds.

Getting started. It is a good idea to list the reasons why your bird club would like to have a sanctuary. Here are some: 1. It gives pleasure to club members. 2. It attracts birds, even groups of birds, such as herons, waterfowl, coniferous woodland species, other woodland birds, or meadowland birds. 3. It provides opportunities for education and research. 4. It preserves a habitat, plant, or animal rare or unique to your locality. Listing reasons such as these will help the members of your club decide the kind of sanctuary they want.

Size. A bird sanctuary must have plants to supply natural food and attract insects and animal food. It must have shelter and water, flowing water if possible. The ideal site includes a variety of habitats, such as meadowland, forests, and brush. If it contains bogs, sand dunes, swamps, or marshes, there is a decided advantage. The passage of time will produce succession from one type of habitat to another. Lakes and ponds gradually fill in to become marsh, then wet meadow, then brushy field, then forest. Do not let these natural changes discourage you. Small dams can be built to create a pond or lake that will start the cycle anew.

COMINGS AND GOINGS. West. The imposing
name Phainopepla identifies an attractive sable-colored bird of
the Southwest, a member of the Silky Flycatcher family. The
birder often perceives first a single low-pitched and loud *wheep*.
Once the Phainopepla making the sound is located, the bird is
seen in all its elegance as it sallies forth in search of insects.
Phainopeplas inhabit arid regions and breed in mesquite brush
and in vegetation growing along streams and rivers—some birders insist that Phainopeplas raise one family in mesquite and,
later, another along the banks of streams. From June to August
you will find Phainopeplas worth a trip to see, because they are
always fun to watch.

Ranges of Phainopepla: *Year-round range*
                        Breeding range

NOTES

AUG 12–18

Visitor from Siberia
Attracts Eager Birders
To Jamaica Bay

ACCIDENTALS
AND
INTRODUCED
SPECIES

ACTIVITIES. On a topographic map, mark the type of vegetation characteristic of each birding spot you visit. Woodlands, for example, can be labeled coniferous, larch, oak, mixed, maple, etc. This information is helpful when you are looking for specific species that prefer a particular one of these habitats. Keep the map up to date by adding newly constructed roads and the like. And when woodlands are cut down, add that information as well. Most important of all, draw in your own walks, the pathways and trails that lead to spots you have found good for birding. By the way, xerography is great for copying maps for friends, but be sure the markings you add to your map are in a reproducible color.

In the winter of 1977–1978 an Ivory Gull appeared at Salisbury, Massachusetts, and about 5000 birders came from as far away as Virginia to observe the northern visitor. Joseph Taylor of Honeoye, New York, has been known to travel 5000 miles and more to see a rare accidental bird. Joe has held the North American record for seeing the greatest number of species in the wild.

HOUSE SPARROW. *This familiar bird, formerly called the English Sparrow, belongs to the Old World family of weaverbirds. It was introduced to the United States at Brooklyn, New York, in the mid-nineteenth century and is now found from coast to coast in the United States and Canada. Aggressive and more adaptable to life in our cities and to proximity to human habitations than are most of our native species, the House Sparrow has usurped the habitats where Chipping Sparrows, Song Sparrows, Field Sparrows, Purple Finches, Verdins, Bushtits, and other birds would otherwise be in residence now.*

ACCIDENTALS & INTRODUCED SPECIES. Birds may extend their ranges without much disturbance of local populations. But some species do cause damage. About 1900 the Great Black-backed Gull of the northern coasts of Europe and northeastern North America began moving south. It now breeds as far south as the coast of North Carolina. This movement has disrupted the Herring and Ring-billed gulls and the rarer Lesser Black-backed Gulls, as well as terns and various shorebirds.

Accidentals are birds far from their regular range. Some have escaped from captivity and are too few in number to establish viable colonies. Accidentals occur infrequently, and birders will travel far to see them. Some recorded in the West are the Reddish Egret, Baikal Teal, Iceland Gull, Heloise's Hummingbird, Prothonotary Warbler, and Hooded Warbler; in the East, the Red-billed Tropicbird, Cape Petrel, Little Egret, Corn Crake, Kiskadee, and Red-legged Thrush.

Introduced birds are those that were brought into an area by otherwise well-intentioned persons, escaped from cages, or were released by a dealer who found it was illegal to keep them. The list of introduced species includes the Domestic Pigeon (Rock Dove), European Starling, House Sparrow, House Finch (from the West to the East), Common Myna Bird, and Ring-necked Pheasant.

Accidentals and introduced species may soon outnumber or replace native species, because the aliens may have no natural enemies in a new territory or may carry disease or parasites fatal to local species. Sportsmen seeking new game species in the United States have successfully introduced the Chukar, Black Francolin, Gray Partridge, and, with less success, the Indian Peafowl. Hawaii has lost many native birds, some because of the introduction of the Chukar, Gray Partridge, Erchel's Francolin, Chinese Quail, Pectoral Quail, Painted Button-Quail, King Quail, Red Jungle Fowl, Reeve's Pheasant, Copper Pheasant, Ring-necked Pheasant, Green Pheasant, Peafowl, and many nongame species.

COMINGS AND GOINGS. Summer is hardly in full swing, and suddenly birds are beginning to migrate south. Plovers and other shorebirds are among the earliest to depart, and the first in line among them are probably those that were unsuccessful in nesting. One of the plovers is the Lesser Golden Plover, a species no birder wants to miss. It migrates both north and south along the Pacific coast and through the central United States and Canada. Except for a few strays, Lesser Golden Plovers are seen along the Atlantic coast only in autumn. They breed along the Arctic coasts, but you may find them stopping over near muddy edges of streams, swamps, ponds, and lakes, even near sewage disposal plants.

➤ *Migration routes of Lesser Golden Plover*

March–May   *March–April*
July–August   *July–Mid-September*   *July–September*

NOTES

AUG 19–25

DISTRIBUTION

ACTIVITIES. In eastern, central, and western parts of the United States and Canada, many species of birds are now beginning to flock, among them starlings, blackbirds, swallows, and some sparrows. Flocking behavior is complex and interesting, an intriguing focus for a special birding trip. Do the flocks you see contain several species? When disturbed, do the birds take off from the ground or from trees? Do the birds display particular flight patterns? For example, how far does the flock fly before setting down again? And how high? You can watch flocking almost anywhere—city parks, suburban lawns, country meadows, marshes, beaches, farmers' fields—wherever birds congregate. The flights are often spectacular.

Explorers of the 15th to 19th centuries brought back tales of weird birds in strange places. The first reports of ostriches, penguins, dodos, and other birds were not believed at first by the less credulous. In fact, birds have occupied all parts of the earth even though few species have adapted successfully to life in the polar lands, whether north or south. Yet, each new land discovered by explorers had its quota of nesting birds, even the most remote regions of Antarctica.

DISTRIBUTION. If you find a bird that is not supposed to be in the area you are in, double-check your identification before calling fellow birders to see the rarity. It is no fun to have the club know-it-all tell you that Lark Buntings get no closer to Connecticut than Nebraska.

The total range of a species throughout the year is defined as its distribution. A distribution map usually shows breeding and wintering ranges as well as the area through which a species migrates. Arrows may indicate routes of migration, especially if there are seasonal differences in routes. Some maps use isochronal lines (see page 50) to show times of migration, at least in spring. The maps in field guides commonly show ranges with little detail. A map showing the distribution of the Osprey, which ranges along water courses and close to lakes, ponds, and oceans around the world, would have so small a scale that it could not indicate much about where the species breeds in the United States and Canada. To be useful, distribution maps in field guides must show the boundaries of states and provinces, and even then someone may complain that a range limit in Nebraska is too far east.

Factors in distribution. You may think birds can fly anywhere in the world, but there are barriers to long flights. Many birds are weak fliers and would find it impossible to travel great distances, many species seem fearful of flying over bodies of water no matter how small, and many fly only when necessary. If a species is satisfied with food and accommodations where it is established, what would impel it to go to strange lands?

Climate is also an effective barrier. Again, many species avoid strange foods. Some, such as the family of warbler-sized white-eyes of southeastern Asia, East Indies, and southwestern Pacific, are apt to fly off in any direction when their homeland gets too crowded and some manage to find an inhabitable island. The Cattle Egret reached South America from Africa on its own and spread over much of the New World.

COMINGS AND GOINGS. **East.** Largest and most

widespread of the black-headed gulls is the Laughing Gull. As one might expect, its call notes are *ha-ha-ha*, becoming shriller and faster (perhaps funnier) during the mating season. Since Laughing Gulls do not mature until their third year, many individuals can be seen in summer away from the nesting colonies. Because this gull is not tolerant of cold weather, its range northward in summer and winter may be curtailed. But the Laughing Gull is slowly expanding its range, despite competition with the Herring Gull for nesting sites and food. Like all gulls, the Laughing Gull is attracted to garbage dumps, which are good places for watching other species as well.

▬▬▬ *Year-round range of Laughing Gull*

NOTES

Zoogeographical regions. Before the Age of Exploration, Europeans believed that the animals they knew at home were found all over the world. About a century ago zoologists realized that different regions often have basically different assemblages of animals and that the world can be divided sensibly into regions. Alfred Russel Wallace (1823–1913), codiscoverer of evolution with Charles Darwin (1809–1882), proposed six zoogeographical regions, as shown on the accompanying map. These divisions enable zoologists to discuss the distribution of birds against a rather simple background based on geographical barriers to diffusion in the geological past and, to some extent, in recent times. The Palearctic and Nearctic regions are similar and share 48 families of birds, so modern practice may use the term Holarctic Region to cover both.

Birds common or peculiar to the Holarctic Region are loons, grouse, auks, waxwings, hawks, owls, woodpeckers, thrushes, jays, Old World flycatchers and warblers, and weaverbirds. The Nearctic Region has turkeys, New World vultures, vireos, wood warblers, blackbirds, and orioles. The Neotropical Region—with more than 1,500 species—in addition to parrots and macaws, has rheas, tinamous, sunbitterns, oilbirds, potoos, motmots, toucans, antbirds, woodcreepers, cotingas, and others. The Ethiopian Region has its unique birds: Hammerhead Stork, Secretary Bird, mousebirds, turacos, and helmet shrikes. The Oriental Region has many pheasants, parrots, fruit

ZOOGEOGRAPHIC REGIONS

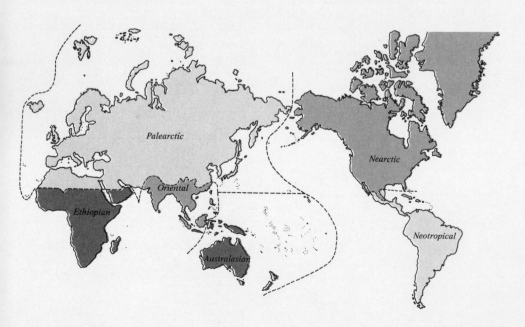

pigeons, flowerpeckers, and lories that are found only there. The Australian Region has cassowaries, emus, kiwis, lyrebirds, birds of paradise, bowerbirds, and others. Perhaps you will be fortunate enough to see these birds someday.

In describing the distribution of birds, several terms are used by zoologists: *cosmopolitan,* occurring on every continent; *cosmomarine,* occurring in every ocean; *pantropical,* occurring in tropical regions. These terms are especially useful in describing the distribution of families and orders but less useful in describing the distribution of genera and nearly useless for species.

In 1910 a zone map of North America was published based mainly on isotherms. It divides the continent into seven zones: Arctic, Hudsonian, Canadian, Transition, Upper Austral, Lower Austral, and Tropical. Bird ranges can be described as being in one or more of these zones for any state or states or even for areas within states. These zones serve well but omit the factor of vegetation, which is an important clue to bird distribution. Ecotone maps were then developed in which North America is divided into 18 sections, or ecotones, based on the dominant vegetation, such as coniferous forest, grassland, creosote-bush desert, and sagebrush, and then is subdivided into 29 provinces.

Remember that few bird species are found throughout a particular zone or ecotone, so the range of a bird is best described by an individual map or description.

LIFE ZONES   ECOZONES

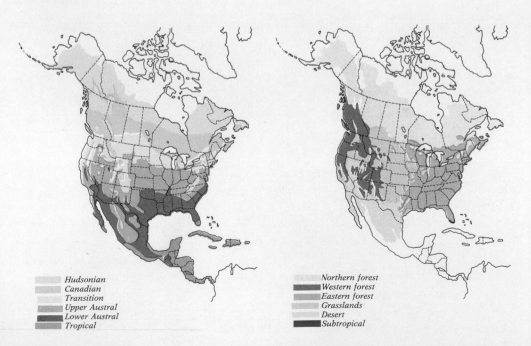

Hudsonian
Canadian
Transition
Upper Austral
Lower Austral
Tropical

Northern forest
Western forest
Eastern forest
Grasslands
Desert
Subtropical

143

AUG 26–SEPT 1

Seed-cracker.
Cardinal: powerful bite.

COMMON NAMES

ACTIVITIES. Practice estimating the numbers of birds you see in flocks and groups. Compare the estimates. Here's a hint: Count the birds in a quarter or other fraction of the flock and then multiply to get the total. If geese fly overhead in V formation, count one leg of the V and then estimate the length of the other leg. If the two legs are equal, multiply your original count by 2. If the second leg is half as long as the first, add half again to your count. Another hint: Observe a perching group of birds through large-mesh screening. Count the birds in one square of the mesh and multiply by the number of squares in which birds appear. You can also practice with other birders, asking them to make their own estimates of a particular flock. There is no way of making precise counts, but practice will improve your technique.

COLLOQUIAL NAMES FOR BIRDS

Eel-tricker. *Red-throated Loon: adept at catching eels.*

Bad-luck Bird. *Common Loon.*

Hell-diver. *Common Loon: quick-diving ability.*

Mother Carey's Chicken. *Storm-Petrels: a sailor's name for these birds, which presage storms, probably a corruption of* madre cara, *"mother dear," referring to the Virgin Mary.*

Thunder-pumper. *American Bittern: pumping call.*

Whistler. *Common Goldeneye: wings whistle in flight.*

Blue Hawk. *Northern Harrier, also called Marsh Hawk: male perceived as bluish.*

Big Blue Darter. *Cooper's Hawk: swift flight after prey.*

Blue Peter. *Purple Gallinule: appears to walk on water.*

Clam-cracker. *American Oystercatcher: feeds on clams.*

Dogtail. *Spotted Sandpiper: habitually wags its tail.*

Big Striker. *Common Tern: strong diver after fish.*

Rain Crow. *Black-billed and Yellow-billed cuckoos: thought to forecast rain.*

Monkey-face. *Barn Owl: face resembles monkey face.*

Cat Owl. *Screech and Great Horned owls: ear tufts resemble cat ears.*

Bull-bat. *Common Nighthawk and Whip-poor-will: wings in flight during courtship aerial diving sound like bawling bull.*

Wicker-whacker. *Common Flicker: call notes make whicker sound.*

Bridge Robin. *Phoebes: commonly nest under or close to bridges.*

Bee-Betty. *Kingbirds: habit of eating bees.*

Spider Wren. *House Wren: eats spiders.*

Bogtrot. *Wood Thrush: common in swamps.*

Butcherbird. *Shrikes: impale prey on thorns.*

Cottontail. *Bobolink: white rump patch.*

Elm Sparrow. *American Goldfinch: feeds on elm seeds.*

COMMON NAMES. Waldo Lee McAtee (1883–1962), while working for the U.S. Fish and Wildlife Service, recorded the colloquial and local names of all birds in the United States and Canada. His files included tens of thousands of names. A few he noted for the American Coot are mudhen, baldface, blue marsh-hen, chicken-bill, Chinese mallard, ivorybill, pelic, and moor-hen. Names were standardized on publication of the American Ornithologists' Union *Check-list of North American Birds* (latest edition 1983), and the names in that list now are officially called "English names."

Confusion resulted from use of colloquial names when they were applied to species of an area, state, or region. As time passed, one colloquial name for each species began to be accepted, and it was called the "common name" to distinguish it from the scientific name. The American Ornithologists' Union (AOU) took on the task of standardizing these common names, which meant using English, since English is spoken in both Canada and the United States. In Latin America common names are in Spanish, and French may be added one day in recognition of its use in Quebec. The AOU accepted an English name for a full species only. Thus, where the Check-list once recognized a Baltimore Oriole and a Bullock's Oriole, they now are known to be one species, the Northern Oriole. Yet it still is acceptable to refer to the western subspecies with more orange on its head as Bullock's Oriole and the black-headed eastern subspecies as Baltimore Oriole.

Though English names of bird species are conventionally referred to as common names, careful writers style English names like proper names, with each part of a name carrying an initial capital letter. Thus when we write *chickadee*, we mean any one of a number of species of chickadees. When we write *Black-capped Chickadee*, we refer to a particular species. Sometimes the word *common* is part of a bird's English name, as in *Common Moorhen. Common* usually means that the bird occurs throughout a large range.

COMINGS AND GOINGS. East. Where two spe-

cies that are genetically close are found together during the breeding season, birders are apt to find crosses, or hybrids, of the species. The Blue-winged and Golden-winged warblers are good examples of this phenomenon. By checking *American Birds*, you can find where the "Brewster's" and "Lawrence's" hybrids occur, and a trip to an appropriate area will test your birding skill. Between late May and June or early July, you may find a nest that has been filled and tended by the two parent species. We once found an example of such a nest in the middle of a wild strawberry field, enabling us to munch berries while watching the birds.

Breeding ranges: *Blue-winged Warbler*
                   Golden-winged Warbler

NOTES

When colonial Americans began to name birds, they copied British names extensively even where the species, genus, or family was not the same. It became necessary eventually to standardize these names in both Britain and America. American names had to be altered to conform with usage and the science of ornithology, and a few British names had to be altered or modified by adjectives. The American Ornithologists' Union finally published "official English Names" as part of its 1983 Check-list. It is hoped that all American birders will follow the official AOU nomenclature even though they may not agree with all the formulations.

Changes in English names in the 1983 Checklist reflect the latest scientific evidence. For instance, the Short-billed Marsh Wren now is called the Sedge Wren, since it is a bird of the open fields, wet or dry, grassy or sedgy. In South America it is found mainly in sedge meadows and fields. Since this leaves only one bird called a Marsh Wren in North America, it need not be called the Long-billed Marsh Wren; Marsh Wren alone will do.

On pages 204–215, we list by their English names all the birds seen in North America north of Mexico. Learn to use these names instead of the names you grew up with, which may be regional and wrong as species names. Since you cannot separate the subspecies Northern Yellowthroat from the subspecies Maryland Yellowthroat by a look in the field, just call it a Common Yellow-

ORIGINS OF SOME BIRD NAMES IN FIELD GUIDE ORDER

BIRD NAME	ORIGIN OF NAME
Pied-billed Grebe	Particolored bill—part one color, part another
Eared Grebe	Plumes or patches of feathers arising from or covering location of ears on sides of head
Horned Grebe, Great Horned Owl	Plumes or other feathers on upper sides of head, where horns would grow
Laysan Albatross, Laysan Rail	After Laysan, a western islet of the Hawaiian Islands
Cory's Shearwater	After Charles B. Cory (1857–1921), American collector and ornithologist
Buller's Shearwater	After Sir Walter Lawry Buller (1830–1906), New Zealand lawyer and ornithologist
Manx Shearwater	After Isle of Man, in the Irish Sea
Leach's Petrel	After William E. Leach (1790–1836), English naturalist
Wilson's Storm-Petrel, Wilson's Plover, Wilson's Warbler, Wilson's Phalarope	After Alexander Wilson (1790–1813), American ornithologist born in Scotland
Magnificent Frigatebird	After the swift, graceful, wooden warships of the 18th and 19th centuries
Northern Gannet	Birds of the booby family, thought to be related to geese, with *gannet* a corruption of *gander*
booby	Name of members of the Sulidae, considered stupid (boobies) because they allowed men to club them to death
cormorant	Corruption of *corvus*, Latin for "crow," because of the black color of the bird; six species breed and winter in the United States and Canada
Anhinga	From Portuguese, borrowed from Tupi, an Indian language of Brazil's Amazon region

throat. House Sparrow is considered more correct than English Sparrow. As a birder, it is important for you to learn to speak the language other birders use.

Origins of some bird names. Anyone using a field guide will notice that the birds are not arranged alphabetically nor, apparently, in any other recognizable order. Actually they are. The order is the one dictated by ornithology, which means that birds that resemble one another anatomically are placed together. In American field guides, in addition, the species considered most primitive are given first and those most advanced are given last. In Great Britain and some other countries, this order is reversed. However the listing is done, the origins of bird names are always of interest.

HARLEQUIN DUCK

LEACH'S STORM-PETREL

BIRD NAME	ORIGIN OF NAME
Brant	In the United States and Canada, a small dark goose that breeds in the arctic and migrates southward; origin of the name much discussed but ultimately must be termed unknown
Barnacle Goose	Long ago believed to have developed from barnacles in northern seas
widgeon	Also spelled *wigeon;* origin of the name much discussed, one candidate being the West Indian duck *vigeon,* but ultimately must be considered unknown; you can see the American and Eurasian widgeons
scaup	Ducks whose call resembles the sound *skawp;* another possibility is the term *scalp,* an old English name for a bed of the shellfish on which scaups feed
Harlequin Duck, Harlequin Quail	Reflecting their clownlike appearance
eider	Through the Dutch, German, or Swedish names for these sea ducks, all from Icelandic *aethur*
Steller's Eider, Steller's Jay	After Georg Wilhelm Steller (1709–1746), German naturalist who explored the arctic with Vitus Bering
merganser	This fish-eating duck takes its name from modern Latin: *mergus,* "diver" (or "waterfowl"), and *anser,* "goose"
California Condor	From a Spanish word, *cóndor,* meaning "vulture," from *kúntur,* a word in Quechua, a Peruvian Indian language
Crested Caracara	From Spanish and Portuguese, deriving ultimately from *caracará,* a Tupi word thought to be imitative of the bird's call
Gyrfalcon	From Old French *gerfaucon;* the derivation of the initial syllable is not clear, but it is thought to be from *gîr,* Old High German for "greedy"

BIRD NAME	ORIGIN OF NAME
Aplomado Falcon	*Aplomado,* Spanish for "lead-colored"
Plain Chachalaca	*Chachalaca,* Spanish, from Nahuatl, imitative of the loud, harsh, strident sounds the bird makes
ptarmigan	Probably from *tàrmachan,* a Gaelic word of uncertain meaning
Gambel's Quail	After William Gambel (1819–1849), American bird collector, who worked especially in California
egret	From the Old French word for "heron"
bittern	From a Latin word for "bittern" and "bull," presumably because the European Bittern makes a bellowing sound. There are two: the American and the Least bitterns.
ibis	A Greek word of Egyptian origin
Greater Flamingo	From a Portuguese word derived from *flamma,* "flame," suggesting the color of the bird
crane	From an Old English word, *cran,* derived from a much older Indo-European word for this bird; the machine called a crane got its name from its resemblance to the long-necked bird
Corn Crake	*Crake* is based on a Scandinavian word imitative of the sound of croaking
Black-necked Stilt	Stilts, long poles attached to one's feet, were in use in England as early as the 15th century, making stilt a logical name to apply to these long-legged birds
Eurasian Dotterel	From a Middle English word meaning "losing one's mind"; the bird was considered stupid because it was so easily caught, so there is the mistaken assumption that its name derives from *dolt*
plover	From the Middle French *plovier,* derived from the Latin *pluvia,* meaning "rain," possibly because these birds were thought to presage rain
godwit	One of the calls of the Hudsonian and Marbled godwits is *godwit,* but the origin of the name is unknown; a mistaken etymology has it that the name is derived from *God's wit;* a more reasonable claim is made for its derivation from *god wicht,* Old English, meaning *good creature,* because the bird was often eaten as a special dish
curlew	Probably from the plaintive calls of two European species, rendered in Middle French as *courlieu*
Willet	Probably from the call of the bird, said by many to resemble *will-will-willet*
phalarope	From the Greek words for "coot" and "foot," since the lobed feet of the phalarope resemble the feet of the coot
Common Snipe	Probably an ancient name of Scandinavian origin, perhaps imitative of the snipping or snapping sound made by its bill when the bird is feeding

BIRD NAME	ORIGIN OF NAME
Rufous-necked Stint	*Rufous* is from *rufus*, Latin for "red"; *stint*, spelled *styne* in Middle English, is a common English name for any of the smaller sandpipers
Thayer's Gull	After John Eliot Thayer (1862–1933), amateur ornithologist who left his collection of birds to Harvard
Heerman's Gull	After Adolphus Heerman (1827–1865), well-known collector of birds and eggs
Ross' Gull	After Sir James Clark Ross (1800–1862), British arctic explorer, who searched (1848–1849) for John Franklin (see next entry)
Franklin's Gull	After Sir John Franklin (1786–1847), arctic explorer who died during an ill-fated search for a Northwest Passage
Clark's Nutcracker	After William Clark (1770–1838), leader with Meriwether Lewis of an expedition to explore northwestern U.S.
Verdin	From French *verdin*, equivalent of Yellowhammer, a European bunting, applied to this yellow-headed relative
Red-whiskered Bulbul	Based on an ancient Arabic word for an Old World songbird, perhaps the nightingale
Bewick's Wren	Named by John J. Audubon after his friend Thomas Bewick (1753–1828), English engraver who illustrated bird books
thrasher	Also given as *thrusher*, both corruptions of *thrush*
Bendire's Thrasher	After Charles Emil Bendire (1836–1897), U.S. Army major and collector of western birds and eggs
Le Conte's Thrasher, Le Conte's Sparrow	After John Lawrence Le Conte (1825–1883), noted U.S. entomologist and biogeographer
Townsend's Solitaire, Townsend's Warbler	After John Kirk Townsend (1809–1851), U.S. ornithologist, who collected many new species in the West
Swainson's Thrush, Swainson's Hawk, Swainson's Warbler	After William Swainson (1789–1855), unlucky English author, artist, and naturalist, who lost his entire bird collection while en route to New Zealand
Veery	Origin unknown, perhaps imitative of the bird's song or descriptive of its flight pattern
pipit	Imitative of the weak and short flight calls of these birds, especially of the Water Pipit, the most widely distributed of our seven species
Sprague's Pipit	After Isaac Sprague (1811–1895), U.S. illustrator
Phainopepla	Based ultimately on a Greek word meaning "shining robe," because of the glossy black plumage of the bird
myna	From Hindi *maina*, the Common Myna of India
vireo	Based ultimately on a Latin word, *virere*, meaning "to be green"; applied first to the Greenfinch of Europe and Asia, then to American vireos

BIRD NAME	ORIGIN OF NAME
Hutton's Vireo	After William Hutton (fl. 1840s), little-known U.S. collector around Washington, DC, and in the West
Bell's Vireo	After John Graham Bell (1812–1889), U.S. collector and taxidermist, companion of John J. Audubon
Prothonotary Warbler	A prothonotary is the chief clerk, or notary, of any of various courts of law, in a papal court bedecked in a bright yellow cowl or robe; the breeding male Prothonotary Warbler is resplendent in deep, bright yellow, and the female is only slightly less colorful
Brewster's Warbler (hybrid)	After William Brewster (1851–1919), New England naturalist; Brewster thought he had identified a new species when he collected it in 1874
Bachman's Warbler, Bachman's Sparrow	After Rev. John Bachman (1790–1874), U.S. naturalist, collector of southern U.S. fauna
Virginia's Warbler	After [Mary] Virginia Anderson, wife of a U.S. Army surgeon, who collected for S. F. Baird
Lucy's Warbler	After Lucy Baird Hunter (1848–1913), daughter of S. F. Baird
parula	Latin diminutive of *parus*, "titmouse"; the Northern Parula and Tropical Parula are warblers
Grace's Warbler	After Grace Coues, sister of Elliot Coues (1842–1899), noted U.S. ornithologist; S. F. Baird named this warbler for her
Blackburnian Warbler	After Anna Blackburne (1726–1793), English botanist who maintained a natural history museum in Lancashire, where she displayed many American birds
Kirtland's Warbler	After Jared P. Kirtland (1793–1852), U.S. scientist, founder of Cleveland Academy of Natural Science and Cleveland Medical College
Yellow-breasted Chat	*Chat* from the chattering sound made by this largest of North American warblers
MacGillvray's Warbler	After William MacGillivray (1796–1852), Scottish ornithologist and author, a friend of John J. Audubon, who named the bird
redstart	From the color and the word *start*, an obsolete term meaning "tail"; European redstarts have red tails; the American Redstart and the Painted Redstart, which are warblers, do not
Bobolink	Imitative of its song, originally given as *Bob o' Lincoln*
grackle	From Latin *graculus*, the European jackdaw, a small crow, thus the Boat-tailed Grackle, Common Grackle, and Great-tailed Grackle
oriole	Derived from Latin *aureum*, "gold," the color of the Eurasian Golden Oriole, which is very similar to the Northern Oriole; in addition, there are the Altamira Oriole, Audubon's Oriole, Scott's Oriole, and Spot-breasted Oriole

ORIGIN OF NAME

BIRD NAME	ORIGIN OF NAME
Scott's Oriole	After Winfield Scott (1786–1866), hero of Mexican War
tanager	Through Spanish and Portuguese, deriving ultimately from *tangara*, a Tupi Indian bird, thus the Hepatic Tanager, Summer Tanager, Scarlet Tanager, and Western Tanager
Pyrrhuloxia	From the former scientific name of the bird, based on Greek *pyrrhoúlas*, "red bird," and *loxós*, "oblique," referring to the shape of its bill
grosbeak	From the French *grosbec*, "big bill," giving us the Rose-breasted Grosbeak, Black-headed Grosbeak, Blue Grosbeak, and Evening Grosbeak
Common Redpoll, Hoary Redpoll	Redpoll is literally "red head," *poll* being an old word for head or the hair of the head.
Pine Siskin	*Siskin* is of European ancestry, appearing as the name of a bird in many languages; it is apparently of Slavic origin
Lawrence's Goldfinch	After George Newbold Lawrence (1806–1895), American ornithologist
Dickcissel	Imitative of the bird's song, which it repeats incessantly after arriving at its nesting ground in spring
towhee	Imitative of one of the calls of the Rufous-sided Towhee; there also are the Green-tailed Towhee, Brown Towhee, and Abert's Towhee
Abert's Towhee	After James William Abert (1820–1897), U.S. Army officer, collector for S. F. Baird
Baird's Sparrow, Baird's Sandpiper	After S[pencer] F[ullerton] Baird (1823–1887), noted U.S. zoologist
Henslow's Sparrow	After John S. Henslow (1796–1861), English naturalist and teacher, friend of Darwin and Audubon
Vesper Sparrow	*Sparrow* as a bird name goes back ultimately to Greek, and *vesper* to Latin, meaning "evening," reminding us that the Vesper Sparrow tends to sing toward evening
junco	Derives ultimately from Latin *juncus*, name of a kind of rush; North American juncos, nevertheless, are forest birds, rarely grassland birds
Botteri's Sparrow	After Matteo Botteri (1808–1877), a Yugoslavian zoological and botanical collector in Europe and Mexico
Harris' Sparrow, Harris' Hawk	After Edward Harris (1799–1863), U.S. amateur naturalist, friend of Audubon
Lincoln's Sparrow	After Thomas Lincoln (1812–1883), Maine farmer and friend of Audubon
McCown's Longspur	After John C. McCown (1817–1879), collector especially in western Texas, U.S. Army and Confederate officer
McKay's Bunting	After Charles L. McKay (d.1883), U.S. Army soldier and collector in Alaska for U.S. National Museum

SEPT 2–8

*Turdus
migratorius*

CLASSIFYING BIRDS

ACTIVITIES. Shorebird migration is beginning in earnest now, so take a trip to the shoreline of any large body of water, salt or fresh, for a birding treat. Do not overlook the possibility of a visit to a sewage plant with open water. As we point out on page 57, such sites are not dirty or smelly, and they are especially attractive for birds. Many shorebirds migrate along marine shores, so now is also a good time to become acquainted with state and national wildlife refuges along the coasts of the United States and Canada. Be sure to carry a telescope and sturdy tripod for watching birds on the other side of the open water, and a camera could be useful for photographing footprints and other animal signs as well as the birds themselves.

Over 9000 bird species have been named and classified so far. The classifications have remained reasonably stable, but it is possible to make changes when firm evidence is accepted by most ornithologists. For example, species have been moved to different genera or placed within different families, orders, or other divisions.

Sometimes entire groups, such as families, have been moved into other, or new, categories. For example, the blackbirds, orioles, cardinals, grosbeaks, tanagers, wood warblers, and many Emberizine sparrows once were placed in different families, but on careful analysis they were found to merge sufficiently with each other to be subgroups of one family, the Emberizidae.

CLASSIFYING BIRDS. Carl von Linné, the Swedish botanist known as Linnaeus, devised a practical system of classifying biota. His system was based on anatomy, physiology, and functions of body parts. He placed little emphasis on appearances, which had led predecessors astray. Whales, for example, had been classified as fish instead of as mammals. Herons and cranes had been lumped together (even Linnaeus made that mistake). What Linnaeus developed was a system of grouping all plants and animals in a logical hierarchy, with each step in the hierarchy possessing a distinctive suffix. Here is the hierarchical classification for the American Robin; the major subdivisions are in boldface type. The scientific name of the American Robin, thus, is *Turdus migratorius.* Note that both words are always given and always italicized. Note also that the genus is capitalized, but not the species.

HIERARCHY OF ANIMAL CLASSIFICATION

Kingdom—Animal
Phylum—Vertebrata
Subphylum
Superclass
Class—Aves (Birds)
Subclass
Infraclass
Cohort
Superorder
Order—Passeriformes
Suborder
Infraorder
Superfamily—Muscicapoidea
Family—Muscicapidae
Subfamily—Muscicapinae
Tribe—Muscicapini
Subtribe—Muscicapina
Genus (plural: genera)—*Turdus*
Subgenus
Species—*migratorius*
Subspecies

COMINGS AND GOINGS. **East.** Two rather plain, uncommon, and secretive warblers, the Worm-eating and Swainson's, are found in canebrakes and rhododendron thickets. Both feed on the ground, preferring insects to worms. They are seen most easily after nesting, because by then their numbers have been augmented by the year's crop of new birds. A feeding flock of these warblers sounds like wind rustling dry leaves. Search for them among the rhododendrons of the mountains and other high country, and while there, listen for the croak of the Raven, a bird found in the East almost exclusively in mountains. Two good spots are Great Smoky Mountains National Park and Skyline Drive in the southern Appalachian Mountains.

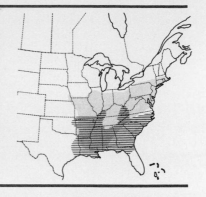

Breeding ranges: *Worm-eating Warbler*
                    Swainson's Warbler

NOTES

SEPT 9–15

Chaetura pelagica

SCIENTIFIC NAMES

ACTIVITIES. Now, when birds begin their autumn molt, is a good time to learn more about this event. As a bird flies overhead, you may see gaps in both its wings. This usually means that a flight feather has been lost from each wing at the same time. A gap in but one wing may indicate accidental loss of a feather or two. Tail feathers may also drop off now, one or two at a time. Because molting makes flight somewhat harder for birds, they may behave secretively, to avoid being noticed by predators. If you keep track of a bird that comes regularly to your feeder, you will see it lose feathers from time to time as new ones grow. You may also see feathers lost where birds gather to feed or roost. Consider starting a collection of feathers, a hobby of many birders.

When Linnaeus devised his system, most western scientists still wrote and understood Latin or Greek, so descriptions of new species were written in Latin. This practice has been discarded, but scientific names still use Latinized forms of modern words. Scientific names are written in the English alphabet, so Russian and Chinese words, for example, are transliterated into English and then given proper Latin suffixes. If a word is misspelled in an original species description, it continues to be spelled that way. Latin is not the language of any modern nation, so there is no basis for chauvinist argument.

Scientific names are useful for birders traveling abroad who wish to find from a foreign-language bird guide whether a bird they see is the same as one back home. Common names may be misleading, because they may be identical or similar in various languages even though the birds named may be different. The American Robin, for example, is not the same as the European Robin (Erithacus rubecula). The Swallow of England (Hirundo rustica) is the Barn Swallow of the United States and Canada. In France the bird is called Hirondelle de cheminée, meaning chimney swallow. Our chimney bird is the Chimney Swift (Chaetura pelagica), which is not a swallow at all and is not seen in France. The scientific names in your field guide can help you sort out the problem.

SCIENTIFIC NAMES. The scientific name of a species places a plant or animal in its genus and assigns it a species and, sometimes, a subspecies name. A genus is a grouping of closely related species, for example, thrushes. Strict rules are followed in describing a new species so that it can be placed correctly in its genus. The species name must be given a Latin or Greek ending that agrees grammatically with the genus name. Just as mathematicians anywhere can read equations written by colleagues who may speak other languages, ornithologists anywhere will understand scientific names.

Naming a species. The first person to describe and name a species is considered the author of its name. Thus the name *Squatarola squatarola* (Linnaeus) tells us the species was first described by Linnaeus. The parentheses indicate that Linnaeus did not place it in the genus *Squatarola*. It was placed in that genus later by another person. When it is found that someone else has described the species first, that person's name is substituted. The full citation for the American Robin is *"Turdus migratorius* Linnaeus [or Linné], 1766, Syst. Nat., ed. 12, 1, p. 292." What this says is that the species was first described by Linnaeus in 1766 in *Systema Naturae*, edition 12, volume 1, page 292. Linnaeus took his description of the bird from Mark Catesby, an English naturalist active in the American colonies about 40 years earlier, who called our robin the "Fieldfare of Carolina."

The scientific name. A bird name always has at least two parts. The first is the genus, and the second is the species. In zoology the genus always carries an initial capital letter. The species never does. A species can never be named correctly merely by use of the second part of the scientific name, as that name may have been used also for a member of another genus. A third word is sometimes added to indicate a subspecies or race, as in *Turdus migratorius confinis,* the American Robin subspecies of southern Baja California.

COMINGS AND GOINGS. **East.** Not far from

home there are probably one or more National Wildlife Refuges that include big marshes or swamps among their natural attractions. And there are state and private preserves that have wetlands. From points overlooking the wetlands during spring and autumn, birders can see thousands, even millions, of migrating birds. The migrating birds include ducks, geese, swans, herons, bitterns, loons, grebes, rails, plovers, sandpipers, blackbirds, and warblers. Visit these choice spots as often as you can. There are no better places for sharpening your skill in bird identification.

- *An important wetland in a National Wildlife Refuge*

NOTES

SEPT 16–22

BIRDS OF
THE WORLD

ACTIVITIES. If you have sharp ears, during autumn evenings you can sit quietly on a terrace, hilltop, or rooftop and listen to migrating birds calling to each other in flight. It is almost certain that birds use their voices to hold together the flock or an individual family. Some birders have learned to recognize particular species by the pitch and quality of their notes. With practice, the sounds can even give a birder a rough count of the number of birds flying overhead. Most people who enjoy the outdoors are familiar with the barking, or honking, of Canada Geese, but there is much more to hear if other night sounds do not drown out bird calls.

SPECIAL FAMILIES. *Just one family of birds lives only in North America, and the family has only one species, the Wrentit (below). It is a shy bird common on the U.S. Pacific Coast. In the Old World there is also only one family, the Prunellidae, that lives there exclusively. It is represented in England by the Hedgesparrow (above), but the family has about a dozen species and ranges all the way to Japan.*

BIRDS OF THE WORLD. When the Age of Exploration shattered archaic notions of geography and the monstrous plants and animals of myth and legend, naturalists began to discover that each major continent had somewhat different flora and fauna. Eventually, as noted earlier on pages 142–143, scientists divided the world into six major regions, based on the relative uniformity of vertebrate animal life. The Nearctic Region, the one in which you live, has 62 families of birds, one peculiar to the region; the Palearctic, 69 families, one peculiar; the Neotropical, 86 families, 31 peculiar; the Ethiopian, 67 families, 7 peculiar; the Oriental, 66 families, one peculiar; the Australian, 58 families, 15 peculiar. Madagascar, a subregion called Malagasy, has four families found only in that subregion.

Zoogeography and numbers. Regions that lie mainly in the tropics have a greater number of colorful species than other regions do, because the flamboyant flowers of the tropics make dull camouflage less necessary. Though there are fewer species in the cooler climates, the numbers of individuals are about the same as long as there is an adequate food supply. Thus Greenland supports only 56 species while Colombia has 1395.

Marine regions. Marine regions are not as distinct as terrestrial regions. The equatorial belt divides the oceans into two groups, and separate oceans such as the Indian Ocean, Arctic Ocean, South Atlantic, and South Pacific, display unique bird life. Further, since marine species must nest on land and since marine food supplies are most abundant where warm and cold ocean currents meet, oceanic species tend to congregate in a species mix instead of being isolated in a region.

COMINGS AND GOINGS. West. In the large National Wildlife Refuges, autumn migrations often are more spectacular than spring migrations, because so many young are swelling the ranks of the migrating birds. By comparing the numbers of immatures with adults of the same species, ornithologists can estimate the annual production of new birds. Different types of wetlands attract different kinds of birds, so it is worthwhile to visit two or more refuges in order to see the greatest variety. The "fall migration" issue of *American Birds* will help you locate the most productive marshes for particular kinds of birds. Another excellent reference is *The Life of the Marsh*, by William A. Niering (1966).

- *An important wetland in a National Wildlife Refuge*

NOTES

SEPT 23–29

BIRDS OF SOUTHWEST OKLAHOMA

BIRDING IN AMERICA

ACTIVITIES. With a thermos filled with a hot beverage, you can enjoy moon watching, a type of birding in which the bird watcher observes night-flying migrating birds as they cross the face of a full moon. Set up a comfortable reclining chair and place a telescope next to you so you can look through it at the moon's disk. You will see the silhouettes of flying birds as they cross the disk. You will be able to categorize them as small, in-between, or large and even be able to identify them as ducks, thrushes, herons, etc. You can determine the direction of flight and judge how high they are flying. Most of all, you can count how many cross the disk. The largest numbers are usually seen just before midnight.

WHERE TO GO BIRDING. *Most parks, wildlife refuges, sanctuaries, and bird clubs publish guides to the best local birding spots. Your birding will be more rewarding if you consult these publications in advance of a visit. You should also stop at the headquarters building before taking to the trails. There you may learn of special birds, perhaps rarities, that experienced birders will travel a distance to see.*

BIRDING IN AMERICA. There are so many excellent birding places in the United States and Canada that you need only hop in your car and take off. But planning of birding trips is facilitated by statewide bird clubs, most of which publish lists of best birding places, with directions for getting to them and information about birds to see in the various seasons. Some clubs provide information about overnight accommodations. Most national parks and wildlife refuges also publish lists of birds that can be seen in each season. Write to them for information.

Two books are indispensable for planning a birding tour, both written by Dr. Olin Sewall Pettingill, Jr.: *A Guide to Bird Finding East of the Mississippi* (2nd ed., 1977) and *A Guide to Bird Finding West of the Mississippi* (2nd ed., 1981). A useful book is *A Bird-Finding Guide to Canada* (1984), by James C. Findlay. It is also useful, when you visit friends or relatives, to let them know of your interest in birds. They may be able to take you to sanctuaries, seashores, or marshes where you will have a good chance to see interesting local birds.

Tours. Birding tours are arranged by touring agencies and advertised in *Audubon, Natural History,* and other nature publications. Such tours, led by experienced birders, are scheduled for seasons when one sees the greatest number of birds. The tours furnish information about clothing, guide books, and other items of concern to birders and members of their families.

If you want to be completely on your own, consult *American Birds,* a magazine containing information useful to the traveling birder. This journal, published bimonthly by the National Audubon Society, reports birds seen in all sections of the United States and Canada. Consult it to find out which birds to watch for when traveling. Or just find your own spots. After all, what makes birding one of the most attractive sports is that anywhere you go, you can find interesting birds and have fun.

COMINGS AND GOINGS. West.

Along rural roads of the southwestern United States and Mexico, even in the suburban atmosphere of Stanford University near Palo Alto, California, you will become aware that many wayside trees and wooden power poles have had holes drilled into them. Look closely: Each hole may be stuffed with an acorn, a pecan, or some other nut. The responsible party is the Acorn Woodpecker. No one knows why it behaves in this way. The Acorn Woodpecker feeds on insect grubs, so perhaps grubs infest the layaway nuts or acorns. At any rate, the range of the Acorn Woodpecker always includes oak forests. Keep your eyes open for the telltale holes. The Acorn Woodpecker is fascinating to watch.

Year-round ranges of Acorn Woodpecker

NOTES

SEPT 30–OCT 6

EXTINCT AND ENDANGERED BIRDS

ACTIVITIES. It is time to open your fast-food franchise for feathered friends. Attract the long-range travelers, and the locals will join them. If you have been feeding all year long, try different menus now (see pages 10–12 for ideas). Talk with other birders about their recent successes in attracting new visitors. You may want to introduce a new type of feeder or try new locations for your present feeders. A change in location of even a few feet can sometimes make a tremendous difference in the number of birds attracted. A tip: Rodents are attracted by fallen birdseed, so check your house walls and foundation for entry holes that rodents might find once cold weather sets in. Patching now saves trouble later.

Many bird species became extinct with the dinosaurs. Archaeopteryx *appeared in the Jurassic—150 million years ago—and left no known immediate descendants in the fossil record.* Gallornis, *the next oldest known fossil bird, came from the Cretaceous—about 130 million years ago. Many ornithologists believe it was a toothless bird ancestral to the flamingos.* Enaliornis, *which arrived about 85 million years ago, is placed among the toothed, flightless, and superficially loonlike Hesperornidae. One species,* Hesperornis regalis, *grew to a length of 5 feet.*

At that time a shallow, inland ocean extending from the Gulf of Mexico to the Arctic Circle, was home to various aquatic reptiles, such as plesiosaurs and ichthyosaurs. Pteranodons and other pterosaurs (winged reptiles) glided overhead. Also in these seas were a ternlike bird, Ichthyornis *(not an ancestor of the terns or gulls), and* Baptornis, *like* Hesperornis *a flightless diver. Some of these divers went in their own evolutionary direction and developed heavy, solid bones useful in diving.*

The Later Cretaceous fossils include possibly ancestral forms of spoonbills, flamingos, storks, and ibises, as well as progenitors of loons, rails, and a large order that includes the shorebirds, gulls, and the auks. The Tertiary fossils—from 70 million to 1 million years ago—begin with the appearance of more modern birds. By 30 million years ago many modern genera had arrived, including Milvus *(kites),* Pterocles *(sandgrouse),* Bubo *(owls), and* Asio *(owls).*

EXTINCT & ENDANGERED BIRDS.
Long before people came on the scene, uncountable numbers of plant and animal species became extinct. Natural disasters, such as volcanic eruptions and exploding meteorites, may have accounted directly for the disappearance of many species. These occurrences, in a kind of domino effect, may have resulted as well in the extinction of many other species. Whatever the reason, when many species are wiped out in a short time, the interdependence of plant and animal life may become severely disrupted and require restructuring. Some scientists believe, for example, that a sudden disaster toward the end of the Cretaceous Period affected many plants and animals and caused the relatively quick disappearance of the dinosaurs.

People today are inducing drastic changes in the environment that threaten many species—perhaps humanity itself. An analogy may be drawn from the history of goats established on ocean islands by sailors who wanted to have a convenient source of food during stopovers. Left uncontrolled, these goats soon ate all the vegetation on some of those islands and starved to death, as did most of the other animals on the islands. Can reasoning animals, such as humans, act like those goats and, by destroying too much, destroy themselves? The answer to this question, in light of human history, is that they probably can.

Recently extinct birds. North of Mexico, the Labrador Duck, Heath Hen (an isolated subspecies of the Greater Prairie Chicken), Great Auk, Passenger Pigeon, Carolina Parakeet, and, probably, the Ivory-billed Woodpecker have become extinct. This was due largely to the activities of humans, but American Indians were an exception. They lacked the means to destroy large segments of their habitat or decimate wildlife. Indians may have lived in balance with the natural world not because they consciously sought to do so but, ironically, because they were unable to do much about changing things.

160

COMINGS AND GOINGS.

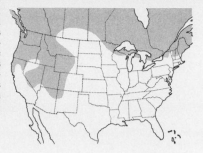

Saucy, pert, raucous, and unafraid, the Gray Jay has earned a host of colloquial names. Some call it the Camp Robber, because the Gray Jay has a habit of stealing food and small objects from cabins and hunting camps. Others call it Whiskey Jack, not because of its hoarse calls but because of the Indian name *Wiss-ka-chon*, which was soon corrupted to Whiskey John and then, inevitably, to Whiskey Jack. At times, particularly in winter, the Gray Jay wanders outside its range, and sometimes individual birds have been brought south as pets by vacationers.

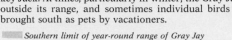 *Southern limit of year-round range of Gray Jay*

NOTES

In the Hawaiian Islands, 14 species disappeared between 1850 and 1932, and at least 10 more have since become endangered. About 40 percent of Hawaii's native forest has been destroyed because of urbanization and large-scale agriculture, which has diverted land from production of natural foods needed by birds to growing pineapple, sugar cane, and other crops for humans. While all this has been going on, 33 species, including the House Sparrow, European Starling, and Common Myna, were introduced into the islands. Because of the closed island habitats, these introductions were particularly damaging to the native birds of the Hawaiian Islands.

The Maoris and their predecessors in New Zealand destroyed about 15 species of moas. These birds, believed to have been flightless, ranged from about chicken size to 13 feet tall. Dodos and Great Auks were exterminated by sailors, who killed them for food.

The rate of bird extinction appears to be keeping pace with technological advance. Since about 1680, when the last Dodo was slain, more than 300 species have become extinct. Since 1900, a total of 200 species have become extinct, most as a result of habitat destruction. The Passenger Pigeon might have become extinct even earlier had our 19th-century forebears possessed today's weapons. Modern sportsmen can go far afield after game species, such as elephants, leopards, and Indian rhinos. Their den walls display trophies of threatened species taken from places to which only 50 years ago hunters could not go. Some people hunt with cameras, but if you are among them, take care. Some species have a low tolerance for disturbance, especially during breeding seasons.

THE EXTINCT DODO OF MAURITIUS ISLAND IN THE INDIAN OCEAN

Endangered species. Wildlife organizations try to protect birds by issuing warnings about endangered species. For the United States and Canada, the list of recently extinct and endangered birds includes the following names:

SOME ENDANGERED BIRDS OF THE UNITED STATES AND CANADA

Hawaiian Goose (Nene) *(Nesochen sandvicensis)*. Thirty reported in 1951. Due to program involving captive birds begun in 1950, there now are several hundred birds.

California Condor *(Gymnogyps californianus)*. Nearly extinct. Last five in wild in 1985 made captive birds. Encroachment on habitat and alterations of environment by people.

Whooping Crane *(Grus americana)*. Never common, but formerly more widespread. Flock at one time down to 28 birds. By 1985, as a result of strict protection and artificial breeding, there were over 100 birds, captive and wild.

Eskimo Curlew *(Numenius borealis)*. Perhaps a few birds of this once numerous and heavily hunted species still survive in the wild. Last North American specimen taken in 1932. Five years later, sighted on eastern Long Island, New York, and near Buenos Aires, Argentina. Hunting is probable cause of near extinction.

Ivory-billed Woodpecker *(Campephilus principalis)*. No reliable reports since 1972. Probably extinct in U.S. Destruction of habitat, mature forests with many large trees, probable cause.

CALIFORNIA CONDOR

EXTINCT BIRDS OF HAWAII

Hawaiian Rail *(Porzana sandwichensis).* Last specimen 1864. Last seen island of Hawaii 1884.

Laysan Rail *(Porzana palmeri).* Disappeared 1823–1836, Laysan Island. Introduced rabbits reduced food.

Amaui *(Myadestes chaenis).* Extinct about 1825.

Oahu Oo *(Moho spicalis).* Not seen after 1837.

Hawaii Oo *(Moho nobilis).* Last report 1934.

Kioea *(Chaetoptila angustipluma).* Last report 1859.

Lesser Koa Finch *(Rhodacanthus flaviceps).* Last collected 1891.

Greater Koa Finch *(Rhodacanthus palmeri).* Last collected 1896.

Kona Grosbeak *(Chloridops kona).* Always rare. Extinct 1894.

Greater Amakihi *(Hemignathus sagittirostris).* Last seen 1900. Habitat destruction.

Hawaiian Akialoa *(Hemignathus obscurus).* Last recorded 1890s.

Kauai Akialoa *(Hemignathus procerus).* Last reported 1967. Probably extinct.

Molokai Creeper *(Paroreomyza maculata).* Last seen 1962. Probably extinct.

Ula-ai-hawane *(Ciridops anna).* Extinct since 1890.

Hawaii Mamo *(Drepanis pacifica).* Extinct since 1898.

Black Mamo *(Drepanis funerea).* Extinct since 1907.

Crested Honeycreeper *(Palmeria dolei).* Last reported 1907.

EXTINCT BIRDS OF THE CONTINENTAL UNITED STATES AND CANADA

Labrador Duck *(Camptorhynchus labradorius).* Apparently always rare. Hunted. Last recorded 1875, Long Island, New York.

Heath Hen *(Tympanuchus cupido cupido).* A subspecies of the Greater Prairie Chicken. Hunted heavily. Last one died on Martha's Vineyard, Massachusetts, in 1932.

Great Auk *(Pinguinis impennis).* Killed in large numbers to fill larders of sailing vessels. Last seen off Newfoundland in 1852.

Passenger Pigeon *(Ectopistes migratorius).* Slaughtered in great numbers up to 1871, when population crashed. Indians killed many by burning forests in which birds bred. Thousands were shipped by rail as cheap food. Last one seen in wild in 1889. Last one died in Cincinnati, Ohio, Zoo, September 1, 1914.

Carolina Parakeet *(Conuropsis carolinensis).* Last reported in wild in April 1904. Possible sighting in 1920. Both in Florida. Last one died in Cincinnati, Ohio, Zoo, 1914.

OCT 7–13

HAWK MIGRATION

ACTIVITIES. Do not delay. This is good hawk-watching time, and a particularly good site for this pleasurable activity is a ridge that runs in a generally north-south direction, against which winds blow often. Wind creates the updrafts on which hawks ride. A treeless summit, even if only a rocky promontory, is also a definite asset for the hawk watcher, since it provides a 360-degree view. But if you cannot find an ideal place from which to watch, you might settle for a comfortable spot in an open field, where you can stretch out on your back with binoculars handy. The sky may seem empty at first, but suddenly along will come the first hawk and your fun will begin.

HAWK FLIGHTS IN THE UNITED STATES AND CANADA

Migrations do not run on strict calendars, with weather the principal variable. As a result the following listing provides only a general indication of hawk viewing periods, with the south seeing birds earlier than the north.

SPECIES NAME	SPRING DATES/ AUTUMN DATES
Osprey	L Feb/L Apr M Sep/M Nov
Northern Harrier	Feb/M May Aug/Nov
Sharp-shinned Hawk	Apr/M May L Aug/L Oct
Cooper's Hawk	Mar/M May L Aug/L Oct
Northern Goshawk	irregular
Harris' Hawk	not migratory; flocks in Aug/L Oct
Red-shouldered Hawk	Feb/E May M Sep/M Nov
Broad-winged Hawk	Mar/E May L Aug/E Oct
Swainson's Hawk	Mar/E May Sep/M Nov
Red-tailed Hawk	Feb/M May L Aug/L Nov
Ferruginous Hawk	Mar/Apr Sep/Oct
Golden Eagle	Apr E Oct/Nov
American Kestrel	Mar/L Apr Sep/L Nov
Merlin	Feb/M May Sep/E Nov
Peregrine Falcon	Feb/M May Sep/L Dec
Prairie Falcon	Feb/M Apr M Sep/M Oct

E= early, L= late, M= middle

HAWK MIGRATION. If you choose the right viewing spot, you can see spectacular flights of migrating hawks. At Hawk Mountain Sanctuary on the Kittatinny Ridge, near Hamburg, Pa, for example, flights of 15,000 to 21,000 hawks have been observed on a single autumn day. At Braddock Bay, just northwest of Rochester, New York, on the shoreline of Lake Ontario, 12,000 hawks were seen on one spring day. But a good place to observe hawks migrating in spring may not be the best place to watch them in autumn.

Fortunately, there are many excellent viewing spots in both seasons throughout the United States and Canada. For example, coastlines often are great for observing hawk migrations during autumn and spring. Check local bird clubs, which identify places for watching hawks, and study maps in bird journals and nature magazines.

Kettles. Like all birds, hawks need to conserve energy during migration, so they fly with the wind when possible or seek out thermal updrafts on which they can soar. When hawks find a wall or column of rising air, caused by wind blowing against the side of a mountain chain or by updrafts of hot air rising from shorelines, hundreds of soaring birds may collect in what are called kettles, groups of birds spiraling upward. Sometimes, however, the wind is strong enough to push birds along in a more businesslike way, so large numbers fly overhead quickly. In either case, when the weather is right, you can see tremendous flights. But look especially for the kettles.

Other birds. In addition to the varieties of hawks, birders at hawk watches during migration periods may spot ospreys, eagles, ducks, herons, and quantities of small birds. What makes the experience so exciting is that you can see many different kinds of birds in a short time, and experienced birders are nearly always on hand to help you identify them. People at hawk watches seem always friendly. So plan to have a good time and learn a good deal about birds.

COMINGS AND GOINGS. West. Motorists will

streak through deserts on interstate highways, seeing, hearing, and feeling nothing. How much better to drive slowly early in the morning or late in the afternoon, when the sun is not oppressive. During these times of day, and on moonlit nights as well, the deserts are often alive with sound and movement. Desert birds are relatively easy to see, and any stream, pond, lake, or spring is a magnet in all seasons for such interesting birds as the Harris' and Zone-tailed hawks, Gambel's Quail, Inca Dove, Greater Roadrunner (a ground cuckoo that feeds on snakes and lizards), Northern Pygmy and Elf owls, Black Phoebe, Bridled Titmouse, Verdin, Cactus and Canyon wrens, and three thrashers: Bendire's, Curve-billed, and Crissal.

Deserts of the United States

NOTES
_____

_____

_____

_____

_____

_____

_____

_____

_____

_____

_____

_____

_____

_____

_____

_____

_____

_____

_____

_____

_____

_____

_____

_____

```
Powell Sanctuary              march 18, 1996
E. Reilly, G. Carruth          9 AM–11 AM
  9/10 CLOUD COVER    38°F – 43°F
  WIND; CALM TO 5 MPH
B-c. CHICKADEE  45-50   MAINLY AT FEEDERS
W-b. NUTHATCH      7        "     "    "
RUFFED GROUSE      1    WHITE TRAIL IN
                         SPRUCE WOODS
SWAMP SPARROW      1    EDGE OF POND
AMERICAN GOLDFINCH 12   WINTER PLUMAGE
AMERICAN CARDINAL 2♂,1♀  AT FEEDERS
```

KEEPING RECORDS

ACTIVITIES. Farmers in the United States and Canada are either harvesting or preparing for winter. Even in the south there is a pause in the annual cycle. Since birds are born gleaners, trips to farmland may reward you with species you have not yet seen this year. Fields not completely harvested, especially those protected against the bitterest winds, are ideal for winter birding. Mark these places on your birding maps and keep your eyes peeled for Horned Lark, Black-billed Magpie, Chihuahan Raven, Bushtit, Northern Wheatear, Fieldfare, Wrentit, Water Pipit, Sprague's Pipit, Pyrrhuloxia, Dickcissel, Bachman's Sparrow, Vesper Sparrow, Lark Bunting, Baird's Sparrow, Harris' Sparrow, juncos, McCown's Lapland, Smith's and Chestnut-collared longspurs, meadowlarks, Brewer's Blackbird, Common Grackle, Bronzed Cowbird, redpolls, and goldfinches.

Serious bird watchers keep journals of their observations. A field trip account is useful for describing in consecutive order what is seen during a day. On pages set aside for each species, a species account is made of information gathered on a particular day. If you follow this procedure, your records may become useful for professional ornithologists.

KEEPING RECORDS. A record of birds you see, and the dates and conditions of your sightings, will increase the fun you get from birding. *The Bird Watcher's Diary* is designed to help you get started as a faithful recorder. On pages 204–215 is a checklist of North American birds, with spaces for dates and places of first sightings. Over the years you will enjoy looking back to see when and where you learned particular species.

Seasonal record keeping. The weekly sections for notes in this book are intended primarily for records of birds seen at your feeder. Enter the date on which a bird species first arrives in spring and record the last date on which you see it. You may also want to keep a notebook of species you see at your feeder every day. By transferring these dates to this book, you will know which species you can expect to see at your feeder during each week of a year.

Field record keeping. On a birding trip, it is helpful to keep an index card in your shirt pocket or field guide. In the upper right-hand corner, write the date, including starting and finishing times. In the upper left-hand corner, write the name of the park or road where you are walking. On the first line, record the weather conditions; on the other lines, each species you see. Estimate the number of birds of each species and, as appropriate, their sexes. As your card file grows, you will have a valuable guide to a new year's round of birding.

Printed checklists and cards are available listing birds you can expect to see in your part of the country. These make excellent personal records, and you need only check off birds' names and sex and note their numbers.

However you keep track of your sightings, the information you gather will give you an up-to-date record of your birding activities. You will increase your participation in the pleasures of birding and have a means of evoking memories of noteworthy days spent observing attractive and interesting species in the field.

Daily Field Checklist

412 Birds of Eastern North America

Date: _____ Total: _____

Observers: _____

Weather: _____

File Key: ___ Date: ___ Place: ___

Locality: _____ Time: _____

	✓	✓
Loon, Common		
Loon, Arctic		
Loon, Red-throated		
Grebe, Red-necked		
Grebe, Horned		
Grebe, Eared		
Grebe, Least		
Grebe, Western		
Grebe, Pied-billed		
Fulmar		
Shearwater, Cory's		
Shearwater, Greater		
Shearwater, Sooty		
Shearwater, Audubon's		
Petrel, Leach's		
Petrel, Wilson's		
Pelican, White		
Pelican, Brown		
Booby, Blue-faced		
Gannet, Northern		
Cormorant, Great		
Cormorant, Double-cr.		
Cormorant, Olivaceous		
Anhinga		
Magnificent Frigatebird		
Heron, Great Blue		
Heron, Green-backed		
Heron, Little Blue		
Egret, Cattle		
Egret, Reddish		
Egret, Common		
Egret, Snowy		

COMINGS AND GOINGS. Chickadees, titmice, and their relatives range throughout North America. Among the 11 species in the United States and Canada, the Black-capped, Mountain, and Carolina chickadees have the largest ranges and are most similar in appearance. You can identify the Black-capped and Carolina chickadees chiefly by their songs and ranges. You can distinguish the Mountain from the Black-capped by the white eye stripe of the Mountain Chickadee. In Canada, the Boreal Chickadee, identifiable by its brown cap, predominates. We have seen it in the suburbs of New York City.

Year-round ranges: Black-capped Chickadee
═══ Carolina Chickadee
⫿⫿⫿ Mountain Chickadee
━ ━ ━ Southern limit of winter range of Boreal Chickadee

NOTES

_____

_____

_____

_____

_____

_____

_____

_____

_____

_____

_____

_____

_____

_____

_____

_____

_____

_____

_____

_____

_____

_____

OCT 21–27

OCEANIC BIRDS

(See page 45 for an explanation of dynamic soaring.)

ACTIVITIES. How about scheduling a birding tour for your next vacation? Such tours have become increasingly popular. Led by experienced ornithologists, groups go anywhere in the world, even to the Arctic and Antarctic and behind the Iron Curtain. You can find out about such tours by consulting natural history and birding magazines. Many bird watchers have discovered that they can have fascinating and educational vacations with groups of people who share their interests. Interest is increased by doing some reading before departure time to become familiar with species that will be encountered. One of us led a birding tour to Russia and southeastern Asia and can attest to the friendly receptions encountered everywhere and the good time the birders shared.

OCEANIC BIRDS. True oceanic birds spend most of their lives gathering food from the sea, returning to land only for nesting and for rearing young. Oceanic birds have adapted remarkably to life on or over marine waters. They can drink the salty water because their tear glands excrete excess salt. Their flight adaptations enable many to remain aloft long hours, supported on their long slender wings and broad tails. (See page 45 for an explanation of dynamic soaring.) Albatrosses and petrels, for example, only occasionally alight to gather food and to rest. They show remarkable mastery of flight even in violent storms, although as soaring birds they cannot fly easily through the windless tropical doldrums. It is not surprising, therefore, that so many of the oceanic birds are found in the southern oceans, where they apparently originated.

True oceanic birds include penguins, albatrosses, petrels and shearwaters, storm-petrels, diving petrels, tropicbirds, frigatebirds, and a few species of other families. They nest mostly on isolated barren oceanic islets or on rocky escarpments of larger islands well offshore. Other semipelagic birds, such as gannets and boobies, cormorants, phalaropes, sheathbills, skuas and jaegers, gulls and terns (especially noddies and sooties), skimmers, auks, and sea ducks, are occasionally or seasonally seen far out at sea.

COMMON TERN

RING-BILLED GULL

LEACH'S STORM-PETREL

COMINGS AND GOINGS. West.

Two nonmigratory magpies are seen in North America, similar except for bill color and range. The Yellow-billed Magpie, found exclusively in the Central Valley of California, has not only a yellow bill but also a dash of yellow under each eye. The Black-billed Magpie has no yellow at all. Some ornithologists believe that the Yellow-billed migrated to North America first, then was pushed down by glaciers from central Canada and the United States. When the glaciers began to recede, it moved north and west of the Rockies and the Sierra Nevada until stopped by competition from the Black-billed Magpie.

Year-round ranges: Black-billed Magpie
                       (winter range extends eastward)
                       Yellow-billed Magpie

NOTES

_____

_____

_____

_____

_____

_____

_____

_____

_____

_____

_____

_____

_____

_____

_____

_____

_____

_____

Gulls and terns, in fact, seldom are found far from land, except for noddies, which are more inclined to wander over ocean areas and nest on remote islands and islets. Even penguins, because they cannot fly, must stay close to their nesting areas. Skuas, jaegers, phalaropes, and cormorants nest inland but are often seen far out at sea during their migrations and wintering.

True oceanic species may remain at sea for as long as 5 to 11 years, or until they are fully mature. They usually fly over the confluences of warm and cold oceanic currents, where there are great concentrations of their food—invertebrates, fish, and other vertebrates.

Observing oceanic birds. Almost any time of year is the right time for watching birds at sea, since they travel about the oceans all year long in huge oval paths, clockwise in the Northern Hemisphere, counterclockwise in the Southern Hemisphere. Some remain in only one ocean or hemisphere.

Pelagic trips, as ocean birding excursions are generally called, are usually scheduled from the United States and Canada between August and November. Advertisements for them appear in newspapers and in periodicals published by bird clubs. Not all birders can take cruises to where the oceanic species congregate, but owners of deep-sea fishing boats or other oceangoing vessels have discovered that dedicated birders will pay to be taken to good viewing spots. The trips generally begin early in the morning and end in the afternoon. Birders on these trips may see petrels, storm-petrels, boobies, gannets, possibly albatrosses, and even the inshore birds, such as gulls and terns, murres, auks (in winter), and sea ducks.

PELAGIC BIRDING. *As long as the weather is not very stormy, you can go to sea nearly anytime during the year to watch oceanic birds. The year-round flight paths of the Laysan Albatross in the Pacific Ocean and of the Greater Shearwater in the Atlantic Ocean are typical.*

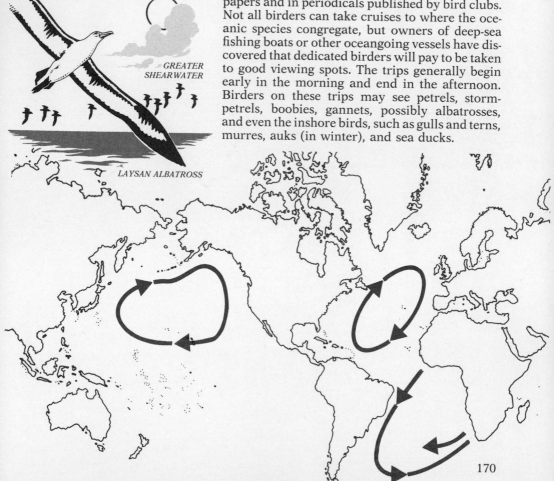

GREATER
SHEARWATER

LAYSAN ALBATROSS

If you go on one of these voyages, dress appropriately—it is usually cooler at sea than on land. When traveling with a group, one birder may be named official recordkeeper, but you may wish to keep your own records as well. If you cannot go out in a boat or are prone to seasickness, try onshore birding after a big windstorm. Oceanic birds are often blown a distance inland.

Identification. Field guides help in identifying oceanic species, but *Seabirds: An Identification Guide* (1983), by Peter Harrison, is especially recommended for its excellent pictures and drawings as well as maps and other helpful information. It is not easy to use field glasses or a telescope to make identifications while being tossed by ocean waves, but practice will bring proficiency.

Before you embark, use your field guide to create a list of birds you expect to see. Make notes about how to tell similar species apart. Estimating bird size will present some difficulty, since you will not have familiar objects to compare them with. Try to compare birds new to you with species of known size, and remember that ratios of wing to tail to head as well as methods of flight are important clues. Shearwaters, for example, earned their name from their habit of flying close to the surface of water, even into wave troughs. Folk etymology attributes "petrel," especially "storm-petrel," to "St. Peter's birds" because of the perceived ability of petrels to walk on water. The birds are actually paddling on the water while in flight.

Effects of island living. Most oceanic birds nest on isolated islets or islands where they have few enemies. Possibly as a result of this relative safety, incubation and fledging times are long. For example, the Black-footed Albatross incubates for 63 to 67 days, and the young fledge in 20 to 25 weeks. In addition, the species may not begin breeding until the ninth year. The incubation period of the Laysan Albatross is 62 to 67 days. Fledging takes about 25 weeks, and the birds mature in about 7 years. The Northern Fulmar has an incubation period of about 56 days. Fledging takes 42 to 56 days, and the birds mature in about 7 years. Storm-petrels take at least 2 years to reach maturity. Because many species nest in burrows on remote islands, such information is unknown for many albatrosses, petrels, storm-petrels, and other species.

Unfortunately, even the remote oceanic birds are endangered by the actions of humans and the pollution they cause. The Short-tailed Albatross, which formerly nested in great numbers on the island of Torishima, off Japan, is now rare because it was slain for its feathers, sought after as decoration for women's hats.

UNDERWATER FLYERS. *Found only in the Southern Hemisphere, the Diving Petrels are a family of ocean birds with necks, wings, and tails shorter than those of other petrels. They dive into the water with wings beating rapidly and they often emerge still flapping vigorously. It takes little imagination to see in them a strong clue of how ancestral penguins must have looked and behaved.*

OCT 28–NOV 3

BIRD LISTS

ACTIVITIES. This is a good time to find out how birds make their nests. Collect an abandoned nest. Note its location and habitat, for example, the vegetation in which the nest is sited, height above ground, and depth and diameter of the nest. Then weigh the nest. If you do not know which species built it, consult Hal Harrison's *A Field Guide to Birds' Nests Found East of the Mississippi* (1975) or *A Field Guide to Western Birds' Nests* (1979). Now pull the nest apart, count the pieces, and identify the material used. A nest built by a Long-tailed Tit, found in Europe and Asia, had 2457 feathers. A nest of an Altamira Oriole had 3387 pieces of vegetation; that of a Purple Finch, 753 pieces of grass. Can you see why the nest of an American Robin or Barn Swallow may outweigh the adult bird more than 30 times?

BIRD LISTS. Unlike the *AOU Check-list of North American Birds,* on which the list that appears at the back of this book is based, or commercial checklists of birds of a large area of the United States and Canada, a bird list usually covers the species of a relatively small area—a park, wildlife refuge, or sanctuary. For example, a daily field checklist of the birds of eastern North America lists the names of 412 species in taxonomic order without further comment. By comparison, *Birds of Brigantine National Wildlife Refuge* contains 269 species but notes their seasonal status and indicates birds that breed within the refuge.

There are bird lists that cover areas larger than a sanctuary but smaller than an entire section of the country. One is the *Checklist of New York State Birds,* which lists about 280 species that have been sighted and verified. The name of each bird is followed by a code indicating whether the bird is common or rare, its seasonal status, where it breeds within the state, and the habitat in which it is typically found. Bird clubs in the United States and Canada, as well as government agencies, prepare similar bird lists.

BIRDS OF BRIGANTINE

This folder lists 269 species of birds that have been identified on Brigantine National Wildlife Refuge since it was established in 1939.

Their value. Bird lists enable birders to keep track of the status of birds, especially their abundance and variety. Common species in time may become rare. A species may suddenly appear and become common or regular. Such information, usually more timely than that given in bird books, is useful because changes in fauna may be correlated with vegetation growth and human activities.

Bird lists are also valuable for planning field trips. For lists write to local or state bird clubs or to the headquarters of the national parks and wildlife refuges in regions you plan to visit. Lists are also available for areas abroad. When you receive a list, check the species you would like to see and note the seasons in which they are present.

By knowing in advance of a trip that a particular species is likely to be in the area you are visiting, you may study it in your field guide and improve your chances of identifying it.

COMINGS AND GOINGS. This map of the winter range of the Green-winged Teal serves to introduce you to the unpredictable winter movements of ducks generally. The northern boundary of the winter ranges of ducks and some other birds is determined by the varying amounts of ice on ponds and streams and is therefore rarely the same from year to year. Unfrozen, rapidly moving water will hold a population of ducks in the coldest weather, provided there is food enough to support them. So if there is open water in winter in your neighborhood, check it for ducks.

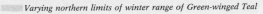 *Varying northern limits of winter range of Green-winged Teal*

NOTES

BIRD ECOLOGY

ACTIVITIES. We have never met a bird watcher who has not collected books about birds. On page 198 we discuss books for your basic bird reference library, but now that uncertain weather is approaching, you might want to check out some nature classics that make for excellent reading. Henry David Thoreau's *Walden* is always worth rereading. But do you know W. H. Hudson's *Book of the Naturalist, Adventures Among Birds,* and *Far Away and Long Ago*? And what about the most famous bird book of all, Gilbert White's *Natural History and Antiquities of Selbourne*? Other books of interest are R. P. Allen's *On the Trail of Vanishing Birds,* John Burroughs's *Wake Robin,* J. S. Huxley's *Bird-watching and Bird Behavior,* R. C. Murphy's *Logbook for Grace,* and O. S. Pettingill's *Bird Watcher's America.*

BIRD ECOLOGY. Ecology is concerned with how plants and animals interact with one another and with nonliving systems. Nonliving systems include chemical factors, such as the carbon, oxygen, nitrogen, and water cycles. They also include physical factors, such as climate, terrain, and the impact of day and night. The living and nonliving systems collectively may be called an environment, which includes people and their effects. The environment of the entire earth is too big to study at once, so ecologists narrow their studies to particular ecosystems.

An ecosystem, a relatively restricted group of plants, animals, and nonliving systems, is defined by a geographical habitat, such as marsh, pond, stream, or desert, or by an even narrower division, such as evergreen forest, hardwood forest, cold desert, freshwater marsh, or saltwater marsh.

Although there are many subdivisions and subsubdivisions of geographical areas, there are two chief approaches to studying an ecosystem: (1) study of one species throughout its life cycle, often called its life history, and (2) study of a community of species during a period of time, say, one day and night or a complete year. In the first approach, a single plant or animal may be studied in all its habitats and in relation to all the species within its ecosystem. In the second approach, as few as two interacting species—often many more —may be studied. Finally, since scientists find it useful to specialize, an ecologist may approach the study of an ecosystem in a particular way. For example, an ecologist may study the flow of energy through an ecosystem; another, the population dynamics within it; and a third, the human impact on it.

No matter how small, every ecosystem has a food chain. This is true even for an ecosystem as small as a tiny pool of water. Most ecosystems have a multitude of interacting food chains. At the bottom of almost every food chain are plants. Next come the herbivores, the animals that eat plants. Then come several stages of carnivores, eaters of the eaters of the first planteaters.

You will find it interesting to compose a food chain for your favorite birding area. Probably humans should be placed at the top. Check over the list of birds and other animals you have recorded in the area and sort them into predators and plant eaters. Then rank them according to size. Remember that a lack of predators on your list may be balanced by immigration of these animals from neighboring areas. Remember also that big predators usually require large areas for their feeding range. And where an ecological niche is left vacant by wild animals, feral dogs and cats will take over.

174

COMINGS AND GOINGS. West.

The Wrentit sparks considerable argument among ornithologists. Some consider it the only known species in the family Chameidae, found mostly in northern Baja California and in California, with some extending farther north. But the *AOU Checklist* places the Wrentit in Timaliinae, the subfamily of Babblers, which is part of Muscicapidae, a vast family—more than 350 species—of Old World flycatchers, thrushes, and others. The Wrentit is secretive, but you can see it at a bird feeder, so keep an eye peeled for this small bird within its small range.

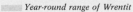 *Year-round range of Wrentit*

NOTES

175

For example, a simple food chain may comprise grasses and herbs, the sparrows that eat the seeds of the grasses and herbs, and the hawks that eat the sparrows. The chain is usually represented as a pyramid because, using the same example, the grasses and herbs are most abundant, the sparrows 1000 times less abundant, and the hawks even less abundant. But most birds do not eat just one kind of food, so a complex diagram has to be constructed to show the paths through which energy made available by plants works its way to the top of a bird food pyramid.

Life histories. From this brief sketch it is easy to understand how complex is the ecology of even a single bird species. Ornithologists must study all aspects of its life history, including physiology, behavior, food, enemies, and other factors to understand how the species fits into an ecosystem. In 1919 Arthur Cleveland Bent (1866–1954) began writing a series of bulletins published by the U.S. National Museum in Washington, D.C., *Life Histories of North American Birds* (23 volumes). It is a lively compendium of ecological data gathered by amateur and professional birders. Even though recently gathered information is not included in Bent's accounts, you will find no better introduction to the ecology of birds you see at your feeders. As you identify birds on your walks and trips, read Bent's accounts. You will find out about habitats, plumages, courtship, nesting, eggs, young, food, migration, voice, and enemies, and you will begin to appreciate how ornithology depends on thousands of reporters, not only professional scientists but also careful amateurs, who discover and record facts about birds.

Studies in greater depth than Bent's about the life histories of individual birds are instructive and fun. One of the most famous is *The Herring Gull's World* (1953), by the British ethologist Nikolaas Tinbergen. Another classic is Margaret Morse Nice's *Studies in the Life History of the Song Sparrow* (Part I, 1937; Part II, 1943). Handy collections of life histories in one or two volumes include *Bent's Life Histories,* edited and abridged into two volumes by Henry Hill Collins in 1960; G. G. Simpson, *Penguins* (1976); P. A. Johnsgard, *Ducks, Geese, and Swans of the World* (1978); and Jean Delacour, *Waterfowl of the World* (4 volumes, 1954–1964).

GREEN-BACKED
HERON

TROUT

WATER
FLEAS

ALGAE

LIVING PYRAMID. *Because energy dissipates as it flows along a food chain, fewer and fewer animals can exist at each successive stage. If this were not true, there might be as many hawks as mosquitoes! This pyramid shows that a mass of algae is needed to support the water fleas, which in turn are food for a smaller number of trout. In their turn the trout support only one Green-backed Heron.*

FOOD CHAIN. *Most food chains begin with a plant, in this case algae. A primary consumer (a plant eater, or herbivore), such as a mayfly nymph, eats the plant. Then follow additional levels of consumers (the meat eaters, or carnivores), ending in the highest, a carnivore that usually is not preyed on by any other animal.*

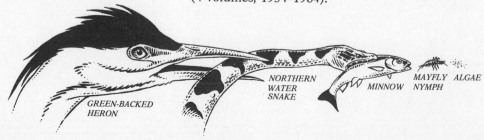

GREEN-BACKED
HERON

NORTHERN
WATER
SNAKE

MINNOW

MAYFLY
NYMPH

ALGAE

Living communities. A second way to understand the ecology of birds is to fit together the roles of all the plants, animals, and nonliving systems in an ecosystem. An excellent introduction to this approach is the series of 14 books sponsored by the U.S. Department of the Interior, *Our Living World of Nature* (1966–1972), published jointly by McGraw-Hill and World Book. Each volume, written by an eminent scientist and profusely illustrated, covers the ecology of a particular habitat, such as desert, forest, river, seashore, and ocean. Other introductions to the ecology of living communities are found in the Institute of Ecology's *Man in the Living Environment* (1970) and Allee, Emerson, Park, Park, and Schmidt, *Principles of Animal Ecology* (1949).

Ecology and the protection of birds. Ecological studies of a single bird species show which species of plants and animals are most important in its life and survival. Few, if any, bird species are dependent on only one kind of plant or animal. Most depend on groups of plants and animals, and for most bird species, variety is the key to survival. Knowing the species of plants and animals a species depends on may help people preserve endangered species. For example, having learned all they could about the ecology of the Whooping Crane, ornithologists initiated an effort by many kinds of scientists that has increased the number of cranes from only 18 surviving individuals to the present population of more than 100.

Your enjoyment of birding will increase as your knowledge of ecology increases. Ecology, the how, where, why, and when of birds, is like baseball: Fans who know the players and statistics take the greatest pleasure in the sport. In similar fashion, your pleasure as a birder will grow as you learn more about the lives of birds.

FOOD WEB. *With few exceptions every animal in a food chain eats more than one species of food. Thus, energy flowing to the highest-level carnivore passes through a complex web of consumers. This strengthens the ecosystem: Breaking one strand of a web does not destroy the web but breaking one link would destroy a simple food chain.*

BIRD ART

ACTIVITIES. Have you thought of collecting pictures of birds? Pictures in field guides are too small to satisfy. Big pictures provide better views of birds, so developing your own collection will be useful as well as fun. Professor Arnolds Grava, a friend of ours, has collected pictures of birds throughout the world and now has more than 8000, most of them in color and filed in taxonomic order in loose-leaf notebooks. His goal is to have a picture of every known species. Watch for reproductions of paintings and bird photographs in magazines, even in advertisements. Advertisers know that excellent bird pictures in full color attract attention.

BIRD ART. Until about 20,000 years ago, bird art apparently was restricted to bone and ivory carvings. Possibly 5000 years before then, an artist of the Stone Age etched the likeness of a bird on a piece of antler. At about the same time, another artist carved one end of a spear-thrower into an excellent likeness of a bird, probably a Black Grouse. Etchings on pottery and figurines of baked clay became fairly common about 5500 B.C. Wall paintings in Egyptian tombs of 3000 B.C. show many identifiable birds, such as falcons, geese, ducks, and ibises. The Harappan, earliest civilization of India, depicted birds on pottery.

In the early New World, eagles, turkeys, and other large birds were etched on rocks by Indians. In the southwestern United States, thunderbird carvings and pottery designs predominated. Many birds appeared in the artwork of the Mayas, Aztecs, Mixtecs, and other peoples of Mexico and Central America. The Incas and their predecessors in South America wove bird designs into their fabrics and produced much pottery decorated with bird figures and motifs. The Chimu Indians of Northern Peru designed adobe buildings with seabirds shown in deep relief on the walls.

Later art. John James Audubon (1785–1851) was undoubtedly a great naturalist and the best of the early American bird artists. His *Birds of America* (1827–1838) and its beautiful paintings are known by everyone interested in birds. Editions have been published even into the twentieth century, and his name is further commemorated in the name of the National Audubon Society. Another noted ornithologist, called the father of American ornithology, although less accomplished an artist, was Alexander Wilson (1766–1813), born in Scotland, who illustrated and published *American Ornithology* in seven volumes (1808–1814). Modern artists of note include Louis Agassiz Fuertes, who illustrated many bird books; Allan Brooks; Arthur Singer; Roger Tory Peterson; Albert Earl Gilbert; George Miksch Sutton; William C. Dilger; and James Fenwick Lansdowne.

FROM MYTH TO REALITY. *The Peruvian decoration (above), taken from a frieze of a building, shows a bird with the eyes and jaws of a cat. The lifelike field sketch (below) by Louis Agassiz Fuertes, one of the greatest of American bird artists, shows a Greater Roadrunner and a California Quail in a desert setting.*

COMINGS AND GOINGS. In winter the southern limits of the Snowy and Boreal owls are determined by a factor different from that determining the northern limits of ducks. These northern owls move south when their natural food becomes scarce in Canada. If their populations expand while their food supplies contract, they will move farther and farther south in search of prey. The two owls hunt different prey, so it is unusual for both of them to forage equally far south in the same season. The Snowy Owl seems to prefer coastal areas in winter. We have seen members of this species skimming the surface of the water for food 300 or more miles at sea.

░░ *Usual winter ranges of Snowy and Boreal owls*
■■■ *Occasional southern limit of winter ranges of both owls*

NOTES

NOV 18–24

NOTIFY F & WILD WASHINGTON 368-5029

BIRD BANDING

ACTIVITIES. Keep an eye on the weather when you are watching birds. It is particularly important to record how birds behave during stormy weather, those you see through a window as well as those you observe in the field. Bad weather is sometimes characterized as "for the birds," but many birds do find such weather hard to cope with. They typically become less active but, like people who deliver the U.S. mail, must get through their appointed rounds. For birds this is a matter of survival. Yet while birding in a swamp during a heavy downpour, one of us pressed close to a large tree for shelter and there found a White-throated Sparrow with the same idea.

BIRD BANDING. The Greeks probably banded birds in order to send messages, and it is certain that Julius Caesar used pigeons for this purpose. Early naturalists are thought to have learned something about the routes these birds took from start to destination. In modern times, John James Audubon, for example, wrapped silver wire about the legs of fledgling phoebes to find out whether the birds returned to the same northern nesting site the following spring. Two did.

The first large-scale organized bird banding in the United States was undertaken in 1909 by members of the American Bird Banding Association. In 1920 their work was taken over by the U.S. Biological Survey, now part of the Department of the Interior. Banding in Canada is controlled by the Canadian Wildlife Service. Techniques of bird banding have improved over the years, and millions of birds have been banded in the two countries, with a good percentage recovered and studied. A great deal of the information is collected at the Patuxent Research Refuge, near Laurel, Maryland, where it is under continuing analysis, lately with the help of computers. Other countries have started bird banding associations of their own—banding is called ringing in England—and the international exchange of information has increased knowledge of the global status of birds.

Why band birds? What banding has revealed about the life histories of birds has exceeded expectations. Ornithologists now know more certainly how long many bird species live. They have better information about migration routes and seasonal schedules. They are more certain about the status of bird populations, especially endangered and threatened species. And since individual birds, not flocks, are banded, ornithologists gain accurate information about the progress and schedule of molts, whether mates migrate together, and whether a species is monogamous. They also learn the diseases and food preferences of birds by season and locality.

There is a dubious report of a parrot in England which lived 104 years. An Andean Condor in the Moscow Zoo lived 72 years there; a Siberian Crane lived 62 years. Maximum ages for banded wild birds are the following:

YEARS	SPECIES
23	Canada Goose
16	Mallard
14	Peregrine Falcon
28	Herring Gull
9	Mourning Dove
10	Barn Owl
16	Barn Swallow
14	American Crow
15	Blue Jay
9	Black-capped Chickadee
5	House Wren
10	American Robin
20	European Starling
(captive) 28½	Northern Cardinal
8	Song Sparrow

COMINGS AND GOINGS.

The waxwings are omnivorous, eating vegetable matter—mainly berries—and insects, which they catch on the wing, as the flycatchers do. Even with insects gone, therefore, waxwings can live far north in winter, feeding on dried fruit and berries. The Cedar Waxwing is a wanderer, moving from spot to spot not on a schedule but according to the availability of food. The Bohemian Waxwing has similar habits but is even more erratic in its winter wanderings, at times going far outside its normal wintering range to reach the East Coast. The two species sometimes travel in the same flock, numbering typically 20 to 30 birds. So keep a sharp eye out.

Winter ranges: *Cedar Waxwing*
             Bohemian Waxwing

NOTES

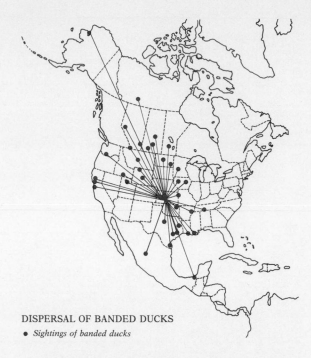

DISPERSAL OF BANDED DUCKS
● *Sightings of banded ducks*

TRACKING DUCKS. *The Tufted Duck carries a Fish and Wildlife Service band that enables ornithologists to trace its movements. For example, the map (right) shows the dispersal of banded ducks of various species from Cheyenne Bottoms, Kansas.*

The study of population dynamics, which is concerned among other things with the numbers of birds, would be severely hampered without the data supplied by bird banding. Estimating the numbers of birds in the field while watching birds can be quite sophisticated, but it is still an art, not a science. Many birds are banded when they are only 3 or 4 weeks old, ready to leave the nest. When seen in the field or recaptured during later years, these banded birds not only show how many years a species can live but also contribute to better estimates of their numbers and more precise knowledge of fluctuations in population from year to year.

The study of migration routes has also become more effective as a result of bird banding. Ornithologists have learned that birds do not necessarily follow the same pathways each year. They also have learned how severe weather conditions can affect choice of routes, sometimes changing them by only a few miles and sometimes by much greater distances. Migrants may move southward or northward on a broad front, straddling rivers and valleys, and at other times travel on a narrow front, even one side of a river valley. By weighing banded birds, ornithologists can determine weight loss during migration. This information helps explain how birds cope with bad weather during migration, whether it delays or slows flights, and whether large numbers are lost because of storms.

Bands recovered from birds in Europe, Asia, Africa, South America, the West Indies, Australia, and New Zealand as well as all over North Amer-

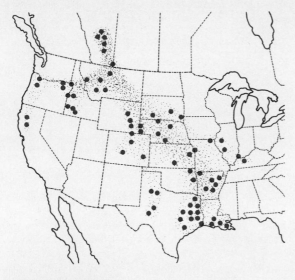

AUTUMN MIGRATION OF
MALLARDS

ica have been sent to Patuxent. When banding
data are entered in the computers, it is possible to
determine whether migration is normal and
whether other bird populations are normal for
any season. The data also enable ornithologists to
track changes in routes and to study population
trends over long periods. Sudden losses of birds in
an area may first be noted in these computer print-
outs, and steps can be taken to correct the problems. Even losses due to failure of natural food
supply may be studied.

Techniques of banding. To band a bird, one must
capture the bird alive, and government permits
are required to do this. Banders must present reasons why they should be granted a permit,
whether federal, state, or provincial; supply references; and indicate whether proper reference
books, an expert, or a museum bird collection can
be consulted. Forms for giving information of
where and when the bird was first banded and
where it was captured are sent to banders and to
the people who recover bands. The U.S. Fish and
Wildlife Service, in Washington, D.C., manufac-
tures bands of suitable size with the address in
Patuxent where recovered bands or information
about birds is to be sent. Plastic bands of various
colors and widths are available for those wishing
to identify certain birds by sight as part of a movement or dispersal study. Combinations of colors
on each leg make it possible for ornithologists to
perform controlled studies, and the bands may be
keyed to show such information as sex and exact
place of banding.

*If you find a dead or injured banded bird
other than a domestic pigeon or chicken,
report the find to the appropriate agency.
This can be done by mailing the band
itself to the address shown on the band or
by mailing the number and other data
from the band. If no address appears on
the band, send the information to this
address:*

> *Bird Banding Laboratory
> Department of the Interior
> Washington, D.C.*

*Include your name, address, where and
when the bird or band was found, and
how the bird died. You will receive a card
telling you where and by whom the bird
was banded and other information of
interest.*

NOV 25–DEC 1

TIPS FOR FIELD TRIPS

ACTIVITIES. Frozen lakes and ponds offer an opportunity to penetrate swamps and marshes that are hard to explore in warm weather, even by boat. Now is the time to clean out the duck nesting boxes you set on poles in the wetlands of your nature preserve. Search for nests you could not reach in summer. Look carefully. Even in cold weather there is a chance of encountering a bit of open water, perhaps near the outlet of a pond, where you might spot wintering ducks that are foraging for food. And for those of you who live too far south to enjoy really cold weather, winter is a good time to travel north for hiking and birding in frozen woods as well as for indulging in more strenuous winter sports.

Important: Sudden fast motions startle birds more than do loud noises or bright, flashy colors. Birds like bright colors.

TIPS FOR FIELD TRIPS. Whether on a short walk or a long trip, you will enjoy birding more if you dress comfortably and know how to spot birds. Here are some tips to help you.

Clothing. Light clothing is more comfortable and often warmer than heavy clothing. If the weather is very cold, wear several light sweaters or jackets and if you get overheated while walking, you can easily shed a garment or two. Sturdy, comfortable walking shoes are important. If you expect to visit bogs or marshes, wear waterproof footwear. It is also a good idea to carry insect repellent in season.

Binoculars, cameras, or other equipment will bang and thump, impeding your stride, if you hang it all around your neck. Fasten equipment out of the way on straps with quick-release snaps sewn to your field jacket. Bush jackets or safari jackets, with their large outside pockets and places for handy loops and straps, are considered ideal for birders.

Spotting birds. Windy days, when birds seek shelter, are not good for birding. In addition, leaves and branches dance about, making it hard to locate birds and to focus your binoculars on them.

Try to approach your lookout with the sun at your back. Most birds will hide behind tree boles or branches to avoid you, which means you will have to change position to see and identify them. Sometimes you will want to ask another birder to identify a bird before you move to get a better look. Birders may have difficulty communicating when different birds are in the same tree and observers become excited about the birds they have spotted. Birders then are responsible for making their own identifications and telling the others exactly where the bird is.

Learn to use your binoculars. Beginners often miss a good bird because they have not learned to focus quickly. Keep your eyes fixed on the bird, and move the binoculars until the bird appears in the lenses. Make sure the lenses have not misted over, and keep them clean.

COMINGS AND GOINGS. **East.** The area around

Miami, Florida, is particularly congenial for immigrants, birds as well as people. Most of the exotic birds there have escaped from captivity, and as long as there are enough of both sexes, they have little difficulty in becoming established. The Red-whiskered Bulbul, for example, a native of Asia, escaped from cages in 1960 and is now resident in Miami parks and suburbs. The Java Sparrow, native to Java and Bali, as well as the Budgerigar, Hill Myna, and others, native to such faraway places as Australia, India, and Africa, have also become naturalized.

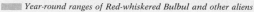 *Year-round ranges of Red-whiskered Bulbul and other aliens*

NOTES

DEC 2-8

FIELD EQUIPMENT

ACTIVITIES. Plan your participation in the important Christmas count (see page 190). After signing up at your local bird club, make a trial run over the section assigned, checking roads, determining which species are about, and noting the terrain and vegetation. Make sure your clothing is ready and your equipment in working order. Even if you have to stay at home during the count, you can participate. Add fresh suet and tidbits of fruit and nuts to your feeder some days in advance of the count to attract as many different species of birds as possible and encourage visits to the feeder on the big day. And when the day arrives, do not be shy about reporting what you see. A single individual of an uncommon species is sometimes counted at a feeder, but two or more observers are preferred for reports of rarities.

FIELD EQUIPMENT. When buying field equipment, including clothing, look for lightness combined with sturdiness. Light equipment may be less sturdy than heavy equipment, so you will have to make your choice based on the kind of birding you do. If you watch birds near home, you will not need equipment as sturdy as you might buy for strenuous backpacking trips.

Binoculars. Field glasses and binoculars help birders see and identify birds easily and quickly. Field glasses are cheaper than binoculars, ranging from $15 to about $100. They consist of two parallel tubes, each with inner sliding tubes equipped with simple lenses. They are good for observing birds in a yard or at a feeder. Since they usually magnify only 5 or 6 times ($5\times$ or $6\times$), they are not adequate for most field birding.

Binoculars have prisms inside the tubes. The prisms reflect the light that enters the instrument so that the distance the light travels between the eyepieces and the objective lenses is greatly increased, thus enabling greater magnification than possible with field glasses. The higher the power, the bigger and heavier the glasses. Binoculars, which range from $4\times$ to $20\times$, are more expensive than field glasses—about $50 to $900 or more. For birding, $6\times$ to $10\times$ is generally used, and it is useful to know that the higher the power, the steadier the birder's hands must be.

MAGNIFICATION. Looking at a bird through 7X binoculars means that the bird appears to be seven times closer than it appears when seen with the naked eye. Note that as the power of binoculars increases, a bird at the same distance from you appears closer, therefore larger. To change magnification, you must either change your binoculars to a lower or higher power or use a zoom lens. Unless the manufacturer of the binoculars supplies special lenses, such as wide-angle lenses, the field of view decreases as the magnification increases, making it more difficult to find and hold the bird in view. This is a good reason for testing binoculars in the field before you make your final selection. You want to be sure they meet your requirements.

7X binoculars   8X binoculars   9X binoculars

COMINGS AND GOINGS.

West. Dippers are birds of cool streams, either in the north or in mountains. Of four species, only one is found in North America. In winter the American Dipper may move to lower altitudes, but even at −40°F it may plunge into mountain torrents and walk underwater along the stream beds, looking for aquatic insect larvae. Various rails walk about the bottoms of quiet swamp pools throughout the year, but the dippers, which are distantly related to robins and thrushes, are the only perching, or land, birds known to do this. Look for them along streams in summer or winter; when you come upon them in cold weather, you will find their behavior most astonishing.

Year-round range of American Dipper

NOTES

_____

_____

_____

_____

_____

_____

_____

_____

_____

_____

_____

_____

_____

_____

_____

_____

_____

_____

_____

_____

_____

A new type of binoculars, called roof prism binoculars, which can cost anywhere from about $500 to $1200, is now available. The arrangement of prisms further increases the distance that light travels within the glasses so, for the same power as other binoculars, they are smaller and lighter. Roof prism binoculars do not employ sliding tubes, so they are sealed against water and dust. Field glasses and ordinary binoculars are sometimes sealed, though often imperfectly.

Although the depth of field is relatively shallow in roof prism glasses, they are probably the best for birders. A shallow depth of field means that as a bird moves about, the birder has to keep adjusting the focus to keep the image sharp. This is a small penalty for having such clear, light, and efficient birding glasses.

Be sure to buy glasses whose lenses and prisms are coated with a mist of magnesium fluoride on all surfaces. This coating prevents undesirable reflections that would reduce the clarity of the image. If you buy your glasses from a reputable dealer, you will be able to trust the legend "Fully Coated" that is stamped on the glasses.

Tip on Center-Focusing: If you have been using a pair of binoculars for a long time, you instinctively know the direction in which to turn the focusing wheel for close-up viewing or distance viewing. In buying new binoculars, make sure the wheel turns in the direction you are used to. If it turns in the opposite direction, it may take you a long time to focus the new glasses quickly. The trouble may be worth it if you are replacing your glasses with an extra-special pair.

What the numbers mean. Most binoculars have numbers, such as "7× 35 7.3°," stamped on the frame. These numbers mean that when you are looking through properly focused glasses, the objects you see are perceived as being seven times closer to you, the objective lens is 35 millimeters in diameter, and the angle of vision is 7.3 degrees. This means that at 1000 yards from a bird you are watching, your width of view is about 133 yards.

Buying binoculars. When buying binoculars, shop at trustworthy stores that will permit you to try the binoculars. To know which kind to order, borrow glasses of various sizes from your friends and test them. You will soon learn which suits you best.

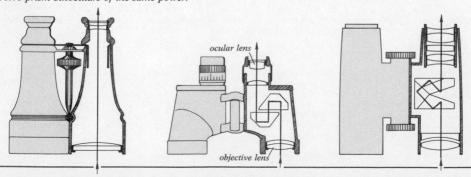

TYPES OF BINOCULARS. *In field glasses (left) the light travels a short distance from the objective lens to the ocular lens. To achieve high magnification, the two lenses must be placed far apart, as in the long brass telescopes once used by mariners. In Porro prism binoculars (center) the light travels farther, permitting higher magnification in a glass of about the same size as field glasses. In roof prism binoculars (right) the arrangement of prisms enables the light to travel in a more confined space, so the binoculars can be smaller and lighter than Porro prism binoculars of the same power.*

ocular lens

objective lens

Buy glasses manufactured by reputable firms, for example, Zeiss, Leitz, Bausch and Lomb, Swift, Busnell, Nikon, Questar, Meade, and Brunton. Cheap glasses, which often cause headaches and eyestrain, usually cost more in the end. Get a warranty with new glasses. Make sure the warranty is issued by an American or Canadian firm or distributor—do not accept other warranties. Make certain there are local repair services.

Do not buy heavy glasses, because they seem to get heavier and heavier on long field trips. Check sturdiness by making sure there are no loose pieces, especially inside. Look hard for scratches, particularly on lenses. Make sure you can focus the glasses easily and that they are properly aligned. Focus on a dark object and note whether any colors appear in the lenses. Cheap optics may show color at the edges of the lenses. Another good check is to look at stars with the glasses held in a firm stand. If your glasses have excellent optics, the stars at the edges of the lenses should be as well focused as those in the center.

Glasses are available with individual focusing for each eyepiece. It is more practical, however, to buy center-focus glasses, in which both left and right optics are focused simultaneously by means of a knurled knob between the tubes. Old center-focus binoculars often develop a wobble, which prevents precise synchronized focusing of the two lens systems. To correct this means an expensive repair that is not easily done. Newer glasses have nearly eliminated this problem.

To adjust center-focusing binoculars properly, first focus the left tube with your right eye closed. Then look through the right tube with your left eye closed and focus it until both tubes are in focus together. After proper focusing, record the setting numbers engraved on the right eyepiece and the tube beneath. Check the settings when you use your glasses. If someone else has used them, the setting may have been changed.

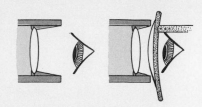

EYE CUPS. *These cups are designed to keep eyes at the optimum distance from the ocular lens. If you wear eyeglasses, you will need shallow eye cups. Some binoculars have rubber eye cups that can be rolled down for those who wear glasses, a convenience you should consider if you share your binoculars with others.*

ALIGNMENT. *Before purchasing a pair of binoculars, check their alignment by focusing on any distant horizontal line, such as the top of a wall or the roof of a house. Then move the binoculars about eight inches away from your eye and see whether the separate images are still aligned. If they are not, the binoculars may cause eye fatigue or headaches during a long field trip.*

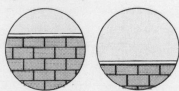

The two images are not aligned

TELESCOPES AND TRIPODS. *Telescopes mounted on tripods are excellent for observing birds across fields and bodies of water. A 20X scope, light and easy to carry, will do for most birding. Zoom scopes enable focusing at 10X to 15X and then, with the same focus, zoom to 20X or more with minor adjustment for finer focus.*

A tripod should be light, sturdy, and easy to set up. If it vibrates in a wind, the image will dance. The legs of a flip-lock tripod flip open and lock at the desired position. Some birders mount scopes on gun stocks and carry them over a shoulder, ready for use. Focusing on a bird with a hand-held scope requires steadiness, but this mount extends the usefulness of a scope. For example, the scope can be used in forests or other confined areas where birds may fly off before a tripod can be set up.

CAMERAS AND RECORDERS. *For those who wish to photograph birds, we recommend Baufle and Varin,* Photographing Wildlife *(1972), which provides excellent advice on how to get started.*

When you hear a song but cannot see the singing bird, you will find it useful to record the song and compare it later with bird songs on commercial records or tapes. Reclusive birds, such as vireos and warblers, are identified primarily by their songs. Fine recorders will pick up only the song you want, but songs recorded on an inexpensive tape deck can also help in making identifications.

DEC 9–15

CHRISTMAS COUNTS

ACTIVITIES. If you have not yet done so, this is a good time to initiate regular visits to museums and zoos, paying particular attention to bird exhibits. Even the smallest museums may have interesting collections or exhibits. Zoos are havens for endangered species, and many have initiated programs for raising and then releasing such species to the wild. In addition to exhibits of birds, often in their natural settings, museums maintain collections of bird skins, books, and other useful reference materials. So here is your chance to learn about familiar birds in unfamiliar plumage and to identify strangers that once appeared in your garden. In addition, you will be able to participate in programs and field trips organized by zoos and museums.

CHRISTMAS COUNTS. Unaffiliated birders and members of bird clubs participate each year in a Christmas count sponsored in the United States and Canada by the National Audubon Society. The society sets a range of dates for this activity and later publishes the results in its magazine, *American Birds*. The dates of the annual count usually fall within the 7 days before and after Christmas, although lately the periods have been extended to 10 days before and after. The count runs officially from midnight to midnight of the day chosen by each local club. The club is responsible for seeing that the counting is as accurate and objective as possible and that it is reported to *American Birds* for publication.

How it works. The area covered by each club is established by the club and registered with National Audubon. It comprises a circle 15 miles in diameter. All birds within the circle are counted, species by species and by total number of individual birds. Birds seen 3 days before and 3 days after the dates set by each club are listed as "in the area during the count week but not on count day." Reports of the circles, being precisely defined, can be compared through the years as to numbers seen and weather encountered. The circles usually are divided by the local club into sections based on road networks, and teams of two or more observers are assigned to each section. Beginners usually are teamed with experienced birders, and the teams keep count of the hours they spend walking, driving, and watching. Birds at feeders within the circle are included in the count.

COMINGS AND GOINGS. West. Whiskered
Screech-Owls and Ferruginous Pygmy-Owls, found throughout
the year in southeastern Arizona and southward into Mexico, are
the size of sparrows. But the world's smallest owl, about 5¼
inches long, is the Elf Owl, found in the same general habitat. It
is entirely nocturnal. Whiskered Screech-Owls and Ferruginous
Pygmy-Owls are usually nocturnal, hiding from the heat of day
in holes or any other shade they can find. All three of these swift,
fierce, diminutive owls, prey on insects. As you can well believe,
it takes sharp eyes to see them.

Year-round ranges:  *Whiskered Screech-Owl*
Ferruginous Pygmy-Owl
Elf Owl

NOTES

DEC 9–15
CHRISTMAS COUNTS

Why make the counts? Christmas counts are designed to be as accurate and reliable as possible in spite of human error in identifying species or in estimating numbers. The counts produce data showing the winter ranges of the species observed. By studying the data, ornithologists have learned, for example, of the spread of the Song Sparrow and other species northward in winter as they have adapted to feeding trays, which supply abundant food during that season.

Because the birds in an area of fixed size are counted each year, relatively accurate estimates can be made of populations and their fluctuations in time and place. Areas can be compared and possible reasons for differences ascertained. Species appearing for the first time in an area are noted, and studies are made of movements over large areas or regions. Total numbers from all the counts indicate whether a species is declining or increasing in population. Sometimes there are surprises that lead to endless speculation, such as birds appearing during winter in an area where they previously were not known to winter. And there is always the possibility of making the first sighting ever of a species in that area.

The reports sent to *American Birds* include latitude and longitude of the center of the circle, elevation in feet, kinds of habitats covered, time of day spent in each habitat, weather throughout the day, snow cover, whether water was open or frozen, status of wild food crops, number of observers, total party hours, miles covered on foot and in vehicles, and other pertinent data. At the end of the count, the official club reporters total the number of species and the number of individual birds. They also list the participants.

Results of a Christmas count, locality by locality, are usually published in issue 4 (July–August) of *American Birds.* Birders all over North America may compare results from various sites and perhaps decide to select a more promising site for the next count in which they participate.

End of count day. Many clubs close the Christmas count by gathering for potluck supper, discussion of the day's events, and submittal of data to the official recorder. Experienced birders may question the accuracy of some reports, but those supervising the count strive to ensure accuracy. (Mistakes rarely go unnoticed by the editors of *American Birds.*) All try hard to be correct, knowing that the count is important for ornithology.

The end of the day is usually merry, as befits the season. Beginning birders make new friends, other trips are planned, and spirits are high because the birders know they have taken part in an international event. You should plan to participate in the Christmas count and thus earn the thanks of all American and Canadian birders.

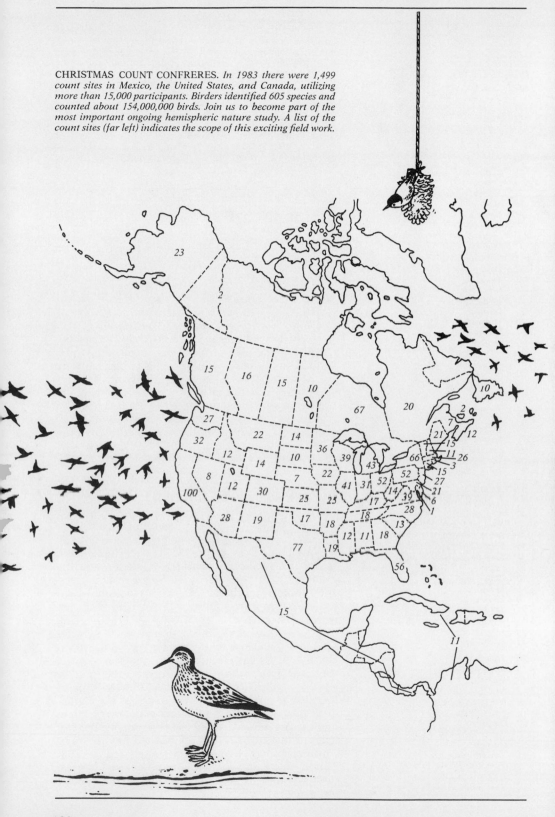

CHRISTMAS COUNT CONFRERES. *In 1983 there were 1,499 count sites in Mexico, the United States, and Canada, utilizing more than 15,000 participants. Birders identified 605 species and counted about 154,000,000 birds. Join us to become part of the most important ongoing hemispheric nature study. A list of the count sites (far left) indicates the scope of this exciting field work.*

DEC 16–22

PLAIN TITMOUSE
—*Louis Agassiz Fuertes*

FIELD GUIDES

ACTIVITIES. The first Christmas trees probably were evergreens growing near a home, church, or temple that were hung with food to attract birds. This is a far better use of trees than stringing them with expensive lights. You might decorate nearby evergreens with suet; surplus kitchen fats; nuts; raisins, apricots, apples, and other dried fruits; various seeds embedded in baked goods; and other goodies, for example, leftover pie crusts or such cereals as oatmeal or farina. Tie your tidbits in brightly colored paper or foil, and watch the birds enjoy them. We pour waste kitchen fats into tin cans and place them in a freezer. When the fats are gelled, we punch a hole in the bottom of the can and thread a wire coat hanger through the fat so that the can may be hung more or less horizontally from a tree branch. Birds love it.

FIELD GUIDES. Since colonial days there have been books describing North American birds, but true field identification guides, as they are known today, first appeared in the 20th century.

Some early books. The first scientific book on North American wildlife was *Natural History of Carolina, Florida and the Bahama Islands* (1743–1748), by Mark Catesby (c. 1680–c. 1750). Catesby, called the founder of American ornithology, described and illustrated 109 species of birds among the plants and animals he wrote about. Another early and exceptionally popular book, especially in France and England, took an exalted view of nature. It was *Travels through North and South Carolina* . . . (1791), by the famous Philadelphia botanist William Bartram (1739–1823), who described 215 species, the largest list of North American birds up to that time.

The 19th century. The first of the great American works devoted solely to birds was *American Ornithology* (1808–1814), a nine-volume illustrated work covering about 279 species. It was written by Alexander Wilson (1766–1813), justly called the father of American ornithology. Then came the even more famous *Birds of North America*, by John James Audubon (1785–1851), first published in London in four volumes (1827–1838) and then in New York City in seven volumes (1860–1861). Audubon painted 497 birds, though some of what he thought were separate species have since been combined. By no stretch of the imagination can these two great works be considered field guides.

In 1832 Thomas Nuttall (1786–1859) published *A Manual of the Ornithology of the United States and Canada* and *The Land Birds*. These books were the first American field guides. In 1872 Elliott Coues (1842–1899) published *Key to North American Birds*. Its last edition appeared in 1903. This is the first book that may be considered a practical field guide, because it provided a scheme for quick identification.

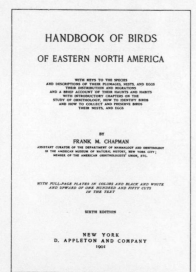

HANDBOOK OF BIRDS

OF EASTERN NORTH AMERICA

WITH KEYS TO THE SPECIES
AND DESCRIPTIONS OF THEIR PLUMAGES, NESTS, AND EGGS
THEIR DISTRIBUTION AND MIGRATIONS
AND A BRIEF ACCOUNT OF THEIR HAUNTS AND HABITS
WITH INTRODUCTORY CHAPTERS ON THE
STUDY OF ORNITHOLOGY, HOW TO IDENTIFY BIRDS
AND HOW TO COLLECT AND PRESERVE BIRDS
THEIR NESTS, AND EGGS

BY
FRANK M. CHAPMAN
ASSISTANT CURATOR OF THE DEPARTMENT OF MAMMALOGY AND ORNITHOLOGY
IN THE AMERICAN MUSEUM OF NATURAL HISTORY, NEW YORK CITY;
MEMBER OF THE AMERICAN ORNITHOLOGISTS' UNION, ETC.

WITH FULL-PAGE PLATES IN COLORS AND BLACK AND WHITE
AND UPWARD OF ONE HUNDRED AND FIFTY CUTS
IN THE TEXT

SIXTH EDITION

NEW YORK
D. APPLETON AND COMPANY
1901

COMINGS AND GOINGS. Although the Northern Cardinal does not occur in every state, it is everywhere a familiar bird because it is widely depicted, particularly at Christmas. It is a year-round resident, though during severe winters it sometimes seeks more clement weather to the south or at lower altitudes. It is now established in Hawaii. An early breeder, it begins its loud *cheer-cheer-cheer* in January or February, even while snow still lies on the ground. The cheerful call does even more than the welcome song of the American Robin to raise the spirits of winter-weary birders.

Year-round range of Northern Cardinal

NOTES

In 1883 Edward Augustus Samuels (1835–1908) published *Our Northern and Eastern Birds.* Originally titled *Ornithology and Oology of New England,* it was for many years the most popular guide to birds of the New England area.

The 20th century. In 1912 Frank M[ichler] Chapman (1864–1945) published his *Color Key to North American Birds.* It was small enough to be carried into the field and helped the beginner by grouping birds according to color. Most of the black-and-white illustrations, where appropriate, included an additional color, indicating where the color appeared on the bird, so if, for example, birders wished to identify a species that contained any blue, they could leaf through the illustrations using blue. This device is still used in some books.

Earlier, in 1895, Chapman had published *Handbook of Birds of Eastern North America,* justifiably considered a 20th-century book. Its final revised edition, the third, appeared in 1939. This book, portable and comprehensive, tremendously influenced professionals and amateurs. It covered about 675 species and contained a color chart but had relatively few illustrations, identification being achieved by description and referral to the color chart. Another early book was *A Guide to the Birds of New England and Eastern New York,* published in 1904 by Ralph Hoffman (1870–1932). Illustrated with pen-and-ink drawings and halftone paintings, it had an identification key based on color and seasons.

In 1906 Chester A. Reed (1876–1912) published the first pocket-sized guides, *Bird Guide* (later titled *Land Birds*). It was soon followed by *Water Birds, Western Bird Guide,* and *North American Birds' Eggs,* as well as by guides to wildflowers, mushrooms, and other flora. All were in a 3¼ by 5½ inch format that could be slipped into a shirt pocket. Selling in the hundreds of thousands, these little books, all in full color, were recognized as the first series of field identification guides in America and became the standard field guides for American birders. There were other field guides to birds, but they usually were restricted in coverage to a city, state, or province.

In 1934 Roger Tory Peterson published *A Field Guide to the Birds* [of eastern North America] (4th ed., 1980). This pioneering guide set a trend for guide books and contributed greatly to making birding popular in the United States and Canada. It was pocket-sized and contained a number of color plates. Every species known in the area was illustrated with a drawing, many in color, with distinguishing field marks pointed out. Emphasizing the field marks in this way not only proved popular but also workable. By now, Peterson has published not only several additional bird guides, such as *A Field Guide to Western Birds*

—*From* Color Key to North American Birds *by Frank M. Chapman*

(2nd ed., 1961), *A Field Guide to the Birds of Britain and Europe* (4th ed., 1984), and *A Field Guide to the Birds of Mexico* (1973), but also guides to other types of wildlife. The Peterson Field Guide Series now has more than 25 titles.

In 1966 *Birds of North America: A Guide to Field Identification* (rev. ed., 1983) was published by Chandler S. Robbins, Bertel Brunn, and Herbert S. Zim, with illustrations by Arthur Singer. In one pocket-sized volume, birds nesting north of Mexico in North America—about 650 species plus 60 regular visitors and 100 casual or accidental visitors—are illustrated in color and described, with ranges mapped on facing pages, making the book especially easy to use as well as comprehensive. This book and the Peterson books are the most widely used field guides in the United States and Canada.

There are other good guides you may wish to add to your library as your interest in birds grows:

Audubon Society Field Guide to North American Birds. Eastern Region by John Bull and John Farrand, Jr. (1977). Western Region by Miklos Udvardy (1977). These two are illustrated with color photographs.

Audubon Bird Guides: Eastern Land Birds (1946, 1949), *Water Birds* (1951), and *Western Birds* (1957), by Richard Pough. These contain more information on habitats than is found in other guides.

Audubon Society Master Guide to Birding (1983), edited by John Farrand, Jr. The three volumes, illustrated with color photographs supplemented by full-color art, contain exceptionally full descriptions and maps.

Field Guide to the Birds of North America (1983). Published by the National Geographic Society.

RECORDS AND CASSETTE TAPES. *Today there are many records and cassettes of bird songs. Cornell University sells records and cassettes with songs arranged in the same sequence as the birds in Peterson's eastern and western bird guides. In addition, records and cassettes are sold by the National Audubon Society and other outlets. All these recordings together do not contain every song, because quite a few have not yet been taped. Many commercial record and cassette dealers handle at least some bird recordings. Also check the book and gift shops of natural history museums.*

VIDEOTAPES. *Now that videocassette recorders are widely available, instruction in how to identify birds has moved from the still life of books to the movement of film. Announcements and advertisements in Audubon and similar magazines describe cassettes of interest to birders. For example, one cassette of the Audubon Society's Videoguide to the Birds of North America is already available; seven are planned.*

The proliferation of field guides, records, and tapes indicates how popular bird watching has become. Perhaps this widespread interest reflects in part a recognition that the existence of American wildlife may depend on all of us.

DEC 23-31

WINTER NIGHTS HOMEWORK

ACTIVITIES. How about taking a course in bird study at a local adult school? Many colleges as well as high schools offer night courses taught by local birders. For those who would rather study at home, an excellent correspondence course is available, *Seminars in Ornithology: A Home Study Course in Bird Biology,* edited by the eminent ornithologist Olin Sewall Pettingill, Jr. For information write to the Laboratory of Ornithology, 159 Sapsucker Woods Road, Ithaca, NY 14850. Colleges and universities offer similar correspondence courses. If no courses are available locally, you might encourage your local bird club to establish a lecture series. Community interest in nature and conservation will increase, and your club will be performing a valuable service.

The chief aim of this book is to present, simply and straightforwardly, the basic facts of bird biology. A second aim is to arouse in the reader a lasting enthusiasm for birds and for the wonderful things they do. If the first goal is attained, reaching the second should be insured by the facts themselves. They make a fascinating story when they are considered in relation to the live, throbbing bird and its problems of existence.

—From the preface to the first edition of The Life of Birds, *by Joel Carl Welty*

WINTER NIGHTS HOMEWORK.

Countless articles and reports dealing with birds have appeared in popular magazines and ornithological journals, and thousands of books about birds have been published. Among all the books, no one can be called the best. But we can recommend books that should be considered for a place on your shelf:

BOOKS

Austin, Oliver L., *Birds of the World* (1983). Lively and well illustrated.

Campbell, Bruce, and Elizabeth Lack (eds.), *A Dictionary of Birds* (1985). A new version of Sir A. Landsborough Thomson's work (see below).

Leahy, Christopher, *The Birdwatcher's Companion* (1982). An encyclopedia of North American birdlife.

Pettingill, Olin Sewall, Jr., *Ornithology in Laboratory and Field* (1984). First published as *A Laboratory and Field Manual of Ornithology.* A classic textbook for serious students.

Reilly, Edgar M., *The Audubon Illustrated Handbook of American Birds* (1968). A popular encyclopedia covering all species of birds of the United States (including Hawaii) and Canada.

Terres, John K., *The Audubon Society Encyclopedia of North American Birds* (1982). A comprehensive reference.

Thomson, Sir A. Landsborough (1890–1977), *A New Dictionary of Birds* (1964). A well-illustrated classic, indispensable for serious amateurs and ornithologists.

Welty, Joel Carl, *The Life of Birds* (3rd ed., 1982). The standard introductory text for college students. Lively, fascinating in content.

COMINGS AND GOINGS. In this book the last week of the birder's year has nine days, enough for some extra birding despite the hectic activities of the holidays. And here is an idea: It has become popular in the holiday season to spend a few days at the shore. If you do so, keep your eyes peeled for special birds: on the Pacific coast, northern gulls, albatrosses, kittiwakes, Pigeon Guillemots, and Ancient Murrelets; on the Atlantic coast, northern gulls, boobies, shearwaters, Sooty terns, Razorbills, Dovekies, and Purple Sandpipers; on the Gulf coast, Brown and White pelicans, frigatebirds, spoonbills, ibises, and Reddish Egrets; and along inland waters, Bald Eagles, wintering ducks and geese, loons, gulls, and jaegers.

Winter birding along the coasts

NOTES

199

There are many books on various phases of bird study, such as attracting birds, behavior, biology, ecology, eggs, evolution, extinction, finding birds, incubation, migration, nesting, and taxonomy. There also are books about particular species, genera, families, and orders of birds. Selected reading lists appear at the end of Leahy's *Birdwatcher's Companion* and Terres' *Encyclopedia* and at the end of each chapter in Welty's *Life of Birds.* And you will find information about new books in reviews and advertisements in the magazines and journals listed next.

Journals and magazines. Beginning birders will probably enjoy popular magazines most but soon wish to become acquainted with the information provided by journals.

POPULAR MAGAZINES
American Birds. National Audubon Society, 950 Third Avenue, New York, NY 10022.

Birding. P.O. Box 4335, Austin, TX 78765.

The Bird Watcher's Digest. P.O. Box 110, Marietta, OH 45750.

The Journal of Field Ornithology (formerly *Bird Banding*). P.O. Box 797, Manomet, MA 02345.

Wingtips. P.O. Box 226, Lansing, NY 14882.

MORE TECHNICAL PUBLICATIONS
The Auk. Journal of the American Ornithologists' Union, National Museum of Natural History, Smithsonian Institution, Washington, DC 20560.

The Living Bird. Cornell Laboratory of Ornithology, 159 Sapsucker Woods Road, Ithaca, NY 14850.

The Condor. Journal of the Cooper Ornithological Society. Los Angeles Museum of Natural History, 900 Exposition Boulevard, Los Angeles, CA 90007.

The Wilson Bulletin. Wilson Ornithological Society, Division of Birds, Museum of Zoology, University of Michigan, Ann Arbor, MI 48104.

ROSS' GEESE

Most magazines of natural history offer articles about birds, reviews of books on birds, advertisements for books and equipment, and other information of interest. Here are a few.

NATURAL HISTORY MAGAZINES
The Canadian Field Naturalist. Ottawa Field-Naturalists Club, Box 3264, Postal Station C, K1Y 4J5, Ottawa, Ontario, Canada.

Audubon. National Audubon Society, 930 Third Avenue, New York, NY 10022.

National Geographic. National Geographic Society, P.O. Box 2895, Washington, DC 20013.

Natural History. American Museum of Natural History, P.O. Box 5000, Harlan, IA 51537.

Scientific American. 415 Madison Avenue, New York, NY 10017.

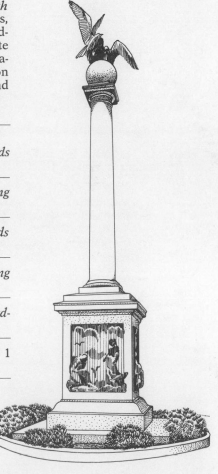

SEAGULL MONUMENT. *This unique tribute to birds stands in Temple Square, Salt Lake City, Utah. It commemorates the timely arrival of flocks of gulls that ate the locusts destroying the crops planted in 1848 by the first Mormon settlers. Two million visitors see the monument each year.*

State and provincial bird societies, as well as local bird and natural history clubs, issue monthly journals or newsletters. An excellent way to find these organizations is through *A Guide to North American Bird Clubs* (1978), Avian Publications, Inc., P.O. Box 310, Elizabethtown, KY 42701. Birders should join their local bird clubs and state organizations, which distribute valuable information on birds of their regions. There are books on the birds of almost all the states, provinces, and larger regions.

Here are books of broad general interest:

BOOKS OF GENERAL INTEREST
Alden, Peter, and John Gooders, *Finding Birds Around the World* (1981).

Dennis, John V., *A Complete Guide to Bird Feeding* [eastern North America only] (1983).

Gruson, E. S., *Checklist of the World's Birds* (1976).

Heintzelman, D. C., *A Manual for Bird Watching in the Americas* (1979).

Kress, S. W., *Audubon Society Handbook for Birders* (1981).

Stokes, D. W., *A Guide to Bird Behavior*, Vol. 1 (1979); with Lillian Q. Stokes, Vol. 2 (1983).

PROBABLE EVOLUTIONARY RELATIONSHIPS
OF
UNITED STATES AND CANADIAN
BIRDS

----- questionable

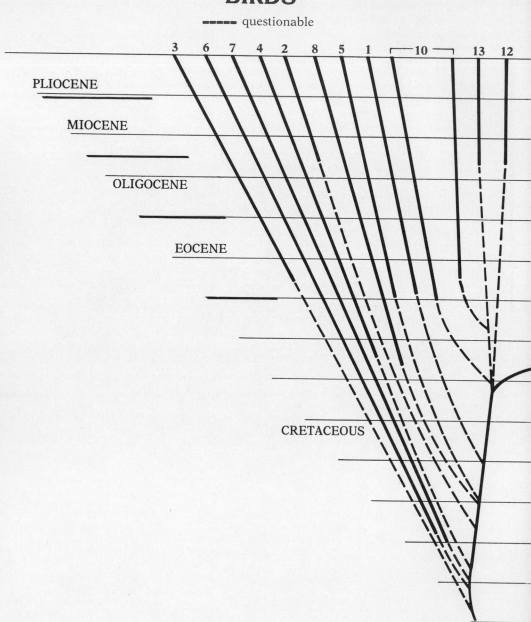

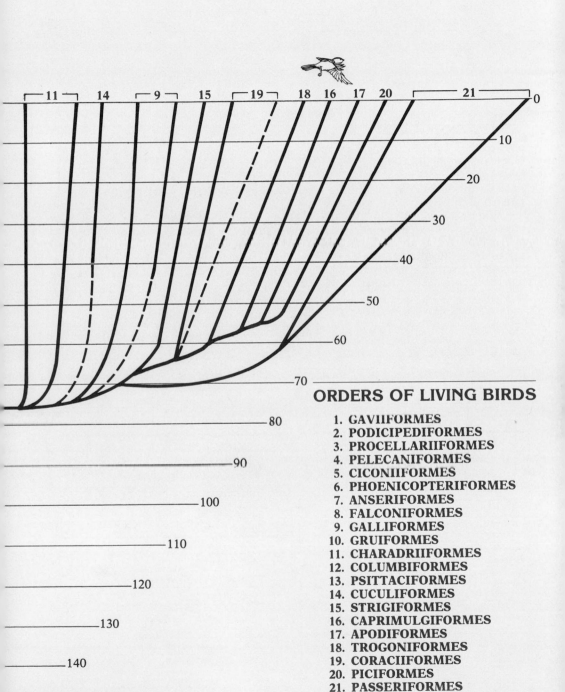

┌─ 11 ─┐   14   ┌─ 9 ─┐   15   ┌─ 19 ─┐ 18 16 17 20 ┌──── 21 ────┐ 0

—10

—20

—30

—40

—50

—60

—70

—80

—90

—100

—110

—120

—130

—140

—150 million years ago

ORDERS OF LIVING BIRDS

1. GAVIIFORMES
2. PODICIPEDIFORMES
3. PROCELLARIIFORMES
4. PELECANIFORMES
5. CICONIIFORMES
6. PHOENICOPTERIFORMES
7. ANSERIFORMES
8. FALCONIFORMES
9. GALLIFORMES
10. GRUIFORMES
11. CHARADRIIFORMES
12. COLUMBIFORMES
13. PSITTACIFORMES
14. CUCULIFORMES
15. STRIGIFORMES
16. CAPRIMULGIFORMES
17. APODIFORMES
18. TROGONIFORMES
19. CORACIIFORMES
20. PICIFORMES
21. PASSERIFORMES

CHECKLIST
OF
UNITED STATES AND CANADIAN
BIRDS

(Based on the American Ornithologists' Union's *Check-list of North American Birds*)

HOW TO USE. The English Names of the birds in this list are arranged in phylogenetic order. They begin with what is thought to be the lowest, or most primitive, species and end with what many consider the highest, or most specialized, species. You should familiarize yourself with this sequence, because most United States and Canadian field identification guides follow it, though not rigorously since the descriptions and illustrations of similar-looking species are often positioned next to each other.

When you identify a bird for the first time, place the date and the locality in the box following the bird's name. In the box preceding the name enter the page number of this diary (or of another notebook) on which you describe the particulars of the sighting (see "Record keeping" in the index). As a space saver, you might find it useful to create a set of symbols for your favorite birding spots: An asterisk (*) could represent your feeder, a plus sign (+) a particular pond or marsh, and so on.

2	Northern Bobwhite 1/4/86 *edge of woods*

Make a note here of the symbols you use.

_225-4/7/91_
_220 - 2/9/91_
_233 - 4/20/92_   _267 - 4/16/95_
_233 - 6/21/94_
_236 - 5/10/94_   _275 5/2/99_
_248 -_

GAVIIFORMES
Gaviidae

	Red-throated Loon
	Pacific Loon
	Arctic Loon
✓	Common Loon
	Yellow-billed Loon

PODICIPEDIFORMES
Podicipedidae

	Least Grebe
✓	Pied-billed Grebe
	Horned Grebe
	Red-necked Grebe
	Eared Grebe
✓	Western Grebe
	Clark's Grebe

PROCELLARIIFORMES
Diomedeidae

	Wandering Albatross (A)
	Short-tailed Albatross
	Black-footed Albatross
	Laysan Albatross
	Black-browed Albatross
	Shy Albatross
	Yellow-nosed Albatross

Procellariidae

	Northern Fulmar
	Cape Petrel
	Black-capped Petrel
	Bermuda Petrel
	Dark-rumped Petrel
	White-necked Petrel

	Mottled Petrel (A)
	Murphy's Petrel
	Kermadec Petrel (A)
	Herald Petrel (A)
	Cook's Petrel
	Bonin Petrel
	Black-winged Petrel (A)
	Bulwer's Petrel
	Jouanin's Petrel (A)
	Streaked Shearwater (A)
	Cory's Shearwater
	Pink-footed Shearwater
	Flesh-footed Shearwater
	Greater Shearwater
	Wedge-tailed Shearwater
	Buller's Shearwater
	Sooty Shearwater
	Short-tailed Shearwater
	Christmas Shearwater
	Manx Shearwater
	Black-vented Shearwater
	Townsend's Shearwater
	Little Shearwater (A)
	Audubon's Shearwater

Hydrobatidae

	Wilson's Storm-Petrel
	White-faced Storm-Petrel
	British Storm-Petrel (A)
	Fork-tailed Storm-Petrel
	Leach's Storm-Petrel
	Ashy Storm-Petrel
	Band-rumped Storm-Petrel
	Wedge-rumped Storm-Petrel
	Black Storm-Petrel
	Sooty Storm-Petrel
	Least Storm-Petrel

PELECANIFORMES
Phaethontidae

	White-tailed Tropicbird
	Red-billed Tropicbird
	Red-tailed Tropicbird

Sulidae

	Masked Booby
✓	Blue-footed Booby
	Brown Booby

	Red-footed Booby
	Northern Gannet

Pelecanidae

✓	American White Pelican
✓	Brown Pelican

Phalacrocoracidae

	Great Cormorant
✓	Double-crested Cormorant
	Olivaceous Cormorant
	Brandt's Cormorant
	Pelagic Cormorant
	Red-faced Cormorant

Anhingidae

✓	Anhinga

Fregatidae

✓	Magnificent Frigatebird
	Great Frigatebird
	Lesser Frigatebird

CICONIIFORMES
Ardidae

✓	American Bittern
✓	Least Bittern
✓	Great Blue Heron
	Gray Heron
✓	Great Egret
	Little Egret
✓	Snowy Egret
	Western Reef-Heron (A)
	Little Blue Heron
	Tricolored Heron
	Reddish Egret
✓	Cattle Egret
✓	Green-backed Heron
✓	Black-crowned Night-Heron
✓	Yellow-crowned Night-Heron

Threskiornithidae

	White Ibis
	Scarlet Ibis (A)
✓	Glossy Ibis
✓	White-faced Ibis
	Roseate Spoonbill

Ciconiidae

	Jabiru
	Wood Stork

A=accidental   E=escaped bird   I=introduced   IH=introduced to Hawaii   ?=in doubt

PHOENICOPTERIFORMES
Phoenicopteridae

	Greater Flamingo

ANSERIFORMES
Anatidae

	Fulvous Whistling-Duck
	West Indian Whistling-Duck (A?)
✓	Black-bellied Whistling-Duck
	Tundra Swan
	Whooper Swan
✓	Trumpeter Swan
	Mute Swan
	Bean Goose
	Pink-footed Goose (A)
	Lesser White-fronted Goose (A)
	Greater White-fronted Goose
✓	Snow Goose
	Ross' Goose
	Emperor Goose
	Brant
	Barnacle Goose
✓	Canada Goose
	Hawaiian Goose
✓	Wood Duck
✓	Green-winged Teal
	Baikal Teal
	Falcated Teal
	American Black Duck
	Mottled Duck
✓	Mallard
	Hawaiian Duck
	Laysan Duck
	Spot-billed Duck (A)
	White-cheeked Pintail
✓	Northern Pintail
	Garganey
✓	Blue-winged Teal
✓	Cinnamon Teal
✓	Northern Shoveler
✓	Gadwall
	Eurasian Wigeon
✓	American Wigeon
	Common Pochard
✓	Canvasback
✓	Redhead
✓	Ring-necked Duck
	Tufted Duck

✓	Greater Scaup
	Lesser Scaup
	Common Eider
	King Eider
	Spectacled Eider
	Steller's Eider
	Harlequin Duck
	Oldsquaw
	Black Scoter
	Surf Scoter
	White-winged Scoter
✓	Common Goldeneye
	Barrow's Goldeneye
✓	Bufflehead
	Smew
	Hooded Merganser
✓	Common Merganser
	Red-breasted Merganser
✓	Ruddy Duck
	Masked Duck

FALCONIFORMES
Cathartidae

✓	Black Vulture
✓	Turkey Vulture
	California Condor

Accipitridae

✓	Osprey
	Hook-billed Kite
	American Swallow-tailed Kite
	Black-shouldered Kite
	Snail Kite
	Mississippi Kite
✓	Bald Eagle
	White-tailed Eagle
	Steller's Sea-Eagle
✓	Northern Harrier
✓	Sharp-shinned Hawk
✓	Cooper's Hawk
✓	Northern Goshawk
	Common Black-Hawk
	Harris' Hawk
✓	Gray Hawk
	Roadside Hawk (A)
	Red-shouldered Hawk
	Broad-winged Hawk
	Short-tailed Hawk
✓	Swainson's Hawk

50

	White-tailed Hawk		Elegant Quail
✓	Zone-tailed Hawk	✓	Gambel's Quail
	Hawaiian Hawk		California Quail
✓	Red-tailed Hawk		Mountain Quail
	Common Buzzard (A)		Helmeted Guineafowl (IH)
✓	Ferruginous Hawk
✓	Rough-legged Hawk
✓	Golden Eagle

GRUIFORMES
Rallidae

Falconidae

	Crested Caracara		Yellow Rail
	Eurasian Kestrel		Black Rail
✓	American Kestrel		Corn Crake
✓	Merlin		Clapper Rail
	Aplomado Falcon		King Rail
	Peregrine Falcon		Virginia Rail
	Gyrfalcon	✓	Sora
✓	Prairie Falcon		Paint-billed Crake (A?)
			Spotted Rail (A)
		✓	Purple Gallinule
		✓	Common Moorhen
			Eurasian Coot (A)
		✓	American Coot
			Caribbean Coot (A)

GALLIFORMES
Cracidae

Aramidae

	Plain Chachalaca		Limpkin

Phasianidae

Gruidae

✓	Gray Partridge	✓	Sandhill Crane
	Black Francolin (IH)		Common Crane (A)
	Gray Francolin (IH)	✓	Whooping Crane
	Erckel's Francolin (IH)

CHARADRIIFORMES
Burhinidae

✓	Chukar		Double-striped Thick-knee (A)

Charadriidae

	Japanese Quail (IH)	✓	Northern Lapwing
	Kalij Pheasant (IH)	✓	Black-bellied Plover
	Red Junglefowl (IH)		Greater Golden Plover
✓	Ring-necked Pheasant		Lesser Golden Plover
	Common Peafowl (IH)		Mongolian Plover
	Spruce Grouse		Snowy Plover
✓	Blue Grouse		Wilson's Plover
	Willow Ptarmigan		Common Ringed Plover
	Rock Ptarmigan		Semipalmated Plover
✓	White-tailed Ptarmigan		Piping Plover
✓	Ruffed Grouse		Little Ringed Plover
✓	Sage Grouse	✓	Killdeer
	Greater Prairie-Chicken	✓	Mountain Plover
	Lesser Prairie-Chicken		Eurasian Dotterel
✓	Sharp-tailed Grouse
✓	Wild Turkey
✓	Montezuma Quail
✓	Northern Bobwhite
✓	Scaled Quail

A = accidental   E = escaped bird   I = introduced   IH = introduced to Hawaii   ? = in doubt

Haematopodidae

- [x] American Oystercatcher
- [ ] Black Oystercatcher

Recurvirostridae

- [ ] Black-winged Stilt (A)
- [ ] Black-necked Stilt
- [x] American Avocet

Jacanidae

- [ ] Northern Jacana

Scolopacidae

- [ ] Common Greenshank
- [x] Greater Yellowlegs
- [ ] Lesser Yellowlegs
- [ ] Marsh Sandpiper (A)
- [ ] Spotted Redshank (A)
- [ ] Wood Sandpiper
- [ ] Green Sandpiper
- [ ] Solitary Sandpiper
- [x] Willet
- [ ] Wandering Tattler
- [ ] Gray-tailed Tattler
- [ ] Common Sandpiper
- [x] Spotted Sandpiper
- [ ] Terek Sandpiper
- [ ] Upland Sandpiper
- [x] Eskimo Curlew
- [ ] Whimbrel
- [ ] Bristle-thighed Curlew
- [ ] Slender-billed Curlew
- [ ] Far Eastern Curlew
- [ ] Eurasian Curlew (A)
- [ ] Long-billed Curlew
- [ ] Black-tailed Godwit
- [ ] Hudsonian Godwit
- [ ] Bar-tailed Godwit
- [ ] Marbled Godwit
- [ ] Ruddy Turnstone
- [ ] Black Turnstone
- [ ] Surfbird
- [ ] Great Knot
- [ ] Red Knot
- [ ] Sanderling
- [ ] Semipalmated Sandpiper
- [ ] Western Sandpiper
- [ ] Rufous-necked Stint
- [ ] Little Stint (A)
- [ ] Temminck's Stint
- [ ] Long-toed Stint
- [ ] Least Sandpiper
- [ ] White-rumped Sandpiper
- [ ] Baird's Sandpiper
- [ ] Pectoral Sandpiper
- [ ] Sharp-tailed Sandpiper
- [ ] Purple Sandpiper
- [ ] Rock Sandpiper
- [ ] Dunlin
- [ ] Curlew Sandpiper
- [ ] Stilt Sandpiper
- [ ] Spoonbill Sandpiper (A)
- [ ] Broad-billed Sandpiper
- [ ] Buff-breasted Sandpiper
- [ ] Ruff
- [ ] Short-billed Dowitcher
- [x] Long-billed Dowitcher
- [ ] Jack Snipe (A)
- [x] Common Snipe
- [ ] Pin-tailed Snipe (A)
- [ ] Eurasian Woodcock
- [ ] American Woodcock
- [x] Wilson's Phalarope
- [ ] Red-necked Phalarope
- [ ] Red Phalarope

Laridae

- [ ] Pomarine Jaeger
- [ ] Parasitic Jaeger
- [ ] Long-tailed Jaeger
- [ ] Great Skua
- [ ] South Polar Skua
- [x] Laughing Gull
- [ ] Franklin's Gull
- [ ] Little Gull
- [ ] Common Black-headed Gull
- [ ] Bonaparte's Gull
- [x] Heermann's Gull
- [ ] Band-tailed Gull (A)
- [ ] Mew Gull
- [ ] Ring-billed Gull
- [x] California Gull
- [x] Herring Gull
- [ ] Thayer's Gull
- [ ] Iceland Gull
- [ ] Lesser Black-backed Gull
- [ ] Slaty-backed Gull
- [ ] Yellow-footed Gull

	Western Gull
✓	Glaucous-winged Gull — *alaska, 7/90*
	Glaucous Gull
	Great Black-backed Gull
✓	Black-legged Kittiwake *alaska/7/90.*
	Red-legged Kittiwake
	Ross' Gull
	Sabine's Gull
	Ivory Gull
	Gull-billed Tern
	Caspian Tern
	Royal Tern
	Elegant Tern
	Sandwich Tern
	Roseate Tern
	Common Tern
	Arctic Tern
✓	Forster's Tern
	Least Tern
	Aleutian Tern
	Gray-backed Tern
	Bridled Tern
	Sooty Tern
	Large-billed Tern (A)
	White-winged Tern (A)
	Black Tern
	Brown Noddy
	Black Noddy
	Blue-gray Noddy
	White Tern
	Black Skimmer

Alcidae

	Dovekie
	Common Murre
	Thick-billed Murre
	Razorbill
	Black Guillemot
✓	Pigeon Guillemot *alaska 7/90*
	Marbled Murrelet
	Kittlitz's Murrelet
	Xantus' Murrelet
	Craveri's Murrelet
	Ancient Murrelet
	Cassin's Auklet
	Parakeet Auklet

	Least Auklet
	Whiskered Auklet
	Crested Auklet
	Rinoceros Auklet
✓	Tufted Puffin
	Atlantic Puffin { ? *alaska 7/90*
	Horned Puffin

COLUMBIFORMES
Pteroclidae

	Chestnut-bellied Sandgrouse (IH)

Columbidae

✓	Rock Dove
	Scaly-naped Pigeon (A)
	White-crowned Pigeon
	Red-billed Pigeon
	Band-tailed Pigeon
	Ringed Turtle-Dove
	Spotted Dove
	Zebra Dove (IH)
✓	White-winged Dove
	Zenaida Dove (A)
✓	Mourning Dove
✓	Inca Dove
	Common Ground-Dove
	Ruddy Ground-Dove
	White-tipped Dove
	Key West Quail-Dove
	Ruddy Quail-Dove
	Blue-headed Quail-Dove (A)

PSITTACIFORMES
Psittacidae

	Budgerigar
	Rose-ringed Parakeet
	Monk Parakeet (EA)
	Hispaniolan Parakeet (A?)
	Orange-fronted Parakeet (E?)
	Canary-winged Parakeet (I)
	Red-crowned Parrot (I)
	Lilac-crowned Parrot (I)
	Yellow-headed Parrot (I)

CUCULIFORMES
Cuculidae

	Common Cuckoo
	Oriental Cuckoo (A)
✓	Black-billed Cuckoo

A = accidental   E = escaped bird   I = introduced   IH = introduced to Hawaii   ? = in doubt

	Yellow-billed Cuckoo
	Mangrove Cuckoo
✓	Greater Roadrunner
	Smooth-billed Ani
	Groove-billed Ani

STRIGIFORMES
Tytonidae

✓	Common Barn-Owl

Strigidae

	Oriental Scops-Owl (A)
	Flammulated Owl
	Eastern Screech-Owl
	Western Screech-Owl
✓	Whiskered Screech-Owl
✓	Great Horned Owl
	Snowy Owl
	Northern Hawk-Owl
	Northern Pygmy-Owl
	Ferruginous Pygmy-Owl
	Elf Owl
✓	Burrowing Owl
	Spotted Owl
	Barred Owl
✓	Great Gray Owl
	Long-eared Owl
	Short-eared Owl
	Boreal Owl
	Northern Saw-whet Owl

CAPRIMULGIFORMES
Caprimulgidae

✓	Lesser Nighthawk
✓	Common Nighthawk
	Antillean Nighthawk
	Common Pauraque
	Common Poorwill
	Chuck-will's-widow
	Buff-collared Nightjar
✓	Whip-poor-will
	Jungle Nightjar (A)

APODIFORMES
Apodidae

	Black Swift
	White-collared Swift (A)
✓	Chimney Swift
	Vaux's Swift
	White-throated Needletail (A)
	Common Swift (A)

	Fork-tailed Swift
✓	White-throated Swift

Trochilidae

	Green Violet-ear
	Antillean Crested Hummingbird (A?)
	Cuban Emerald (A)
✓	Broad-billed Hummingbird
	White-eared Hummingbird
	Berylline Hummingbird
	Rufous-tailed Hummingbird
	Buff-bellied Hummingbird
✓	Violet-crowned Hummingbird
✓	Blue-throated Hummingbird
✓	Magnificent Hummingbird
	Plain-capped Starthroat (A)
	Bahama Woodstar
	Lucifer Hummingbird
✓	Ruby-throated Hummingbird
✓	Black-chinned Hummingbird
✓	Anna's Hummingbird
	Costa's Hummingbird
	Calliope Hummingbird
	Bumblebee Hummingbird (A)
✓	Broad-tailed Hummingbird
✓	Rufous Hummingbird
	Allen's Hummingbird

TROGONIFORMES
Trogonidae

✓	Elegant Trogon
	Eared Trogon (?)

CORACIIFORMES
Upupidae

	Hoopoe (A)

Alcedinidae

	Ringed Kingfisher
✓	Belted Kingfisher
	Green Kingfisher

PICIFORMES
Picidae

	Eurasian Wryneck (A)
✓	Lewis' Woodpecker
✓	Red-headed Woodpecker
✓	Acorn Woodpecker
✓	Gila Woodpecker
	Golden-fronted Woodpecker
✓	Red-bellied Woodpecker
	Yellow-bellied Sapsucker

✓	Red-naped Sapsucker
	Red-breasted Sapsucker
	Williamson's Sapsucker
✓	Ladder-backed Woodpecker
	Nuttall's Woodpecker
✓	Downy Woodpecker
✓	Hairy Woodpecker
	Strickland's Woodpecker
	Red-cockaded Woodpecker
	White-headed Woodpecker
	Three-toed Woodpecker
	Black-backed Woodpecker
✓	Northern Flicker
✓	Pileated Woodpecker
?	Ivory-billed Woodpecker

PASSERIFORMES

Tyrannidae

	Northern Beardless-Tyannulet
	Greenish Elaenia (A)
	Olive-sided Flycatcher
	Greater Pewee
✓	Western Wood-Pewee
	Eastern Wood-Pewee
	Yellow-bellied Flycatcher
	Acadian Flycatcher
	Alder Flycatcher
	Willow Flycatcher
	Least Flycatcher
	Hammond's Flycatcher
	Dusky Flycatcher
	Gray Flycatcher
✓	Western Flycatcher
	Buff-breasted Flycatcher
✓	Black Phoebe
	Eastern Phoebe
✓	Say's Phoebe
✓	Vermillion Flycatcher
✓	Dusky-capped Flycatcher
✓	Ash-throated Flycatcher
	Nutting's Flycatcher
	Great Crested Flycatcher
	Brown-crested Flycatcher
	La Sagra's Flycatcher (A)
	Great Kiskadee
	Sulphur-bellied Flycatcher

	Variegated Flycatcher (A)
	Tropical Kingbird
	Couch's Kingbird
✓	Cassin's Kingbird
	Thick-billed Kingbird
✓	Western Kingbird
✓	Eastern Kingbird
	Gray Kingbird
	Loggerhead Kingbird (A)
✓	Scissor-tailed Flycatcher
	Fork-tailed Flycatcher
	Rose-throated Becard

Alaudidae

✓	Eurasian Skylark (IH)
✓	Horned Lark

Hirundinidae

	Purple Martin
	Cuban Martin (A)
	Gray-breasted Martin
	Southern Martin (A)
✓	Tree Swallow
✓	Violet-green Swallow
	Bahama Swallow
✓	Northern Rough-winged Swallow _Indiana 6/92_
✓	Bank Swallow
✓	Cliff Swallow
	Cave Swallow
✓	Barn Swallow
	Common House Martin (A)

Corvidae

✓	Gray Jay
✓	Steller's Jay
✓	Blue Jay
	Green Jay
	Brown Jay
	San Blas Jay (A)
✓	Scrub Jay
✓	Gray-breasted Jay
✓	Pinyon Jay
✓	Clark's Nutcracker
✓	Black-billed Magpie
	Yellow-billed Magpie
	Eurasian Jackdaw (A)
✓	American Crow
✓	Northwestern Crow

A = accidental   E = escaped bird   I = introduced   IH = introduced to Hawaii   ? = in doubt

143

Mexican Crow	Millerbird
Fish Crow	Wood Warbler (A)
Hawaiian Crow	Dusky Warbler (A)
Chihuahuan Raven	Arctic Warbler
✓ Common Raven	✓ Golden-crowned Kinglet
Paridae	✓ Ruby-crowned Kinglet
✓ Black-capped Chickadee	Blue-gray Gnatcatcher
Carolina Chickadee	✓ Black-tailed Gnatcatcher
✓ Mexican Chickadee	Black-capped Gnatcatcher
✓ Mountain Chickadee	Red-breasted Flycatcher (A)
Siberian Tit	Siberian Flycatcher (A)
Boreal Chickadee	Gray-spotted Flycatcher
Chestnut-backed Chickadee	Elepaio
✓ Bridled Titmouse	Siberian Rubythroat
Varied Tit	Bluethroat
Plain Titmouse	Red-flanked Bluetail (A)
✓ Tufted Titmouse	White-rumped Shama (IH)
Remizidae	Northern Wheatear
✓ Verdin	✓ Eastern Bluebird
Aegithalidae	✓ Western Bluebird
✓ Bushtit	✓ Mountain Bluebird
Sittidae	✓ Townsend's Solitaire
✓ Red-breasted Nuthatch	Omao (Hawaiian Thrush)
✓ White-breasted Nuthatch	Kamao
✓ Pygmy Nuthatch	Olomao
Brown-headed Nuthatch	Puaiohi
Certhiidae	? Veery
✓ Brown Creeper	Gray-cheeked Thrush
Pycnonotidae	✓ Swainson's Thrush
Red-vented Bulbul (IH)	✓ Hermit Thrush
Red-whiskered Bulbul (IH & Fla.)	Wood Thrush
Troglodytidae	Eurasian Blackbird (A)
✓ Cactus Wren	Eye-browed Thrush
✓ Rock Wren	Dusky Thrush (A)
✓ Canyon Wren	Fieldfare (A)
✓ Carolina Wren	Redwing (A)
✓ Bewick's Wren	Clay-colored Robin (A)
✓ House Wren	Rufous-backed Robin (A)
Winter Wren	✓ American Robin
Sedge Wren	Varied Thrush
✓ Marsh Wren	Aztec Thrush
Cinclidae	Greater Necklaced Laughing-thrush (IH)
✓ American Dipper	Melodious Laughing-thrush (IH)
Muscicapidae	Red-billed Leiothrix (IH)
Japanese Bush-Warbler (IH)	Wrentit
Middendorff's Grasshopper-Warbler (A)	**Mimidae**
Lanceolated Warbler (A)	✓ Gray Catbird

✓ Northern Mockingbird	ᵛᵒⁱᶜᵉ ✓ Bell's Vireo
Bahama Mockingbird (A)	Black-capped Vireo
✓ Sage Thrasher	Gray Vireo
✓ Brown Thrasher	Solitary Vireo
Long-billed Thrasher	Yellow-throated Vireo
Bendire's Thrasher	Hutton's Vireo
✓ Curve-billed Thrasher	✓ Warbling Vireo
California Thrasher	Philadelphia Vireo
Crissal Thrasher	Red-eyed Vireo
Le Conte's Thrasher	Black-whiskered Vireo
Prunellidae	Yucatan Vireo (A)
Siberian Accentor	**Emberizidae**
Motacillidae	Bachman's Warbler
✓ Yellow Wagtail	Blue-winged Warbler
✓ Gray Wagtail	Golden-winged Warbler
White Wagtail	Tennessee Warbler
Black-backed Wagtail	Orange-crowned Warbler
Brown Tree-Pipit (A)	Nashville Warbler
Olive Tree-Pipit	Virginia's Warbler
Pechora Pipit	Colima Warbler
Red-throated Pipit	✓ Lucy's Warbler
✓ Water Pipit	Northern Parula
Sprague's Pipit	Tropical Parula
Bombycillidae	✓ Yellow Warbler
✓ Bohemian Waxwing	Chestnut-sided Warbler
✓ Cedar Waxwing	Magnolia Warbler
Ptilogonatidae	Cape May Warbler
✓ Phainopepla	✓ Black-throated Blue Warbler ᵐⁱᶜʰ 6/92
Laniidae	✓ Yellow-rumped Warbler
Brown Shrike (A)	✓ Black-throated Gray Warbler
✓ Northern Shrike	✓ Townsend's Warbler
✓ Loggerhead Shrike	Hermit Warbler
Sturnidae	Black-throated Green Warbler
✓ European Starling	Golden-cheeked Warbler
✓ Common Myna	Blackburnian Warbler
Crested Myna	Yellow-throated Warbler
Hill Myna	✓ Grace's Warbler
Meliphagidae	Pine Warbler
Kauai Oo	Kirtland's Warbler
Bishop's Oo	Prairie Warbler
Zosteropidae	Palm Warbler
Japanese White-eye (IH)	Bay-breasted Warbler
Vireonidae	Blackpoll Warbler
White-eyed Vireo	Cerulean Warbler
Thick-billed Vireo	✓ Black-and-white Warbler

A=accidental   E=escaped bird   I=introduced   IH=introduced to Hawaii   ?=in doubt

✓	American Redstart		Olive Sparrow
	Prothonotary Warbler	✓	Green-tailed Towhee
	Worm-eating Warbler	✓	Rufous-sided Towhee
	Swainson's Warbler	✓	Brown Towhee
	Ovenbird		Albert's Towhee
	Northern Waterthrush		White-collared Seedeater
	Louisiana Waterthrush		Yellow-faced Grassquit (IH)
	Kentucky Warbler		Black-faced Grassquit
	Connecticut Warbler		Saffron Finch (IH)
	Mourning Warbler		Bachman's Sparrow
	MacGillivray's Warbler		Botteri's Sparrow
	Common Yellowthroat	✓	Cassin's Sparrow
	Bahama Yellowthroat (A)	✓	Rufous-winged Sparrow
	Hooded Warbler		Rufous-crowned Sparrow
✓	Wilson's Warbler	✓	American Tree Sparrow
	Canada Warbler	✓	Chipping Sparrow ✓
✓	Red-faced Warbler		Clay-colored Sparrow
✓	Painted Redstart		Brewer's Sparrow
	Slate-throated Redstart (A)	✓	Field Sparrow Mich 6/92
	Fan-tailed Warbler (A)		Worthen's Sparrow
	Golden-crowned Warbler (A)	✓	Black-chinned Sparrow
	Rufous-capped Warbler (A)	✓	Vesper Sparrow
	Yellow-breasted Chat	✓	Lark Sparrow
	Olive Warbler	✓	Black-throated Sparrow
	Bananaquit		Sage Sparrow
	Blue-gray Tanager		Five-striped Sparrow
	Stripe-headed Tanager	✓	Lark Bunting
✓	Hepatic Tanager Madera '92	✓	Savannah Sparrow
✓	Summer Tanager		Baird's Sparrow
	Scarlet Tanager		Grasshopper Sparrow
✓	Western Tanager		Henslow's Sparrow
	Crimson-collared Grosbeak		Le Conte's Sparrow
✓	Northern Cardinal		Sharp-tailed Sparrow
✓	Pyrrhuloxia		Seaside Sparrow
	Yellow Grosbeak	✓	Fox Sparrow
✓	Rose-breasted Grosbeak	✓	Song Sparrow
✓	Black-headed Grosbeak		Lincoln's Sparrow
	Blue Bunting (A)	✓	Swamp Sparrow
	Blue Grosbeak		White-throated Sparrow
✓	Lazuli Bunting		Golden-crowned Sparrow
	Indigo Bunting	✓	White-crowned Sparrow
	Varied Bunting		Harris' Sparrow
	Orange-breasted Bunting (E)	✓	Dark-eyed Junco
	Painted Bunting	✓	Yellow-eyed Junco
	Dickcissel	✓	McCown's Longspur
	Red-crested Cardinal (IH)		Lapland Longspur
	Yellow-billed Cardinal (IH)		Smith's Longspur

Chestnut-collared Longspur	Lawrence's Goldfinch
Little Bunting (A)	✓ American Goldfinch
Rustic Bunting	European Goldfinch (I NY)
Gray Bunting (A)	Oriental Greenfinch
Pallas' Reed-Bunting (A)	Yellow-fronted Canary (IH)
Common Reed-Bunting	Common Canary (IH)
Snow Bunting	Eurasian Bullfinch
McKay's Bunting	✓ Evening Grosbeak
✓ Bobolink	Hawfinch
✓ Red-winged Blackbird	Laysan Finch
Tricolored Blackbird	Nihoa Finch
Tawny-shouldered Blackbird	Ou
✓ Eastern Meadowlark	Palila
✓ Western Meadowlark	Maui Parrotbill
✓ Yellow-headed Blackbird	Common Amakihi
Rusty Blackbird	Anianiau
✓ Brewer's Blackbird	Kauai Akialoa
✓ Great-tailed Grackle	Nukupuu
Boat-tailed Grackle	Akiapolaau
✓ Common Grackle	Kauai Creeper
Bronzed Cowbird	Hawaii Creeper
✓ Brown-headed Cowbird	Maui Creeper
Black-vented Oriole (A)	Molokai Creeper
Orchard Oriole	Oahu Creeper
✓ Hooded Oriole	Akepa
✓ Streak-backed Oriole	Iiwi
Spot-breasted Oriole (I FLA.)	Crested Honeycreeper
Altamira Oriole	Apapane
Audubon's Oriole	Poo-uli
✓ Northern Oriole	**Passeridae**
✓ Scott's Oriole	✓ House Sparrow (I)
Fringillidae	Eurasian Tree Sparrow (I)
✓ Common Chaffinch	Red Bishop (IH?)
Brambling	Yellow-crowned Bishop (IH?)
Rosy Finch	**Estrildidae**
✓ Pine Grosbeak	Red-cheeked Cordonbleu (IH?)
Common Rosefinch	Lavender Waxbill (IH)
Purple Finch	Orange-cheeked Waxbill (IH)
✓ Cassin's Finch	Black-rumped Waxbill (IH)
✓ House Finch	Common Waxbill (IH)
Red Crossbill	Red Avadavit
White-winged Crossbill	Warbling Silverbill (IH)
Common Redpoll	Nutmeg Mannikin
Hoary Redpoll	Chestnut Mannikin (IH)
✓ Pine Siskin	Java Sparrow (IH)
✓ Lesser Goldfinch	Pin-tailed Wydah

A=accidental   E=escaped bird   I=introduced   IH=introduced to Hawaii   ?=in doubt

INDEX